THE SEARCH FOR QUALITY

Del Goddard is Chief Adviser in the London Borough of Enfield, and is well known, both in the UK and abroad for his work on all aspects of development, including school development plans.

Marilyn Leask is Senior Lecturer in Education at Bedford College of Higher Education and has worked with schools throughout the country on the DES-funded School Development Plans Project based in Cambridge.

THE SEARCH FOR QUALITY

Planning for Improvement and Managing Change

DEL GODDARD

and

MARILYN LEASK

P·C·P
Paul Chapman
Publishing Ltd

Paul Chapman Publishing Ltd
144 Liverpool Road
London
N1 1LA

British Library Cataloguing in Publication Data
    Leask, Marilyn
    Search for Quality: Planning for Improvement and
    Managing Change
    (Education Management Series)
    I. Title II. Goddard, Del III. Series
    371

ISBN 1 85396 190 6

Typeset by Inforum, Rowlands Castle, Hants
Printed and bound by Athenaeum Press, Newcastle upon Tyne

A B C D E F G H   9 8 7 6 5 4 3 2

CONTENTS

PART II: LESSONS FROM HISTORY

PART III: IMPROVING QUALITY THROUGH UNDERSTANDING DEVELOPMENT

PREFACE

The high level of concern expressed by parents, teachers and politicians about the quality of the education system and the priorities for development in the future led us to write this book. We too are concerned – concerned that confidence in the education system be re-established so that parents, teachers, students and politicians can feel confident that they share the same goals; and concerned that the lessons to be learned from the history of change in education be understood, and not ignored, in the pressure for reform.

The capital of a nation depends on improving the quality of the education of each generation. The quality of education depends not only on the quality and motivation of the teaching force but also on the motivation of the children. Both of these are directly influenced by the values and attitudes of society.

In modern societies, values and attitudes are passed on to children by the adults responsible for parenting, through the media and by schools. We question whether parents and those in the media are sufficiently conscious of their wider role in ensuring the well-being of society at large. Society's aspirations are such that improvement fuels demands for further improvement. An industrialist was discussing the drop in ability of the 16-year-olds he employs. As the discussion progressed, it became apparent that part of the problem was related to the higher aspirations of young people. Twenty years ago, he was recruiting school-leavers who had five or more O-levels; nowadays, many young people with these qualifications are opting for higher education, leaving those who have attained less to apply to his firm. But the demands his industry makes on young people are much greater than they were twenty years ago!

This then is the central dilemma for a modern education system. The technological nature of society requires those who would previously have taken unskilled work to become skilled workers. This requirement for higher attainment applies at virtually all levels in society. In order for society to move forward, young people require an education that will enable them to meet the challenges of the future. For these reasons, constant review and adjustment of the education system and of education provision has become the norm for our society.

In order to meet this demand for constant review we propose action on three fronts:

1. *That change be planned coherently rather than in a piecemeal fashion.* Careful consideration of the impact of proposed changes on the whole of the education system, service and provision should be normal practice. Change in the future needs to be based on what has been learned already from what has gone before.
2. *That research and development work be increased to improve current levels of understanding of how professionals and organizations develop.* This work would include detailed examination of the context that supports learning and change. The necessary synergy in the system – whereby the growth of the individual enables the organization to grow and, at the same time, the growth of the organization enables the individual within it to grow – could provide a focus for such work.

   For work in these two areas to be used for the maximum benefit of the education system, we propose action on a third front:
3. *The establishment of a professional council charged with overall responsibility for education.* This council could have as its central brief the duty to bring about change through consultation and consensus – building on the strengths of the past and drawing together advice about the way forward.

The ideas we express have developed from our own involvement and experience in the education system as parents and teachers, in advisory and research work and in working with school governors. Our teaching experience spans all phases of education and our children are currently at primary school, secondary school or university.

We hope that what follows in this book will provide food for thought for all concerned with improving the quality of education and that some action will follow.

Del Goddard, Marilyn Leask
January 1992

Authors' note – using this book

The book covers different aspects of the improvement process and the four parts are designed to be read independently if the reader so wishes.

Readers who do not know the context of the UK education system will find that 'Part II: Lessons from History' provides essential background reading. Others will be able to move straight on to 'Part III: Improving Quality through Understanding Development', which draws on the experiences of many schools and LEAs that have been consciously planning and managing improvement in the education system.

Although the authors have worked closely together in writing this book, Del is primarily responsible for writing Part III and Marilyn is primarily responsible for writing Parts I, II and IV.

Reading about improvement is the easy part. The advice those experienced in the process give is to *think big – start small*. In our experience, the goodwill, motivation, understanding and training of those who are to implement change are the central ingredients in successfully managed change but they are all too easily neglected or taken for granted.

ACKNOWLEDGEMENTS

The seeds of ideas and understandings can lie dormant for long periods to germinate only when conditions are right – such are the origins of many of the ideas and understandings expressed in this book. They have come from conversations and from experiences with children, students, teachers, parents, governors, civil servants, politicians and others concerned for the quality of education. To acknowledge all these people by name would be impossible – often an idea has become fully formed in our minds only long after the experience or conversation which planted the seed has passed from memory. Nevertheless, we thank them for their contribution. The work of colleagues in the national teachers' centres network as well as all those colleagues who have shared their ideas with us in INSET sessions is particularly acknowledged.

Ian Terrell and Ann Wignall both contributed to the book and we thank them for allowing us to use their work. We would like to thank our families for their patience and forbearance as well as the following colleagues who provided us with inspiration and support and who, in some cases, were also our teachers: Charles Beresford, Glenda Jones, Prof. David Hargreaves, Dr David Hopkins, Gordon Hutchinson, Martin Rainsford, Prof. Helen Simons, Clare Woroniecka and Barbara Wynn.

PART I
DEFINING QUALITY

1
THE ELUSIVE IDEAL: QUALITY IN EDUCATION

Introduction

Quality is a very difficult term to define. But however it is described, the only way that quality can be achieved is by the development of high-quality learning and teaching in schools and classrooms. Few would disagree with this statement, but teaching methods and curriculum content are controversial issues. Both are the subject of continuing debate.

In education, the lack of a strong professional base of understanding about learning and teaching means that teachers have a restricted amount of research data to support their professional judgment, and both politicians and the public (from whatever base of experience) feel able to enter into the debate about teaching. In recent times, the education debate has almost deliberately been taken out of the professional arena with the Secretary of State for Education making pronouncements on practice apparently based on personal preference and political philosophies rather than hard evidence.

The consequence of this uninformed method of policy-making is that changes tend to be unco-ordinated and the confidence in the education system of teachers, the community, parents and politicians, is eroded.

Quality – a moving target

'Quality in education is somewhat problematical: like beauty, it lies in the eye – or rather the mind – of the beholder' (Clift, Nuttal and McCormick, 1987, p. 202). A high-quality education system is essential to the health and future of a nation. Yet the definition of quality appears to shift according to the values of those who hold influence and power in the system and the values of different communities in society. In any case, views about content and teaching approaches change over time. What was deemed high-quality educational provision at the beginning of the twentieth century is seen as limited and narrow as the twenty-first century draws near. The amusing story of the 'sabre-tooth' curriculum (Peddiwell, 1939) is a reminder of the dangers of ossification of the curriculum. The prehistoric community in the story become fixated on teaching youngsters how to deal with 'sabre-toothed tigers' and fail to adapt to new challenges when the sabre-toothed tigers die out.

Whilst the detail of what is to be taught and learned cannot be prescribed once and for all, some measure of agreement in society is necessary about what the education service is expected to achieve. Aspects of the National Curriculum provide a useful framework for the curriculum but it will require regular updating if it is to avoid 'ossification'. There is probably consensus that basic skills (e.g. numeracy and language skills, interpersonal skills and problem-solving skills) are essential for all children – but agreement at the level of detail of how these should be taught is harder to achieve. There are too many variables in the teaching and learning process for certainty in this area.

Quality and purpose

What is quality? Behind this question lies the fundamental issue of the purpose of education. Is it about what people want or need? If so, who defines the wants and the needs?

There is a fundamental problem in defining the purpose of education. Modern democratic pluralistic societies require education systems to work towards potentially contradictory outcomes. On the one hand young people are to be educated to support society's collective values and to contribute economically to society; on the other hand, the individual is to be allowed the choice and the freedom to do what they want. Herbert Read (1958, p. 2) summed up this central dilemma more than thirty years ago:

> [In education] there are at least two irreconcilable possibilities: . . The first view assumes that each individual is born with certain potentialities which have a positive value for that individual and that it is his proper destiny to develop these potentialities within the framework of a society liberal enough to allow for an infinite variation of types. The second view assumes that whatever idiosyncrasies the individual may possess at birth, it is the duty of the teacher to eradicate them unless they conform to a certain ideal of character determined by the traditions of the society of which the individual has involuntarily become a member.

This dilemma is reflected in the complexity of teachers' accountability. Teachers often face a conflict of values in their work – they are placed in positions where their practice can be at odds with their beliefs about what is right.

There have been attempts recently to apply the British Standard for Quality, *BS 5750*, and notions of 'Total Quality Management' (TQM) to education. But these definitions of quality are not necessarily applicable to education. Take, for example, the British Standards Institute definition (1987, p. 4): 'Quality has a number of different meanings but BS 5750 looks at it through the fitness for purpose . . . is the service provided designed and constructed to satisfy the customers' needs?' The Department of Trade and Industry defines quality in the booklet, *Total Quality Management*: 'Quality then is simply meeting the customer requirements' (undated, p. 3).

In education, the requirements of the customer are not defined in a uni-dimensional relationship. Quality looked at through the eyes of parents, students, government, local communities and business has different characteristics. One of the reasons why the definition of quality in education is very difficult is the variety of assumptions and values that underpin the curriculum and schooling. Some are explicit, many are implicit, some are to do with learning and a number are to do with social control and advantage.

Why not measure outcomes?

The debate on quality often focuses on standards of attainment in examinations as these are thought to be easily comparable. But these results show an individual's attainment in only one aspect of achievement and are the outcome of a process stretching back many years. This is not to say that examination results (or reading levels or the results of other tests) are not important in their own right. But good results for one individual at one point in time provide no guarantee that similar results will be achieved for those following or that the same individual will achieve good results in the future. It is the structures and processes underlying the achievement of these educational goals which ensure success and it is the improvement of these underlying processes and structures which ensures quality.

The necessity for a shift in focus from the quality of outcomes to the quality of the process of education can be illustrated by drawing an analogy with the success of a football team. Although the team may win most of their matches one season there is no guarantee they will do so next season. The continued production of high-quality football depends on the underlying processes for ensuring quality: for example, team motivation and training programmes. In education, it is the individual student's and teacher's levels of motivation, skill, knowledge and vision which influence the quality of teaching and learning and which ensure positive outcomes.

These underlying processes involve all the systems, structures, institutions, teachers and students with whom the individual comes in contact as well as the individual's family, local community and society in general. A young person's approach to learning is affected by much that is outside the school's sphere of influence (for instance, the media and the expectations of the local community).

Lifelong learning

There is growing recognition that if the challenges of the future are to be faced, then a creative, resourceful and adaptable people is required – able to respond to changing circumstances throughout their working lives. The work in the UK of the Technical Vocational Education Initiative (TVEI – 1983 onwards) has been based on this precept (Grubb Institute, 1989) as was the Royal Society for the encouragement of Arts, Manufactures and Commerce (RSA) campaign, *Education for Capability* (1980–91). The concept of a learning society was also recognized in the work of UNESCO (Lengrand, 1975) and in the USA in the influential report, *A Nation at Risk*, which states that

> educational reform should focus on the goal of creating a Learning Society. At the heart of such a society is the commitment to a set of values and to a system of education that affords all members the opportunity to stretch their minds to full capacity, from early childhood through adulthood, learning more as the world itself changes.
> (National Commission on Excellence in Education, 1983, p. 13)

If this view is held to be sound, one measure of quality in an education system entering the twenty-first century must be the extent to which students are enabled to 'learn to learn'. That is the extent to which students are enabled to carry on learning throughout their lives and the extent to which they can apply their learning to solve problems in other situations.

Thus whilst the outcomes (e.g. examination results) at one point in the individual's education may appear to indicate that a high-quality education has been experienced, the real evidence of such quality will be produced over the individual's lifetime. The 'hot-house flower' approach to teaching and learning – where students are force-fed a high-content diet to enable them to pass examinations – may not provide an adequate preparation for their own independent learning in the future – yet may, in the short term, provide high-quality outcomes.

This long-term effect causes problems for those seeking easy solutions to the quality debate. Quick-fix remedies for the problems of education are unlikely to be effective in the long term. Yet if the longer-term view is taken, society requires the assurance that quality education will be provided. If, as is suggested, measuring outcomes is only partially satisfactory in providing an indication of quality, then what processes should be in place to ensure high-quality education is delivered? What principles should underpin such a system and what structures are required to support the education service in this work? In this book we seek to address these issues.

Processes supporting improvement of quality

The debate about what should be taught is a continuing one. Society has to find a means of undertaking that debate, of informing it and of arriving at sufficient consensus for the service to operate.

For this reason, we put to one side the debate about what should be taught. We believe that the root of the improvement of quality lies in the structures of the education system and the processes guiding and developing the work of the education service. We look back over time to establish the lessons to be learned from the past and we put forward proposals for the future based on an analysis of what has gone before.

We start from the premises that there is no single view, at the level of detail, about what constitutes high quality in education – that there is no easy answer which satisfies all. Peters (1977) discusses the problems of defining quality in some depth, and readers interested in a philosophical discussion about the nature of quality in education are recommended to read his work. What we do say is that the apparently easy solution of judging quality by outcomes only is insufficient because quality outcomes are the result of a process taking many years.

Five key components in the process of improving quality that have been particularly neglected in recent times provide the themes running through this book:

1. The influence of society's views and beliefs, actions and priorities.
2. The necessity for consultation and reaching consensus about improvement.
3. A coherent and improved approach to change.
4. The motivation of those involved.
5. The need for increased understanding of the learning process for pupils and teachers and its implications for teaching.

The influence of society: values and beliefs, actions and priorities

The values and beliefs of society as expressed by government, parents, the media, young people's culture, religious groups are, together with the ethos of the school, the most important factors influencing the achievement of young people. But are all of these partners in education working together? What messages do young people in the UK receive from society about the value of education? Aren't they to some extent of the 'don't bother, it's not worth it' variety? Unemployment has dogged the school-leaver and graduate through the eighties and into the nineties as has the fear of war and the view that the planet is doomed. A negative ethos in society can all too easily drain youthful optimism.

Is there any consensus about values in the UK? High-quality education cannot be achieved by schools and teachers alone. The perceptions and values of the pupils affect their motivation and these perceptions and values are shaped by society at large. Gray (1990, p. 9) discusses the formation of values:

> It is often believed that there is only one valid set of values – a mistake that is currently made by the 'total quality' movement. Values are always a personal matter but they concern our most deeply rooted attitudes and practices. Values go deeper than logic and draw on our basic personal instincts – which are either tutored and informed or repressed and uncontrolled – and often something of both.

Schools are expected to perform 'competing functions – custodial, developmental and socialising' (Handy, 1984, p. 32), but what support is given by the media, by parents for this role? 'Sort out the moral climate, not the teacher', reads the headline of an article in the *Guardian* newspaper (11 June 1991). A head of a lower school in the north of England describes the problem:

> Three mothers appeared at my school one lunchtime, demanding to see me. They were angry at me for punishing their children for playing truant the previous day. I had naively believed that the parents' visit was to thank me for my vigilance in noticing a single day's absence, spotting one forged absence note and quickly punishing the pupils for the offence.

The article brought responses from teachers all over the country confirming the prevalence of this attitude. Making Christianity a compulsory part of the curriculum doesn't solve the problem of national values – values are demonstrated through actions. As a society, we have not identified the education of young people as a high priority. Allan Smith, previously a director for the Australian Broadcasting Corporation and Queensland

Educational Television, in an interview for this book has described television and the media in general as the 'third parent'. He commented that Australian figures show young people spending on average twenty-two hours viewing per week and the situation is not very different in the UK. How many parents, he asked, spend even a fraction of that time discussing moral issues with their children?

The provision of qualified teachers and a relevant curriculum alone will not achieve high standards. The children have got to want to learn, to see a purpose in learning, in doing homework rather than going out or watching the television or endlessly playing computer games. Many primary schools work on the basis of nurturing and valuing children as individuals, yet it is questionable whether this attitude to children – of valuing and caring for them – is reflected in society in general.

This raises the issue: How should the partnership between schools and society (including the media) be developed and managed?

Consultation and consensus

In a pluralist democratic society, consultation with the aim of reaching consensus is the process which enables diversity to be accommodated. In the UK, prior to the Education Reform Act in 1988, this democratic process was already operating to some extent – LEA policies on the curriculum, for example, were the expression of will of the community through elected councillors. But the centralization of control over the education system which has steadily increased since the late seventies, has militated against the building of consensus.

A particular dilemma for society is the balancing of provision of choice for individuals with the requirement to establish a framework that prevents anarchy. The balance is crucial but is difficult to maintain. The building of partnerships and collaboration between different groups plays a vital role in maintaining stability and supporting improvement.

This leads to one of the issues we explore in this book: Is there a role for an independent but representative national body which is responsible for establishing consensus and for creating a long-term vision for education?

A coherent approach to change

In the sphere of education, a coherent approach to change has two main dimensions: coherence must be maintained in terms of the way the education system operates as well as in terms of the expectations and attitudes of society (including the media) as a whole.

If an individual is to receive a 'high-quality education' then the work of numerous teachers, schools and others over a period of many years must be of consistently high quality. But education is not only provided at school. The wider learning environment provided by family and society plays a key role in motivating the individual to achieve.

In a modern society, the media role in creating (or destroying) such a learning environment is crucial as is the role of politicians. They need to put long-term considerations before short-term political considerations in order to maintain a balance between the necessary level of change required to ensure the system operates efficiently and their political aspirations. Coherence then becomes a live issue in the debate about what ensures a high-quality education system. Not only do the values and expectations of the young person, the family, the school, society and the teachers need to be mutually reinforcing, but the education system itself must also operate coherently. For this to happen, it is essential that the major components of the education system (e.g. curriculum, INSET, initial teacher training, resources) are considered as a whole when change is proposed.

There is, for example, little point in making substantial changes to the curriculum if insufficient training is provided for teachers to implement the changes. Change must be seen as a holistic process. Changes in one part of the system have an impact on other parts of the system.

This leads to a third issue addressed in this book: Is a piecemeal approach to change appropriate to the context of education in the nineties?

Motivation

Improvements in quality depend on the motivation and agreement of those involved in the service so that existing ways of working are changed. But what motivates teachers?

The model currently used in an attempt to enhance quality is based on extrinsic forms of motivation – inspection, appraisal, league tables of results, performance indicators, individually negotiated salaries. Yet what evidence is there that these motivate teachers?

Everard and Morris (1990, pp. 28–9) discuss the question of what motivates people to work and cite the work of McGregor (1960) in drawing a distinction between 'two views of work – one asserting that people seek fulfillment through work, and the other suggesting that they seek only to satisfy lower level needs'. McGregor's work is included here as we suggest that the education service is currently being managed according to McGregor's X theory – that coercion is the main route to improving quality – whereas the application of his Y theory – that whilst leadership is important, the individual's desire to achieve a high standard is the main motivating force – is more likely to lead to improved quality in education because of the nature of the work and the beliefs of those who choose teaching as a profession.

Everard and Morris (1990, pp. 28–9) summarize McGregor's X and Y theories of motivation and these are included as Table 1.1. This raises a fourth issue considered in this book: To what extent have current education reforms taken account of the importance of motivating teachers and students?

Table 1.1 McGregor's X and Y theories of motivation

Those managers who adopt 'theory X' believe

1. work is inherently distasteful to most people;
2. most people are not ambitious, have little desire for responsibility and prefer to be directed;
3. most people have little capacity for creativity in solving problems;
4. motivation occurs only at the physiological and security levels; and
5. most people must be closely controlled and often coerced to achieve organization objectives.

'Theory Y' managers, on the other hand, believe

1. work is as natural as play, if the conditions are favourable;
2. control of one's own work activities is often indispensable in achieving organizational gains;
3. the capacity for creativity in solving organizational problems is widely distributed in the population;
4. motivation occurs at the social, ego and self-realization levels as well as at the physiological and security levels; and
5. people can be self-directed and creative at work if properly led.

(From Everard and Morris, 1990, pp. 28–9.)

Teaching and learning misunderstood

The teaching and learning process is highly dynamic but this is not widely understood. Teachers, like psychiatrists, work with the mind, and much of their work is unseen. They also work with raw material of unknown and variable quality – the potential of an individual. This makes the judging of a teacher's effectiveness difficult and it means that the impact of poor teaching is insidious – the effects may not be seen for many years. It also allows for superficial judgments about what the work of the teacher involves.

More research into the processes of teaching and learning is necessary so that change can be soundly based on knowledge and experience.

Teachers do much more than transmit knowledge. By their approach to their work they convey messages to children about learning – is it about using knowledge to solve problems or about learning, parrot fashion, someone else's solutions? Is it a short-term or a long-term activity, pleasurable or a trial? Is there scope for individual thought or is there a fixed body of knowledge to acquire?

If a teacher's experience with their own learning is limited then they will pass on this restricted view to those whom they teach. If, however, teachers are actively engaged as learners themselves they will be better able to re-create with their students a learning environment where students experience learning as invigorating and exciting but at the same time painful and mentally taxing.

But can't anyone teach?

'The clever man will tell you what he knows; he may even try to explain it to you. The wise man encourages you to discover it for yourself, even though he knows it inside out' (McNiff, 1988, p. 52). The word 'teacher' is used very loosely in the English language and this gives rise to a false impression among non-teachers about the work of a professional teacher. In England and Wales (but not in Scotland) it is possible to become a teacher without having any qualifications.

Teachers joke that being alive and reasonably willing are used as major selection criteria. This situation has existed for so long that parents and government do not seem to question it (perhaps parents do not even know). After all, the reasoning seems to go, everyone at some point in their lives will have 'taught' ('taught' is often used where people really mean 'trained') someone new skills – new colleagues how to tackle a job or children how to look after themselves. But 'teaching' at this level is a world away from the job of managing the learning of a group of children of diverse abilities and dealing with the issues of progression and continuity and learning on a day-to-day basis.

The Association for Science Education (1991) carried out a detailed analysis of the qualifications of science teachers and their information should interest all who are seriously concerned with quality in education. Professional development for under-qualified teachers in England and Wales should be a priority.

'Inspired' teaching provides a spark that starts off a journey of discovery and learning for the child. Those who do not recognize this creative side to teaching are recommended to read Charles Dickens's *Hard Times* and then to ask themselves, are the 3 Rs enough? Is the 'Gradgrind' model of teaching acceptable for their child?

Have headteachers, LEAs and governors in England and Wales colluded with government in allowing short-term needs – to have 'a body' in front of a class – to override the long-term interests of the children? It is too easy to forget that a poor teacher (qualified or unqualified) may remain in the teaching force for forty years. Surely parents have a right to expect the teachers of their children to be adequately qualified as well as to possess the other skills so necessary in teaching, e.g. expert knowledge in how to motivate children, the ability to enthuse children and to communicate the subject to them, boundless energy, good record-keeping skills, good inter-personal skills with adults?

To return to the question: 'But can't anyone teach?', we must be clear about what are the characteristics of good teaching. 'Effective' teaching can be said to be that which enables students to go beyond the limits of the teacher's learning into a future their skills and abilities will define. Students can of course be drilled so that they can jump mental hurdles for short-term gain, e.g. in examinations. Useful though the National Curriculum is as a framework, there is a possibility that it will encourage such 'drilling' and impose a commonality of experience that denies individualism.

There may have been a time when education was simply about the acquisition of knowledge and skills. However, the rate of development in society now is such that problem-solving – the ability to apply existing knowledge and skills to new situations – is a crucial part of every individual's education. Those being educated need to know how to continue to learn and a central aspect of education for the twenty-first century is about enabling young people to become effective learners for the rest of their lives. Adult learning is as much an issue as children's learning.

Teachers are only too painfully aware of the complexity of the learning process and are thus understandably cautious about unnecessarily restrictive assessments. One headteacher speaks of her son who couldn't read at 7 yet who gained a First from Oxford. National Curriculum assessment would have placed him in a category well below average in English for his age – yet of what relevance was this to his later achievement? Other adults, when pressed, speak bitterly of their failure of the 11-plus – yet these same people have achieved highly in academic fields as adults. Some might say the failure spurred them on but, for those who were spurred on, how many lost belief in themselves?

The complexity of the learning process needs to be understood by legis-lators who are making decisions about the education system. Much is still to be learned about the way people learn effectively and the way in which the brain organizes and utilizes information. Thankfully, each person is different but this means that the effective teacher must use a range of strategies in order to maximize the learning of each individual. Unfortunately, the view that there has to be one right way of doing things pervades teaching as it pervades much of human activity, and intolerance of others' views about approaches to learning is usually a feature of those who fail to understand this complexity of the learning process.

The wide variety of ways in which children learn to read provides just one example of the range of the different approaches teachers need to be able to utilize. Table 1.2 provides an amusing but thought-provoking comment on the range of strategies people use in reading. The letter was written to *The Times Educational Supplement* at a time when a debate about the use of real books versus reading schemes was raging. This debate was stoked by comments made by Kenneth Clark (Secretary of State for Education) and Martin Turner (an education psychologist who produced evidence of falling reading standards) early in 1991 – the first year of national testing of 7-year-olds in the UK. Incidentally, the use in the national tests of 'real books' caused some consternation among those who stuck rigidly to reading schemes in the early years.

Table 1.2   Rxxl bxxks dxbxtx xs pxxntlxss

Whxn wxll thx rxxl bxxks xrgxxmxnt xnd? Sxrxly xt mxst bx clxxr thxt chxldrxn usx a vxrxxty xf strxtxgxxs tx rxxd prxnt xnd thxt xn xndxrstxndxng xf thx rxlxtxxnshxp bxtwxxn lxttxrs xnd sxxnd xs xnly xne xf thx strxtxgxxs.

It muts be fairyl obvoius to aynone raeding thsi lettre that raedres draw on thier konwledeg of how lagnuaeg wroks, thier abitily to recgonise wrods on sihgt and theri capacity to ues contextaul cleus to enabel them to maek senes of what has goen befoer and perdict what is cmoing next.

If Kenne— Cl— and Ma— Tu— can re— th— let— they mu— agr— tha— a mix— appro— is nec—. If th— ar— no— abl— to re— thi— let— the— mu— be stu— or cra—.

(Reprinted with the permission of Peter Donnelly, English advisory teacher. The original appeared in *The Times Educational Supplement,* 29 March 1991.)

The work in developing sound approaches to educational evaluation and action research which has been carried out over the last twenty years provides tools for teachers, their appraisers and inspectors to use in coming to a shared understanding and agreement about the quality of teaching and learning taking place in a classroom. It is time these tools became part of the professional equipment of every teacher. A fifth issue, then, is: How can the teaching and learning process best be supported and developed so that quality is improved?

Whilst legislation may be used to change the structures and organization of the education system, these five fundamental issues provide the foundations on which the legislation builds the system. If the foundations are shallow, the structure will be shaky.

Some definitions

In this book, a distinction is made between *the education system, the education service* and *educational provision*. The term 'the education system' is used to refer to the organizational structures of education through which responsibilities are delegated. The 'system' consists of schools, local education authorities (LEAs) and the Department of Education and Science (DES), which is responsible to the Secretary of State for Education. The term is also used to include national systems of assessment/appraisal/ inspection for students, schools and teachers. The National Curriculum is seen as part of the 'system' providing a framework within which teachers teach and young people learn. An examination of the history of the education system and an analysis of the 'current state' of components of the system is the focus of Parts II and IV of this book.

The term 'the education service' is used to describe the way education is provided (in other words, 'the work done') by those employed in education. The processes and procedures which guide their work within the education system and the contribution of these processes and procedures to the improvement of quality are the focus of Part III.

The term 'educational provision' is used to describe the educational experience provided for the individual by the education system and by society. It includes the 'overt curriculum' of the school – the content taught – and the 'covert curriculum' which includes extra-curricular activities, as well as what is learned from the ethos of the school and the values it is seen in practice to support. The overt and covert curriculum provided by the media and by society is part of this provision as it is influential in influencing the quality of the education received by young people. Educational provision is referred to in general terms throughout the book but the detail and the debate about what should be taught is left for others to pursue.

Defining Quality

Conclusion

How can agreement be reached on what education should be provided? Legislation is often focused on changing the system in order to effect change in either the education service or in educational provision. But the effectiveness of the legislative approach to change is questionable – areas essential to successful change are usually neglected, such as the motivation of those implementing the changes, consultation about change and the provision of training to support change.

In this book we make the case for improvement in the quality of education to be reached through collaboration between the interested parties at each level of the service. It may be that the best way to do this is via a national representative body which would take education out of the political arena – where the focus is inevitably on short-term goals – into a forum where goals can be thoroughly debated and consensus can be reached.

Change is normal

In the search for improved quality over the last decade, legislation has been passed that has swept schools into a whirlpool of change in which good and bad practice have been sucked in without discrimination. The pace and demands for these changes have lowered morale and deskilled teachers. Poorly handled changes have led to disillusionment, good ideas have not been able to be turned into practice or have been jettisoned long before it was reasonable to assess their value. Much of this upheaval could have been avoided if what is known already about managing change had been taken into account.

The desire for improvement should be seen as normal. As attitudes, goals and knowledge in society change, so too is the education system required to adapt. Raymond Williams (1961, p. x) puts this desire for continuous change and reassessment of what is being done in context:

> We are living through a long revolution . . . It is a genuine revolution, transforming men and institutions; continually extended and deepened by the actions of millions, continually and variously opposed by explicit reaction and by the pressure of habitual forms and ideas. Yet it is a difficult revolution to define and its uneven action is taking place over so long a period that it is almost impossible not to get lost in its exceptionally complicated process.

We are still undergoing this revolution: change is part of living – the desire to improve and change is part of human nature. Our aim throughout this book is to contribute to a debate about the ways in which the improvement of the quality of education can be achieved.

Issues for consideration

1. What do you and your colleagues consider to be the hallmarks of a high-quality education system? To what extent are you achieving these in your school? What should be improved?
2. Is there a case for establishing an *independent* but *representative* national body which has the responsibility for developing consensus and, from that, a long-term vision for education?

Further reading

DES (1985) *White Paper: Better Schools* (Cmnd 9469) HMSO, London.
Fullan, M. (1991) *The New Meaning of Educational Change*, Cassell, London.
HMI (1977) *Ten Good Schools: A Secondary School Enquiry*, DES/HMSO, London.
ILEA (1984) *Improving Secondary Schools* (the Hargreaves Report).
Peters, J.S. (1977) *Education and the Education of Teachers*, Routledge & Kegan Paul, London.
Reynolds, D. (ed.) (1985) *Studying School Effectiveness*, Falmer Press, Lewes.
Rutter, M., Maughan, B., Mortimore, P. and Ouston, J. (1979) *Fifteen Thousand Hours*, Open Books, London.
Warnock, M. (1988) *A Common Policy for Education*, Oxford University Press.

2
THE CURRENT CONTEXT

Introduction

In 1991 both major parties in the UK (Labour and Conservatives) issued statements about how they intended to improve quality in education. The Labour plan for an 'Education Standards Commission' was based on the assumption that quality in the education service is improved by making the methods of accountability more rigorous – particularly through inspection (Straw, 1991, p. 1). The Conservative view, expressed through the Citizen's Charter, similarly placed reliance on external methods of accountability for improving quality. The purpose of the charter (Conservative Central Office, undated, p. 3) was defined as being to

- raise the *standard* of public service;
- increase the *choice* available to every citizen;
- *open up* public services to public scrutiny and accountability; and
- improve *value for money* in the public services.

Both pronouncements assume there is a direct relationship between external methods of accountability and quality. The assumption is that if the curriculum is prescribed (through a national curriculum) and the accountability measures are tightly prescribed then high quality will automatically follow.

This approach ignores key variables which must be present for high-quality outcomes to be produced – in particular, the energy of the teachers (which comes from their skills and knowledge, level of motivation, goodwill and self-esteem) together with the energy of young people which stems from their motivation, enthusiasm and belief in the value of education (Figure 2.1). If this energy input is low when change is introduced then much of the effort and money put into changing education will be wasted and improvements in quality will be elusive.

Standards – choice – accountability – value for money: these issues are at

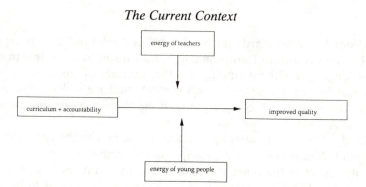

Figure 2.1 Energy inputs and high-quality outcomes

the forefront in the drive for change as the education system enters the 1990s, and the whole of the system and service is affected – schools, LEAs, parents, teachers, governors. So what do these ideas mean in practice?

The rest of this chapter is devoted to a discussion of these four areas, followed by an analysis of the role of the LEA which is being reviewed in the light of the drive for standards, choice, accountability and value for money – a review by politicians.

Standards

Standards are of central concern to teachers, students, parents and govern-ment alike and always will be. But there is uncertainty about how higher standards are to be achieved and indeed what constitutes a high standard.

How do other countries define high standards? Take Italy for example: 'The results of final secondary school exams in Italy show the town which recorded the *worst* results was Turin, where only 94 per cent passed. The south did better: in Palermo 99 per cent got through' (*Guardian*, 26 July 1991, p. 22). What do these results say about Italian standards? Did you feel that standards are too low because most young people were able to achieve the required level? Why, in England and Wales, do the majority of students not reach the standard of A-level? Is it because the examinations are set at too high a level for young people at that stage of their learning or because young people in England and Wales are not at similar levels in their learning in comparison with young people abroad? This question must be urgently addressed.

There is pressure to improve staying-on rates, but if failure is the likely outcome for most at A-level there is little to motivate young people to stay on. The status of this narrow specialist examination at 18 must be seriously questioned. The standard may be high but is it relevant? For example, as the UK moves toward European union, students need to be able to speak other languages without closing off other avenues of study. In Scotland, Eire and France, for instance, each student studies a wider range of subjects (five or more) in comparison with the three subjects most students study at A-level.

Handy (1984, p. 41) sums up a central problem with the system in England and Wales: 'The elitist principle is still embedded in many school systems, elitist in the sense that success has to be rationed to be seen as meaningful. The idea that everyone can succeed is thought to be tantamount to a reduction of standards.' A serious omission from the rhetoric about standards is the consideration of what motivates young people to learn.

In the drive for higher standards, social deprivation is ignored, yet the link between lower attainment in reading and an impoverished home background has been too strongly established to be easily dismissed. The work of Buckinghamshire educational psychologist, Mike Lake (1991), sheds light on the links between achievement and social circumstances. Action to improve standards for these children requires the co-ordination of effort across different public services and is currently an LEA responsibility. If LEAs were abolished, as has been mooted, it is hard to see who would take responsibility for these children. Individual schools are unlikely to shoulder the responsibility – the costs in staff time are better spent with a class, nor is such a local role appropriate to the DES, based as it is in London.

League tables and achievement

The publication of league tables of raw examination results for schools will, it is proposed, lead to higher standards. Yet experience with league tables for colleges within the University of Oxford runs counter to this supposition.

At the same time as legislation is being introduced to ensure schools provide results for use in league tables, the colleges of Oxford University are doing away with the league table of college undergraduate results. This league table – the 'Norrington' table – has been published by newspapers since 1963. Lecturers at Oxford found that the teaching of post-graduates (who don't feature on the table) and research was adversely affected as energies were diverted to undergraduate work. There was also the feeling that interesting but potentially risky candidates for undergraduate places (who might get a brilliant 'First' but also might get a 'Third') were being discriminated against in favour of 'safer' candidates.

Students themselves complained of being 'rusticated' (not allowed to take their exams) because tutors felt their examination results might not bring credit to the college (Unsworth, 1989; *Oxford Magazine*, 1991). Merton College don, D. J. Markwell, argued in a letter to *The Daily Telegraph* (5 June 1991) that league tables damage standards:

> the table's increasing prominence has led to excessive and unhealthy competition, and has made it the enemy of high educational standards in Oxford. The table is also misleading. Perversely, a college's Norrington ranking would be better if a student fails to get a degree (or fails to sit finals) than if he or she gets a poor degree.

This issue of the publication of 'league tables' provides another example of the failure of those introducing change in education to base such change on an understanding of past experience.

Another problem with league tables is that research shows that teacher performance varies from year to year (Reynolds, 1988), and the difficulty of measuring and comparing success is that the full potential of each individual student is unknown and in any case is affected by many things outside the teacher's control.

The work on contextualizing examination results through multi-level modelling (Nuttall, 1991) is worth consideration if meaningful information about the performance of schools is to be provided. With short-term superficial solutions (such as those on league tables) being proposed to solve what are complex problems, the achieving of higher standards is likely to be random and unsustained.

Choice

What does choice really mean to parents and students? Grant-maintained schools are said to be the 'jewel in the crown of parent power' (Conservative Research Department, 1991, p. 3) and City Technology Colleges (CTCs) are claimed to 'improve the opportunities for children in inner city areas' (*ibid.*, p. 5), yet the reality is apparently the opposite. According to reports in *The Times Educational Supplement* of 31 January 1991, grant-maintained schools are doing the choosing. Many pupils and parents in the Conservative-controlled London Borough of Hillingdon, where a large number of secondary schools have opted out, were left with no offer of a secondary-school place whilst others had offers of three or four.

Is not 'free choice' an adolescent illusion? The tension between the free play of market forces and the necessity to plan educational provision has been ignored in recent changes. Parents (in both the public and the maintained sector) know that choice of schools is a hollow notion – schools do not have infinite space – when they are full they turn students away.

In any case, 'choice' is often restricted by location, mobility, and childcare arrangements. As there is no child for whom less than the best is good enough, all schools must be working towards high standards and be provided with adequate resources. Diverting resources to CTCs a hundred miles away or to grant-maintained schools in the next town simply reduces the resources for other schools in an area.

Accountability and inspection

Accountability means much more than having teams of inspectors checking what is happening. The different forms of accountability (moral, professional and contractual) are not widely recognized yet they have a crucial role in the drive to improve standards. In Chapter 8, these issues are explored in depth.

The lack of understanding of accountability issues in education at national level has resulted in simplistic solutions being proposed. Collusion between professionals is given as the reason for introducing the notion of lay people being inspectors of the professions – in the case of education as HMI. Formal inspection systems rather than professional advice and support systems are seen to provide the route to quality (Audit Commission, 1989).

Yet what model is being offered to replace HMI and local inspectorates? The government seems to be pushing audit firms and *ad hoc* collections of individuals as providing a higher-quality alternative to what exists already. The role of auditors as a model needs careful examination, as the work of Mitchell *et al.* (1991, p. 7) reveals:

> companies such as British and Commonwealth, Coloroll, Parkfield, Sock Shop, Johnson Matthey, Eagle Trust, Leading Leisure, British Island Airways, Corton Beacy, Levitt Group, Sound Diffusion, Polly Peck and others have collapsed within weeks of receiving clean audit reports . . . In each case, the auditors were paid handsomely. Yet the individual investor has no recourse against them. In 1990, the landmark case of *Caparo v Dickman and others* revealed that the auditors do not owe a duty of care to members of the public who rely on the accounts in deciding to buy shares.

There is also a secrecy about investigations into the affairs of companies which is unacceptable in education. All HMI reports are published in contrast to the reports of the Department of Trade and Industry investigations, which involve checking the work of audit firms and companies: 'Of the nearly 1,400 company investigations authorized by the Department of

Trade and Industry since 1979 (at vast cost to the nation), the government has only published 18 reports, a secrecy which conceals the true extent of financial manipulations and the way the public might be misled' (*ibid.*) This is hardly a model for improving quality in the education system.

Judging education

There is a dichotomy to be faced in 'judging' education – a teacher may teach to a required standard but not be effective in developing the children's ability to learn. We know of cases where children who were urged by the school to take 13 O-levels were put off learning anything for years after these examinations. Yet in the results league table, the school falls in the top 100 maintained schools in the country. How would a lay inspector have compared this school with one offering 7 or 8 O-levels? What did the parents see? Effective teaching is not as easy to define as it might appear.

The emphasis on formal inspection methods could easily lead us down the path of the now discredited, rigidly inspectorial Australian systems of the 1930s to the 1950s, which Maclaine (undated, pp. 45–6) describes as

> foster[ing] the promotion of the unimaginative and rigidly-formal teacher who was most successful in drilling his pupils in a narrow range of basic subjects. . . . Not only was the method of evaluation faulty, it also conflicted with the growing realization that the school inspector had an important role to play as a professional adviser and educational leader of the teachers coming under his jurisdiction. Yet the requirement of detailed assessments of teachers completely overshadowed the inspector's wider function and, in fact, allowed time for little else. Furthermore, it has been consistently claimed that it inhibited teachers from confiding in the inspector and seeking help with their difficulties. On the contrary, there was the temptation for teachers to 'window-dress' their work, pander to whatever 'fads' the inspector was supposed to have, and cover up their weaknesses. These and other criticisms of the inspectorial system were cogently put forward in the 1930s by the visiting American educators Cramer and Kandel and reiterated some twenty years later by Clegg from the United Kingdom.

How would lay inspectors acquire the ability to recognize effective teaching and effective school management? As with governors, such people could easily end up frustrated and concerned at their inability to do a thorough job. So much of what happens in schools is dependent on the ethos – the unspoken attitudes and responses to situations that the children and staff understand but which are hard to penetrate from the outside.

Anyone who has spent time in a classroom realizes that whilst superficial observations can be made, the detailed examination of the teaching and learning taking place requires careful observation planned in advance, discussions with the teacher and the children, coupled with examination of the children's work and the teacher's plans. The whole context of the school has to be known too. A teacher working with a group of demotivated children may not appear to have achieved the same level of learning with the children as one working with highly motivated children – yet the former teacher may be more effective than the latter.

Decisions about appropriate inspection systems must be based on hard evidence not supposition or guesswork. With reference to the UK, it is worth noting that the HMI system in England and Wales is to be reformed (some say 'privatized') yet the similar approach in Scotland is to be left intact.

Value for money

There is nothing new in current pressures for 'value for money' (VFM) or in a system for 'payment by results' – yet again education policy is revisiting old ground. An ex-Chief HMI, Edmond Holmes, writing in 1911, gives his reflections on the 'payment by results' system after a lifetime of support for it. He speaks of 'that deadly system of "payment by results" which seems to have been devised for the express purpose of arresting growth and strangling life, which bound us all, myself included, with links of iron, and which had many zealous agents, of whom I, alas! was one' (Holmes, 1911, p. vii). With the gradual reintroduction of payment by results during the eighties and early nineties, one is tempted to ask, will the outcomes be different this time?

The VFM approach reflects the government's belief about how teachers are motivated and this is enshrined in the 1988 Education Act. Wignall (1990, p. 51) puts it thus: 'The "framework" provided by the 1988 Education Act . . . includes the introduction of a "value for money" approach with related concepts of economy, efficiency and effectiveness together with the ability to measure success through the use of performance measures, at different levels within the education sector.'

The delegation of budgets to schools as part of local management of schools (LMS) was seen as a way of ensuring value for money – schools had direct control over expenditure and would therefore spend the money more carefully than had been the case before. But defining value for money is not easy in a service where the output in terms of value gained is not easily measurable. Delegating budgets to schools also meant that centrally run initiatives for minority interests could no longer be funded – the loss of children's creative-writing workshops run by Hertfordshire LEA for gifted children provides just one example, loss of music provision across the country provides another. What has been valuable provision for individual gifted children from different schools has been lost among the host of individual school priorities. LEA science centres too have disappeared. Short-term financial considerations have led to long-term loss of high-quality provision which will be difficult to restore.

The evidence is that schools will often act in the best interests of the whole school where these are at conflict with the interests of the individual. Current policy does not recognize that the interests of the individual child are not necessarily synonymous with the interests of the school. Devolving finances from LEAs to schools has, in some ways, actually restricted the choice for the individual.

Performance measurement was linked to the value-for-money cause but the problems of such measurement in education dogged the VFM initiative. Hopkins and Leask (1989, p. 9) define the difficulties with identifying performance indicators as follows:

- There is lack of clarity . . . about who/what is being measured and for whom.
- Efficiency and effectiveness do not necessarily go together. Indicators for both are required and sensitive interpretation is required.
- There is no simple link between inputs and outputs in education; in any case, methods of measuring inputs and outputs are not well developed.
- At the moment, there is probably no 'bottom line' for use in comparing an institution's effectiveness and efficiency. Thus, the process of building accurate performance indicators will take considerable time, effort and resources.
- The socio-economic context within which an institution operates is difficult to define. If this is made explicit – as is suggested so that assessment results can be put in context – it is 'unlikely to be acceptable or constructive of good relations' (DES, 1988). A suggested alternative is to use data on pupil ability at intake as a baseline but pupil expectation and motivation should not be ignored.
- There are serious problems of interpretation.

The problem with allowing the free play of market forces in education means children's education is irreparably damaged as individual schools are allowed to decline. The bankruptcy of some public schools during the early nineties' recession provided examples of the disruption of children's education when a school ceases to be viable.

Clearly the public have a right to know that the money is being spent wisely, but it would seem that much more work has to be done in education to ensure that such pressures for value for money do not damage the education of the children.

Educating a child to university entrance level in the maintained system costs less than a third of the cost of educating them in many public schools. Is that value for money?

The role of the LEA

What is the role of LEAs? International practice does not support the idea of an education system run solely from the centre without delegation to the regions and this issue of centralization and decentralization is further discussed in Part II.

In the UK, the role of the regional authorities (LEAs) has been undergoing review but the debate on the LEA role has been singularly ill-informed. The focus on financial delegation to schools (the late eighties to the early nineties) obscured any wider view of the work LEAs carry out. In this part, we summarize the role of the LEA as a contribution to the debate on the structure of the education system.

The LEA has a number of functions including the protection of children's interests on behalf of the local community. These functions span six major areas:

1. Representing and meeting individual pupil's interests and needs.
2. Representing the interests of the local community.
3. Policy implementation (national and local).
4. Quality assurance.
5. Development and professional support.
6. Strategic planning.

Representing and meeting individual pupil's interests and needs

The LEA has a duty to meet the interests of individual pupils, for example, through organizing primary/secondary transfer, appeals and exclusions, and providing resources for statemented children. The LEA is also responsible for the educational provision for those children who are not in the traditional stable family environment and who require support from the range of services provided through local councils: housing and social services as well as education.

These services currently liaise at the local level on individual cases. Often such children (who may include immigrants and refugees) will not be registered with a school. If there is no one to take responsibility locally, who will look after their interests? An apparent side-effect of LMS is that the number of exclusions of children from schools has risen leaving LEAs to find school places for these children but with the original school retaining the funding for that pupil for the remainder of the financial year (Merrick and Manuel, 1991).

That much of this work of the LEA is hidden from view has caused particular financial problems for LEAs as opted-out schools have to be given, by law, funds for services they are not required or are not able to provide. The case of the educational welfare officer (EWO) provides one example. Whilst schools could certainly buy in the EWO to follow up pupils registered with them, who is going to pay the EWO to follow up those children not registered with any school? And should a school with a higher proportion of pupils who resist attending school have less to spend on books and so on because it has to spend more money trying to get children to school? Similar absurd cases apply to special educational needs provision including the costs of educational psychologists, the cost of statementing children, and the provision required for travellers' children and other special cases.

Representing the interests of the local community

One aspect of the role of the LEA is to bring together the views of the community – expressed through elected council members and community groups – and the views of educational professionals (in the LEA education department) in order to plan appropriate educational provision for children in the area. The LEA has a duty to ensure that sufficient places are available and thus must have the power to make decisions about closing schools and building new schools. The removal of some of these decisions to national level has occurred to some extent already as schools 'opt out' to avoid a local rationalization of provision. However, there will be times when rationalization will not be avoidable. If at this point there is no regional level of decision-making, such decisions would have to be made at national level, yet local knowledge is required if the decisions made are the best in the circumstances.

Policy implementation

LEAs receive grants targeted on the implementation of particular government policies: GEST, WRNAFE, TVEI, National Curriculum assessment and so on. This resource targeting requires the LEA to ensure that national policy is implemented. In the maintained sector, this aspect of LEA work is not a service to be bought in on an optional basis; those receiving the money have a 'duty' to make appropriate provision. However, it appears that when grant-maintained schools have received their share of this money, they have not been required to implement national policy as a condition of receipt. Even more absurd is the case in Avon where a grant-maintained school had to be given a share of Section 11 funding although it had no children who qualified for help from this funding!

A flaw in current thinking is the assumption that, by about 1995, the education system will be perfect and there will be no more government policy to implement – hence the infrastructure supporting implementation of policy can be disbanded. However, it may be worth looking at experience elsewhere before deciding all the problems will have been solved by the National Curriculum and assessment arrangements, the abolition of the LEAs and the restructuring of the inspection service.

Whilst at the moment there is a nationally determined curriculum, the evidence is that other countries which have gone down that route have found it a 'blind alley' and reverted within a short time to regionally determined curricula. The French about-turn in the spring of 1991 is not the only example: no longer will all French children be doing the same thing at the same time. If unnecessary waste is to be avoided, those taking decisions need to be very sure that regional authorities are not required before charging ahead with abolition.

The changes the twenty-first century will bring to education are largely unknown. What is known is that structures will be required that enable change to be managed and challenges to be met as they occur. There will never be a point where it can be said there will be no more national priorities for change in education. Disbanding structures currently used for the implementation of policy could cause serious problems in the future.

Quality assurance

The 1988 Act brought changes to the governance of schools. The widening of powers of locally appointed governors was seen as ensuring that the school reflected the needs and concerns of the community. In addition, the governors have a duty to ensure that the National Curriculum is delivered in their schools. But what do these changes really mean in practice? Lay people are not in a position to make professional judgments about educational practice and nor should they be expected to.

The LEA currently has a duty to inspect non-opted-out schools to 'ensure the curriculum' (in the words of the 1988 Act), but grant-maintained schools and CTCs are under no such locally accountable scrutiny. Indeed, they are given the money which previously was used to fund their LEA inspections. The HMI inspections they, CTCs and public schools receive are funded out of central government funds. This is another anomaly. If inspections are deemed to be necessary then all schools (and thus children) should have similar entitlements.

Development and professional support

In 1978 the DES and the Advisory Committee on the Supply and Training of Teachers (ACSTT) noted in their booklet, *Making INSET Work: In-Service Education and Training for Teachers: A Basis for Discussion*, that 'INSET is currently at take-off point in this country' (1978c, p. 6). They made the case for an annual target of 3% release of teachers for INSET and for teachers to have an entitlement to regular sabbaticals.

By 1991, the level of INSET provision was in a nose-dive. Resources were drastically cut through GEST. Opportunities for professional development were being lost in some areas as the fragmentation of LEA INSET budgets to school level meant that the sums involved are too small to buy meaningful INSET. The notion that there can be economies of (large) scale was forgotten in the desire to delegate spending.

Many LEAs spent some time developing sophisticated systems of 'needs analysis' in order to provide services targeted on the profession's requirements and linked with plans for development both at school and LEA level. Yet there is no evidence of such good practice being followed through the production of a National Development Plan for INSET.

Shadowing a pupil for a day gives an insight into how a school functions, and the Secretary of State for Education and his colleagues may well find such an exercise carried out at LEA level illuminating. However, what they won't so easily discover on a day's visit is the learning environment created for teachers by the LEA.

We argue that it is in a collaborative supportive environment that teachers are enabled both individually and collectively to take on new challenges. If it is accepted that collaboration provides support for learning and that isolation inhibits learning, then the necessity for teachers from different disciplines to be able to meet and work with colleagues from other institutions must follow. This facilitating role is an important aspect of work at LEA level.

Will INSET training no longer be necessary?

Can it be assumed that teachers will know all that is necessary to know for their whole professional life by the end of their training? Even if this was possible, the variety of routes into teaching makes any notion of homogeneous teacher training inconceivable. The assumption that the articled, licensed and possibly non-B.Ed. teachers of the future will require less INSET is optimistic to say the least.

The altruism of LEAs in providing opportunities for teachers to undertake research and development work leading to higher degrees is unlikely to be matched by governors who naturally are particularly concerned with one school and who, in any case, will not have sufficient resources to provide such opportunities. In the past, these teachers have often moved on, taking their new-found expertise to other LEAs or into institutions of higher education. It is likely that a whole area of the research and development arm of the education service will disappear.

Will groups of trainers able to provide appropriate training wait in the wings for their cue? In any case, who will train them and how will they keep up to date?

Oddly enough, at the same time that training structures in education are under threat, employers were offered tax incentives in the 1991–2 national Budget to induce them to recognize the value of training.

Strategic planning

LEAs have a duty to ensure there is appropriate and sufficient provision for the education of members of the local community – schools are opened, closed and reorganized on the basis of local need. Strategic planning is a key LEA role and it is questionable whether this function can be satisfactorily carried out centrally.

Conclusion

Realizing assets

The government is turning the capital invested in resourcing the LEAs into cash for the short-term gain of providing immediate funds for schools. But the 'capital' in an LEA resides in the intellectual capabilities and potential of the staff built up over time. Removing the staff from the LEA frees this 'capital' investment so that the money saved can be diverted as revenue for schools. This is a short-sighted measure with long-term consequences.

Unfortunately, this attitude is the reverse of that of our Victorian predecessors who turned their revenue into capital – investing in institutions which could develop the wealth of the nation further. Will this asset-stripping of LEAs, which are currently charged with providing for the nation's future through overseeing the education of our children, improve the quality of education children receive?

The focus on short-term planning is leading to a volatile situation. The system is being overloaded with change, and U-turns of policy (e.g. over

GCSE, curriculum and assessment issues, funding provision) are a regular occurrence. Stability is urgently needed.

Who will pick up the pieces?

Abolishing LEAs will not, of course, abolish any of the functions they now carry out except the requirement to have local curriculum policies. Someone will have to fill the gaps. It's hard to see what other structure would suit. The 26,000 schools can hardly be managed from one centre (the DES).

Clearly provision would have to be reasonably local – the thought of writing to the DES in London to appeal against Johnny not getting a place at Joyce Bloggs Secondary seems somewhat inappropriate. Similarly, despatching an educational psychologist and an educational welfare officer from London to follow up Johnny's problems smacks of inefficiency, lack of economy and ineffectiveness. Local problems are best solved by those with a knowledge of the local context. Nor will governors fill the gap left by education professionals and elected members. Many of them find their duties onerous enough already (Deem and Brehony, 1990).

To some extent the debate about the future of LEAs has stemmed from the necessity to find political solutions to problems linked with the 'community charge' and underfunding.

If indeed LEAs are abolished, there will still be a need for a department to deal with local issues – i.e. a local education authority by another name but this department will be run directly from the DES in London and not be, as are LEAs, publicly and locally accountable. The central management by the DES of grant-maintained schools provides the model. Brighouse (1991, p. 12) notes this loss of local democracy as 'probably the greatest issue affecting the health of our democracy today'.

Part II provides an abbreviated history of educational change in England and Wales so that the reader unfamiliar with this history can place current developments in education in the context of what has gone before.

Issues for consideration

1. What is the appropriate forum for bringing together professional and political views on change in education?
2. To what extent does a focus on the issues of standards, choice, accountability and value for money provide a useful framework for improving the quality of education?
3. What is the most appropriate structure for the education system in the UK? What should be the responsibilities of each level?

Further reading

Audit Commission (1989) *Assuring Quality in Education: The Role of Local Education Authority Inspectors and Advisers*, HMSO, London.

Brighouse, T. (1991) The uncertain future of local education authorities, *Local Government Policy Making,* Vol. 18, no. 1, July.

Conservative Central Office (undated) *Local Government Brief No. 38: Citizen's Charter*, London.

Conservative Research Department (1991) *The Priorities, Structure and Content of Education*, London, 30 April.

Sallis, J. (1988) *Schools, Parents and Governors: A New Approach to Accountability*, Routledge, London.

Straw, J. (1991) Raising the standard: Labour's plan for an Education Standards Commission (Labour Party press release), London, 25 June.

PART II
LESSONS FROM HISTORY

3
A HISTORY OF CHANGE

Introduction

'The past decade has been a period of unparalleled change in almost every aspect of education!' But which decade? The reader of today could be forgiven for thinking the quotation referred to the eighties or the period going into the nineties, yet it was actually written in 1976 – referring to the period of the mid-sixties to the mid-seventies (Advisory Committee on the Supply and Training of Teachers, 1976, p. 2).

Change is normal. The urge to change and develop is part of the human condition. In order to improve, change has to happen but change on its own does not guarantee improvement. This truism places a duty on those who would bring about change. Changes will improve quality where they are built on an understanding of what has gone before. Education in the 1990s has become a 'hot' political issue but there is a danger that the search for political solutions may focus attention on short-term solutions to what are long-term problems – the requirement for education to adjust continually and to adapt to the demands of an unknown future.

While 'chaos' may enable business to thrive (Peters, 1988), it is less than certain that such management theories apply to education. Perhaps because the teaching and learning process requires some continuity and stability if high quality is to be achieved, there is an expectation that change in education should be coherently planned.

In this chapter we look back over more than fifty years to identify the major events forming education as it is now in England and Wales. Where appropriate, this review encompasses Scotland, Northern Ireland and other countries both in Europe and in the rest of the world. In Part IV, the key components affecting the functioning of the education system are identified and the knowledge of what has gone before is applied in an attempt to identify the future path of development of the education system in England

and Wales. The aim is to draw out lessons which could guide future development. *By learning from accumulated experience, a much sounder education system can be built, which will get closer to meeting the needs of young people as the twenty-first century approaches.*

One of the values of examining the development of the education service lies in the identification of underlying trends and broad goals. Set in this context, the particular events of the eighties and early nineties can be seen in perspective. For example, increasing the age range for education and training has been a recurring concern. In the UK, the system has moved from an 'average duration of school attendance in 1835 of one year' (Williams, 1961, p. 137) to twelve years (plus nursery education) by 1972 – and the pressure to increase this is growing. Such changes reflect the growing technical complexity of society's requirements.

It seems that in recent decades at least, there have been two major pressures for change operating symbiotically. First comes the pressure for improvements in education to meet higher aspirations. It comes in periods of intense activity and sets out new aims, goals and curriculum requirements. These then create a pressure for change which in its turn gives rise to various attempts at managing change which involve considerable amounts of curriculum development and in-service training.

This work leads to increased understanding of the change process which has to be improved so that the new and complex demands placed upon the service can be accommodated. At such times, a wider perspective has to be retained which encompasses all the changes in order to retain coherence in the service.

Many sound innovations up until now have been limited in their implementation because the nature of the change process has not been well understood. Attention has been focused on individual components of the system (e.g. the curriculum) and other complementary components, such as INSET or management processes, have not been developed in conjunction.

It is time for those with the power to influence education to step back and reflect on the achievements to date and to recognize that the development of the service – its expansion and improvement – is a very long-term and continuing process which must be viewed holistically. For any change at a national level to bring about real improvement there needs to be, among those involved,

- broad agreement on the principles underlying a high-quality education service; and
- increased understanding of the processes governing the effective management of change.

Table 3.1 Legislation and major reports

Date	Title	Principal concerns
1859	Newcastle Commission	Elementary education
1870	Education Act	Local-elected school boards made responsible for elementary education
1888	Cross Commission	Elementary education (paved the way for payment by results)
1902	Education Act	Set up LEAs and assisted places
1918	Education Act	Role of central and local government, encouraged nursery provision
1926	Haddow Report	Education of adolescents
1931	Haddow Report	Primary education
1933	Haddow Report	Infant and nursery education
1938	Spens Report	Secondary education
1944	Education Act	Structural changes in the education system
1959–60	Crowther Report	The state of education
1963	Newsom	Education of adolescents of average and less-than-average ability
1963	Robbins Report	Higher education
1965	Circular 10/65	LEAs asked to draw up plans for comprehensive schools
1967	Plowden Report	Primary education
1972	James Report	Teacher education and training
1972	'ROSLA' implementation	Raising of school-leaving age to 16 years
1975	Bullock Report	Language
1977	Munn Report	Curriculum (Scotland)
1977	Taylor Report	Partnership for schools (parent-governors)
1977	Green Paper	*Education in Schools* (Cmnd 6869)
1978	Warnock Report	Special educational needs
1980	Education Act	Assisted places scheme, built on Taylor Report
1981	Education Act	Incorporated recommendations of the Warnock Report; 'statementing' introduced
1982	Cockroft Report	Mathematics
1984	Circular 3/84	Initial teacher training (Council for the Accreditation of Teacher Education (CATE) set up)
1985	Swann Report	Education of children from ethnic minority groups
1986	Education (No. 2) Act	Composition of governing bodies, teacher appraisal
1988	Higginson Report	A-levels
1988	Education Reform Act	A national curriculum, 'local management of schools'
1989	Elton Report	Discipline
1991	White Paper	Further and higher education
1991		Royal Commission on Education chaired by Sir John Cassell
1991	Schools Bill	Inspection of schools, the role of the LEA

Note
Many reports on specific aspects of the curriculum are produced and the findings absorbed into school practice. These have included HMI reports, Assessment of Performance Unit reports, the findings of House of Commons committees, Audit Commission reports, plus reports of committees set up by LEAs, e.g. the Hargreaves Report (ILEA, 1984).

One of the aims of this book is to contribute to a debate about these issues.

Legislation, major reports and significant events

This backward glance is, of necessity, selective. Key events are highlighted to help in the identification of significant trends or concerns.

A glance at the list of reports of major committees set up by the DES and its predecessor and the legislation which has been passed (Table 3.1) shows the continuing concern that governments have about education. It is perhaps a healthy sign that the same concerns regularly come up for review – curriculum and assessment, the age range taught, structures and governance, the training of teachers. It suggests the education system, service and provision is being continually reviewed and adjusted to the ever-changing circumstances and demands of society. Such reports and legislation punctuate a process of continuous examination of education and they set a new direction – but one which has to be reset continually as society changes.

The debate about the raising of the school-leaving age to 16 provides an example of a society reaching agreement. The Spens Report noted, in 1938, that raising the leaving age to 16 was inevitable. Twenty years later, in 1959, the Crowther Report recommended raising the school-leaving age to 16. This recommendation was repeated in the Newsom Report in 1963. The decision to raise the leaving age was made in 1964 but the formal announcement that it would happen was not made until 1968. The decision to raise the school-leaving age was finally implemented with effect from September 1972 (more than thirty years after the Spens Report). The impact of the decision was to create pressure for more change, e.g. towards a common examining system at 16-plus. In a similar way, the 1944 Education Act was also the product of a long period of debate.

But legislation and reports have no effect on their own. They can only have impact if they are associated with an effective change process. 'Brute sanity' doesn't bring about change.

In the past, reports often had little impact because the processes for translating reports into action in the classroom were poorly developed – particularly in England and Wales, less so in Scotland. There was little understanding that implementation strategies had to be planned to ensure that change happened. People's expectations were often too high and effective development was prevented where different components of the education system were not working together. For instance, the Schools Council (1964–84) produced much excellent curriculum development but

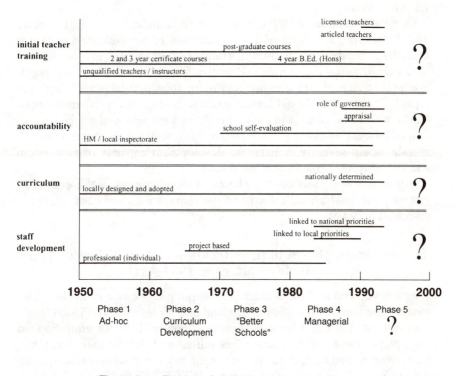

Figure 3.1   Phases of development in education

the structures for implementing curriculum change were weak and the impact of the council's work was muted.

The implementation of the Education Acts of the late 1980s was possibly the first time that an implementation strategy had been linked to legislation – money was set aside to train teachers and to evaluate what was happening. LEAs played a key role in enabling the implementation of government policy though politically this role was denied.

In some respects, this legislation marked a step forward for education but much of the change was focused on certain components: for example, inspection, mangement and the content of the curriculum. As Figure 3.1 indicates, by the late eighties, nearly all the main components of the education system were being actively developed. This offered the opportunity for a coherent approach to the development of the whole system, which was not seized. Within a short time, crucial components in a quality system, such as professional development and school-focused staff development, were in decline.

One vital component of the system which is difficult to chart is morale and motivation. The level of quality achieved in the education system is crucially dependent on relationships between the teachers and the children in the classroom – the morale and motivation of both teachers and pupils probably affects the change process more than any legislation and any report. Teacher morale did appear to drop as the confrontations between teachers and government in the mid-eighties were followed by the imposition of far-reaching change with extremely tight deadlines. Such a drop of morale would severely damage the development capacity of any system and the education system is no exception.

In the following section the phases of development in the education system since 1944 are described and the characteristics of each phase are discussed in detail.

Development phases in the education system in England and Wales – after the 1944 Act

There have been several distinct but overlapping phases in the development of the education system in England and Wales since the 1944 Education Act but there has been no overall conscious plan for education. In each phase, the focus for change has shifted and development has taken place in an almost *ad hoc* way in each of the key components of the system, e.g. curriculum, resources, management, INSET, ITT and so on. Figure 3.1 illustrates the ebb and flow of this development.

There is also a shifting of various powers from central government to regional bodies or schools and back again. LEAs have been an integral part of the structure of the education system since 1902 and, given the size of the system and the responsibilities of LEAs, it is hard to imagine a shift back to total central control if, for example, all schools become grant-maintained.

In this section, attention is drawn to the lessons that could be learned from each phase of this earlier work. Four major phases in the education system since 1944 are identified and these have been dated roughly according to times at which they reached maximum impact in schools. There is some overlap of one phase with the next as the seeds of new ways of working are germinating at the same time as seeds from an earlier approach are still being dispersed to the furthermost corners of the service. Thus the influence of developmental work tends to taper off rather than to end abruptly.

The major phases marking change in the education system in England and Wales are as follows:

Phase 1: the *ad hoc* phase (the mid-forties to the mid-sixties).
Phase 2: the curriculum development and diffusion phase (the mid-sixties to the mid-seventies).
Phase 3: the 'better schools' phase (the mid-seventies to the mid-eighties).
Phase 4: the managerial phase (the mid-eighties to the early nineties).
Phase 5: will this be the 'holistic phase'?

Phase 1: the *ad hoc* phase

For about twenty years after the reorganization of education which followed the 1944 Education Act, change was slow judged by today's standards. There was little curriculum development and what development there was was focused on the professional development of the individual teacher. Improving the quality of the teaching force was seen as the way to improving quality in educational provision.

According to McBride (1989, p. 177) INSET was available to teachers during the fifties with LEAs as the main providers of short courses. Many members of the teaching force had undergone shortened and intensive programmes of teacher training after the war and the LEA short courses were a means of improving this training. Professional development, in the form of long-term secondments, was also available. McBride identifies 1955 as the date when the 'pooling system' started. This was the first major national initiative to direct substantial resources to the development of the service through the development of teachers.

'Pooling' allowed the cost of long-term secondments to be shared between LEAs and the DES – a situation that was changed in 1983 when the DES was no longer prepared to fund such courses without any say over what they were for (Goddard, 1989a). While it was in operation, the pooling system provided substantial resources to support the professional development of the individual teacher and many of those in education today who have higher degrees owe these to secondments paid through the pooling system. Such secondments enriched the store of knowledge and understanding in the education system as a whole rather than developing the work of any particular school. So whilst secondments certainly supported individuals, this was not an approach that could support coherent change in education as a whole or even probably in most individual schools.

A lack of systematic planning

There appears to have been little systematic planning for the development of the education service or widespread recognition of the necessity for developing a whole-system and whole-school approach to managing the changes. Curriculum development and professional development were not co-ordinated. University lecturers, research students and HMI carried out much of the developmental work but there was no identifiable overall strategy or vision. There was, however, considerable concern about the future of education. The Ministry of Education (now the DES) commissioned a report on the state of education – which became known as the Crowther Report (1959, 1960). Among other points, the report (1959, Vol. 1, p. 473) called for a national plan for education: 'We plead then for a forward plan for education. . . . Education after all, should be peculiarly susceptible to forward planning.' This plea went unheard.

In the USA at this time, there was also concern about the quality of education, and the objectives-based curriculum model (which included regular testing of children) was gaining acceptance (McCormick and James, 1988).

This approach was to influence developments in the UK. The next phase was marked by a shift in emphasis from teacher development to curriculum development based on identifiable objectives. Research has revealed that for some teachers this period was a turning point in their careers – they had not been aware of any INSET or professional development opportunities being available before the early sixties but the curriculum development of the sixties started them thinking about and questioning the curriculum.

Phase 2: the curriculum development and diffusion phase

This period, from the mid-sixties to the mid-seventies, was characterized by an expansion in the resources available for education together with a strong emphasis on centralized curriculum development.

The rivalry of the space age sparked off this period of increased resource provision for education both in the USA and in Britain. Thus the pressure for technological development created a pressure for curriculum reform. Becher (1984) identifies this period as the beginning of systematic curriculum development in the UK.

The Newsom Report, *Half our Future* (1963), had highlighted shortcomings in the education of 13–16-year-olds and the Schools Council for Curriculum and Examinations was set up in 1964 in an attempt to improve this situation. (In Scotland, the Scottish Consultative Committee on the Curriculum was established.) Up until this point, there had not been a national body with specific responsibility to oversee the curriculum although the Secondary Schools Examination Council had been set up in 1917. The Schools Council notionally brought both functions together although only for twenty years. Curriculum and examinations responsibilities were separated again in 1983–4 with the formation of the Schools Curriculum Development Committee (SCDC) and the Secondary Examinations Council. Both of these organizations were replaced as a result of the 1988 Act which brought the National Curriculum Council (NCC) and the Schools Examination and Assessment Council (SEAC) into being.

The decision to raise the school-leaving age to 16 meant that the curriculum had to be reviewed to ensure that the education provided was relevant. The vast increase in the population as a result of the post-war baby boom also brought pressures for reform. The Robbins Report (1963) paved the way for unprecedented expansion in higher education in a response to the demands society was now placing on education. The ideal of comprehensive schooling was formalized with DES Circular 10/65 requesting LEAs to submit their plans for the provision of comprehensive education. All of these initiatives provided pressure for change and development.

To some extent, the curriculum development materials produced at this time were intended to be 'teacher-proof' in the expectation that this would achieve the desired goals.

There was also a concern for checking standards and the Assessment of Performance Unit (APU) was set up during this period with the aim of using an objectives model to measure pupil performance in different areas of the curriculum (McCormick and James, 1988).

Piecemeal change

The model used for developing the curriculum (known as the Research Development and Diffusion Model or the Centre–Periphery Model) was based on a misconceived model of how change happened in institutions. There was an assumption that if the product was right, then change was automatic. The model was based on the premiss that the curriculum was the key to improvement rather than the school or the teacher. The central role of the school in the change process was not recognized.

Materials were developed by central teams who then trained the teachers. Colleagues teaching at this time still recall their disappointment that, when they returned to school, they often found they were unable to implement change. Other teachers didn't expect to have to change their practice because someone had 'been on a course'. The necessary attitudes and methods of working within the school that would ensure change happened were missing.

Hence whilst sound curriculum development work went on, implementation was non-existent or short lived. Resistance to change is, of course, still found today with some teachers and in some schools but the planning of INSET based on a 'needs analysis' of institutional and individuals' needs – a strategy commonly used in schools by the late eighties – makes the implementation of the planned changes more likely.

What these early experiences did do was to show that more needed to be known about how change happened in institutions and that the capacity for change varied significantly between institutions. INSET and curriculum packages on their own were not enough to ensure development. Havelock's seminal work (1969) marks a turning point in the understanding of the change process in education.

Resourcing

The period of increasing resources was relatively short lived (1965–75). The destabilizing of the economy caused by the oil crises of the early seventies is usually pinpointed as significant in limiting the resources available for development. Implementation of the provisions of the James Report on teacher education and training (DES, 1972) appears to have been delayed for lack of resources.

INSET and initial teacher training

In retrospect, it is clear that approaches to professional and staff development were underdeveloped when compared with practice in many schools by the mid-eighties. By the eighties many schools had used TRIST (TVEI-related in-service training and later grant-related in-service training (GRIST)) funding to draw up quite sophisticated INSET plans together with systems for identifying school and individual development needs and for implementing change as a result (see Chapter 4 for more details).

The James Report (1972) recommended that all teachers should have an entitlement to secondment. One term every seven years was suggested initially, changing to one in every five years eventually. (Incidentally, the latter has long been available to teachers in Australia as 'long service leave'.) These recommendations were never implemented although although similar proposals were put forward as part of the Advisory Committee for the Supply and Training of Teachers (1978c) proposals for in-service training in 1978. The switch from individual long-term secondments to INSET focused on specific priorities came during the eighties. Goddard (1989a, p. 15) puts this change down to a recognition of the economic dimension (of individual secondments) . . . being forced on the government through the uncapped pool for secondments. The size of the government contribution was growing apace as LEAs began to increase the number of secondees not just to improve the quality of the profession but to use it as a means to offset the salary bill caused by falling rolls, and to supplement the numerical strength of advisory teams. The sum of money available to INSET through the secondment pool was substantial but locked away in one form of INSET that at its best could support major change but in its main mode was mostly geared to the needs of individuals, the traditional approach to educational change.

The DES contributed to the pool and all LEAs put in an equal amount. Thus an LEA with fifty teachers on secondment paid the same as one with five and, although costs to all the LEAs increased with the number of secondments, most of the extra cost was borne by the DES. Goddard (*ibid.*, p. 17) refers to the system as 'an open cheque book from the DES'.

Induction schemes for new entrants into the profession became more common. The work of the Teacher Induction Pilot Scheme (TIPS) provided a lead in this field (Bolam, 1982).

Teachers' centres too opened – initially often as part of the network for training teachers to use new curriculum materials but they soon developed a central role in the provision of a range of curriculum and professional development support that focused initially on the teacher and then the school as the basis for supporting change.

Initial teacher training too was changing. The move to an all-graduate profession gathered momentum during the seventies. The two-year Certificate in Education (Cert. Ed.) course had been replaced by a three-year Cert. Ed. in 1960, and this in turn was replaced by a four-year B.Ed. (Hons) during the late sixties to 1980. But the period was one of contraction in teacher training. Many colleges were closed during the period as part of a rationalization process which was based on less demand for teachers as the birth rate was falling after the post-war high point (McNamara and Ross, 1982). By the end of the seventies, teaching posts in primary education had become hard to find as the numbers of young children dropped. The problem then affected secondary schools from the early eighties.

The theory and practice of evaluation develop

Evaluation of the new curricular initiatives of this period was not initially an inherent part of project design but it was soon realized that evaluation was an integral and important part of curriculum development. The cost of developing new educational programmes in both the UK and the USA led to demands for accountability which resulted in evaluation becoming higher priority. In any case there was concern about standards. Becher (1984, p. 107) describes the setting up of the Assessment of Performance Unit as stemming from a political demand for evidence about standards.

But existing quantitative and product focused methods of evaluation were felt to be limited and unhelpful in developing understanding about why some programmes went well and why others failed. These views led to the development of new approaches to evaluation. This reassessment of evaluation methods culminated in a conference on evaluation methods at Churchill College, Cambridge, in 1972 as a result of which 'illuminative' or qualitative methods of evaluation gained support (Leask, 1988).

Stenhouse's work (1975) on the role of the teacher as researcher sparked off a new direction in the search for quality in schools. The notion of the teacher-researcher, with teachers analysing their own classroom practice in order to understand and improve, had widespread acceptance by the 1990s.

A major shift in focus marked the change to the next phase. Curriculum development through the Schools Council continued but attention turned to developing the processes by which schools and their staff could work together effectively in order to implement change. It had become clear that where schools had no established processes for implementing and support-ing improvement then any proposed changes were doomed to failure. Cur-riculum changes which were 'bolted on' to the existing system rather than integrated into the work of the school withered and died once particular individuals left or the targeted funding and support ceased.

Phase 3: the 'better schools' phase

During this phase (the mid-seventies to the mid-eighties) the focus for change shifted from central curriculum development to strategies for mak-ing the whole school 'better'. This 'better schools' phase had three main facets:

1. A national debate on education including concerns about standards and direction.
2. Research into the characteristics of 'effective' schools.
3. Work at national and international levels on improvement and the change process.

The national debate

There was considerable pressure on the education service to be more pub-licly accountable and for there to be open discussion about education. This demand for increased accountability is often traced back to the then Prime

Minister James Callaghan's speech at Ruskin College (October, 1976) and the accompanying Green Paper, *Education in Schools: A Consultative Document* (DES, 1977). In fact, the speech marked a high point in a debate about what should be taught and how it should be taught which had been ongoing throughout the seventies.

The publication of 'Black Papers' by Cox, Dyson and Boyson had punctuated the previous decade. The purpose of these papers was to rally those with similar beliefs ('right wing' beliefs) so that existing practice in education in maintained (state) schools would be changed (Ahier and Flude, 1983).

Research into the characteristics of effective schools

Rainsford (1989, pp. 14–15) summarizes the work of a number of researchers of the period:

> Research on effective schools in the USA (Purkey and Smith, 1982; Clark, 1984) and the UK (Rutter *et al.*, 1979; Reynolds, 1985; Mortimore *et al.*, 1985) found that differences among schools do affect students' academic progress and that certain internal conditions are typical in schools that achieve higher levels of outcomes for their students.
>
> Purkey and Smith (1982, p. 65) . . . concluded that . . . there is broad agreement on the factors that are responsible for that difference . . .
>
> 1) strong leadership
> 2) high expectations by staff for student achievement
> 3) clear goals and emphasis for the school
> 4) a school-wide effective staff training programme
> 5) a system for monitoring student progress.
>
> Miles and Ekholm (1985) describe nine factors that are representative of the organization of effective schools:
>
> 1) instructionally focused leadership
> 2) emphasis on curriculum and instruction
> 3) external support
> 4) clear goals and high expectations for students
> 5) a system for monitoring performance and achievement
> 6) an orderly, humane climate
> 7) change-supportive norms within the school
> 8) continuing staff development
> 9) parental involvement and support.

The work of a number of these researchers was widely disseminated and must have contributed to the debate about improving the quality of schools.

The White Paper, *Better Schools*, also provoked much discussion about ways of improving the quality of education (DES, 1985b).

Developing understanding of the change process

The development of strategies aimed at bringing about whole-school improvement was a feature of the mid-seventies. Methods of undertaking school-based review were, over a period, extended to embrace the wider notion of school development planning. However, this early assumption, that review would automatically lead to improvement, still lingers today.

In the mid- to late seventies, many LEAs produced school self-evaluation handbooks to guide schools through the process of improvement. The ILEA document, *Keeping the School under Review* (1977), was widely used and referred to. The guidance produced by most LEAs was similar in form. Helen Simons (1987) in documenting these early attempts at school self-evaluation comments that 'by the end of 1980 approximately three-quarters of the LEAs in England and Wales had initiated discussions on school self-evaluation and one-fifth had issued guidelines for schools' (p. 220).

The guidelines produced tended to be in the form of booklets containing long lists of questions and issues to consider which attempted to cover every possible area of school activity. In practice, this process of self-evaluation or review took a very long time – months or even terms – and although the review was often comprehensive it usually produced reflections on what had happened rather than a plan for the future. Because the review was required by the LEA it was seen by some as much an instrument for accountability as a tool for school improvement. In some LEAs the report of the review was publicly available – being circulated to councillors as a matter of course in Oxfordshire.

These early booklets gave little advice, if any, on the process of identifying priorities for change or on the implementation and evaluation of such changes. Consequently the production of a report on the current state of the school was often seen as an end in itself rather than as the means for providing the foundations for change.

The limited value of these tools became clear as school-based review on its own failed to produce desired improvements. Strategies to support the implementation of desired changes and for evaluating change were needed to take this review work further. Schemes to streamline the review process and to support the implementation of change were produced. Most widely used was (and probably still is) GRIDS (Guidelines for Review and Internal Development in Schools) produced under the auspices of the Schools Council Development Committee (McMahon *et al.*, 1984) but another approach is the NFER/IMTEC scheme (Hopkins, 1987).

The majority of schools across the country involved in the DES-funded School Development Plans Project (1989–90) reported using the GRIDS approach to review their work but modifying it to suit their particular circumstances.

School development plans and whole-school planning

The history of an idea is difficult to trace. Ideas expressed at a conference or in print can spread quickly across the world. Such ideas bear fruit at different times, and with different degrees of success depending on the prevailing conditions. So it is with formal school development plans. Heads and teachers had always planned albeit informally. But the notion of producing a formal school development plan had a firm foothold in the UK by 1985 in at least two education authorities (ILEA and Enfield). The idea was to spread rapidly throughout the country as a result of the pressures from two principal sources: 'initiative overload' and the desire for improved whole-school review strategies.

During the early eighties it became clear that schools without established processes for supporting the active management of change would be reduced to a state of crisis management by the volume and nature of legislation and curriculum reform proposed. Indeed as the decade progressed, the term 'innovation overload' was increasingly used to describe the pressure schools were under.

At the same time, the school-based review and school self-evaluation strategies developed during the late seventies were being found to be relatively ineffective in producing school improvement. A strategy was required which would ensure development happened.

Goddard (1989b, p. 2) explains why school development plans were introduced in Enfield:

> [SDPs provided] the way in which the LEA could help make explicit its aim to support schools through a major period of change. This was achieved by focusing on the school, the staff and the curriculum as a whole and through a major INSET programme. It provided help and specific training on the management of change for the heads, INSET co-ordinators and other key members of staff in the service in order to raise awareness that change could be managed by developing the abilities of all staff to work together to manage the process.
>
> Implicit in all of this and in the procedures was a key principle that the school and the staff are concerned with *the creation of a learning environment for everyone.*

The DES funded the School Development Plans Project during 1989–90 with the brief to produce national advice on school development planning (Hargreaves *et al.*, 1989; Hargreaves and Hopkins, 1991).

In some LEAs, where the process of whole-school development was weakly developed, the plan was thought of as an end in itself and was strongly linked to the financial accountability introduced by LMS. Planning was not seen as a means of supporting improvement. The 'plan' became seen as a 'management plan' rather than as a whole-school development plan. It remains to be seen whether such 'management' plans are effective in supporting the process of change.

Teacher-researchers and teacher-evaluators

Tying funding to particular initiatives was a feature of government policy in the eighties and together with this funding went the obligation to evaluate the work done. The funding for TVEI, Education Support Grants (ESGs) and TRIST/GRIST/LEATGS was provided on this basis. Consequently the development of teachers' skills in evaluation became a priority. Courses were developed by advisory teams in LEAs as well as higher education institutions and new practices were developed particularly through the evaluation of INSET and TVEI (Leask, 1988).

Colleagues in higher education involved in the field were particularly concerned that their evaluation work on the curriculum initiatives of the eighties should be useful and used. The ensuing debate about the purposes and methods of evaluation further developed the understanding in the profession of the use of evaluation as a tool for change. The development of evaluation methods by and as tools for the teaching profession is a feature of this phase.

The teacher-researcher movement prompted by Stenhouse's and others' work was gaining momentum. CARN, the Classroom Action Research Network, was formed and it still provides a focal point for teachers re-searching the teaching and learning taking place in their classrooms.

The international perspective on school improvement

Concerns at this point about how to improve the education service were not restricted to the UK. Internationally these led to the setting up of ISIP – the International School Improvement Project. This project, involving 150 people from fourteen countries worldwide, was part of the work of the Centre for Educational Research and Innovation (CERI) which is part of the Organization for Economic Co-operation and Development (OECD). Van Velzen *et al.* (1985) and Hopkins (1987) describe the work of ISIP. The work of the project, and the subsequent work of members of the project, has given rise to a substantial body of literature on the manage-ment of educational change.

A number of countries called in international teams from ISIP to evalu-ate their education service, system and provision and whilst the UK was not among them, the work has had significant impact in the UK. ISIP focused attention on the principles and practice of supporting change at the school level and insights into strategies for the successful support of change were, during the 1980s, available to those implementing change in education in the UK.

Goddard (1989b) attributes the introduction of development planning in the London Borough of Enfield to ideas emerging from ISIP and the work of Per Dalin and Val Rust (1983). This early work drew on the body of literature and practice which is now commonly labelled 'the management of change'. A number of organization development (OD) principles and practices can also be seen to have contributed to the development of practice in this area as have certain management concepts and techniques. These areas are addressed in detail in Part III.

Moving to phase 4: a confusion of purpose

Whilst in some LEAs and schools there had been a steady development of knowledge and understanding about whole-school improvement, for many schools and LEAs whole-school planning was seen as a way of managing the introduction of LMS and the increased local accountability brought by the 1988 Education Act.

In those schools where formal planning processes were already established, the reason for producing a school development plan was clear: *to improve the quality of educational provision.* For schools starting development planning in 1988 and 1989, this focus was blurred. Tackling management and accountability issues became a higher priority than improving the quality of what happened in the classroom. The reasons for this were understandable. The changes of the 1988 Act were fundamental and timescales for implementing change were short. In addition, accountability to inspectors and the community via governors was given a high profile in documents sent to schools following the Act, as was the requirement to manage finance (Leask, 1990a; 1990b).

As a result, in schools where formal planning of school development was new, the idea of whole-school planning was often reduced to the production of a school management plan by a small group of people. The desire to draw up a balanced budget preoccupied many headteachers at the time and a number of official publications reinforced the confusion that a development plan was really the same as a management plan (DES Circular 7/88, the publications of the LMS initiative).

LEAs too were giving advice about plans and asking for copies of schools' plans. In some cases this promoted the idea that the plan was to do with accountability to the LEA. At about the same time the DES-funded

SDP project was providing advice about the role of school development plans in whole-school improvement. This confusion about the real purpose of school development plans still exists in many areas and will exist for some time to come.

Conclusion

Whilst ideas of INSET planning and whole-school development which sprang from the school-focused work of this phase are still, in the nineties, being disseminated to teachers, a managerial model for the operation of the education service is displacing this earlier work. In the next chapter, the changes introduced in this, the fourth phase of change, are discussed.

Further reading

Clarke, P. (1990) *Finding out in Education*, Longman, Harlow.

Maclure, J. S. (1986) *Educational Documents: England and Wales*, Methuen, London (5th edn).

Ministry of Education (1951) *Education 1900–1950: The Report of the Ministry of Education and the Statistics of Public Education for England and Wales for the Year 1950* (Cmnd 8244), HMSO, London.

Rogers, R. (1984) *Crowther to Warnock: How Fourteen Reports Tried to Change Children's Lives*, Heinemann, London (2nd edn).

Simon, B. (1991) *Education and the Social Order 1940–1990*, Lawrence & Wishart, London.

Thomas, N. (1990) *Primary Education from Plowden to the 1990's*, Falmer Press, Lewes.

4
CHANGE TODAY: THE MANAGERIAL PHASE

Introduction

In the political timetable the changes in this phase were initiated in the early eighties, but they grew out of the concerns for standards voiced during the seventies. The main impact of reform was not widely felt until the mid- to late eighties when regulations of the 1986 and 1988 Education Acts came into force.

The period was one of immense change and development for the education system. New approaches to school management were proposed and implemented: accountability, value for money, choice and standards were the issues underpinning government thinking and action. There was a shift of emphasis away from professional development for teachers to structures, resource management and INSET based on supporting the implementation of government priorities.

The concept of 'the self-managing school' (Caldwell and Spinks, 1988) was seen to provide a model of school management for the future. Schools were under pressure (particularly financial pressure) to 'opt-out' of local authority control and become 'grant-maintained'.

Changes in this phase have a different focus from those in the sixties and the seventies. The reforms of the late eighties operated not just on discrete parts of the service such as the curriculum or INSET but across probably the whole range of components of the education service albeit in a disconnected fashion. Areas such as assessment, teacher appraisal, financial management, governance and curriculum received particular attention.

Collaboration or confrontation?

During the eighties, the concern that the curriculum did not match the needs of the day was aired as it had been in previous decades – leading to the 1918 Education Act, the 1944 Education Act and the various reports in between. Similar concerns were expressed in the USA and the National Commission on Excellence in Education was established. This commission produced a report in 1983 – *A Nation at Risk*. One major difference in approach between the two countries appears to have been in relationship to the teachers themselves. In the USA, there was a call for unity in the search for quality: 'This unity, can be achieved only if we avoid the unproductive tendency of some to search for scapegoats among the victims, such as the beleaguered teachers' (National Commission for Excellence in Education, 1983, p. 12).

In the UK, however, the necessity to review the education system tended to be attributed to the shortcomings of the teachers and the schools alone. This had the effect of lowering self-esteem and motivation in the profession and promoting a downward spiral of confidence on behalf of public and teachers.

The changes the educational legislation of the eighties was to bring were fundamental. The 1980 DES publication, *The Educational System of England and Wales*, described (p. 1) the mechanism of control of British education thus: 'A distinctive feature of the British Education Service is that responsibility is distributed between Central Government, the local education authorities and the teaching profession.' This tripartite relationship – one of partnership – was long established but it was brought to an abrupt end with the announcement (12 November 1982) of the setting up of the major curriculum initiative of the early eighties through the Manpower Services Commission – an agency outside the education service. The Technical Vocational Education Initiative (TVEI) was born amid much controversy. The teaching profession and LEAs who had previously shared responsibility with the DES for the education service were not consulted.

Centralization or decentralization?

Differences of viewpoint about the centralization or decentralization of control over curriculum and resources and the relevance or not of regional structures were a feature of international changes in education during the eighties.

Ironically, as the UK was moving to a centralized control over curriculum, France, which had long had such a central control, was adopting a more flexible approach to the curriculum. At the same time in the UK, resources were being decentralized through the local financial management initiative and the role of regional authorities (LEAs) was being weakened. Norway, by way of contrast, was moving to more autonomy for regional authorities (Granheim, Kogan and Lundgren, 1990). Such diversity of approach suggests the necessity for international co-operation so that some common understanding of the advantages and disadvantages of different systems can be reached and unnecessary and costly mistakes may be avoided.

Tensions over the balance of power in the UK between the centre (at the DES) and the regions (LEAs and schools) are reported as early as the late sixties and early seventies. Parkinson claims that the DES was criticized by the OECD as 'adopting increasingly secretive, anti-democratic decision-making procedures . . . the department showed a growing insensitivity to the wishes of its partners in the education alliance as it sought to make unilateral policy choices with minimal public discussion of their rationale or implications' (Litt and Parkinson, 1979, p. 26).

The focus for change

The thrust of reform continued through the eighties and into the nineties. John Major, in a speech to the Centre for Policy Studies in London (1991, p. 3) indicated that the government was driving reforms through on three main fronts:

> Our educational reforms have been driven by three interlocking ambitions. To raise *standards*. To widen *choice*. And to increase the *accountability* of the system to those who use and pay for it. These principles will drive our reforms forward in the 1990s too. For there is still much to be done.

The legislative changes chosen to achieve the government's goals of higher standards, wider choice and increased accountability were wide-ranging and included

- a national curriculum;
- local management of schools (LMS);
- a change in role for the LEAs;
- the move to grant-maintained ('opted-out') schools;
- different approaches to inspection;
- the publishing of information about schools.

The problems associated with this model for improving quality are discussed in Chapter 2. In this chapter, we document major changes taking place.

Cheque-book curriculum development

The early eighties began with a form of curriculum development where those controlling the purse used this power to control the curriculum. The funding of TVEI (in the secondary sector), INSET through the GEST/LEATGS grants (and earlier TRIST and GRIST), and Education Support Grant (ESG) schemes was done on this basis. LEAs had to bid for funds. TVEI provided pressure for pedagogic change and broadening of the curriculum. It provided an impetus for change, overcoming the inertia of a system unused to justifying itself in order to receive funding. This form of 'categoric' funding was apparently first used by the DES in the mid-seventies (Litt and Parkinson, 1979).

Janet Harland (quoted in McBride, 1989, p. 7) suggests that this approach to curriculum development was adopted to avoid the necessity for legislation: 'categorical funding is used when a body which has neither the statutory right nor the means to implement its own policies, seeks to do so through agencies that have both and are prepared to deliver in exchange for the necessary monies. It is a substitute for legislation.'

The new model of curriculum development was crucially different from the research–development–diffusion model used for the Nuffield and Schools Council curriculum innovations of the sixties and seventies. TVEI schemes were locally planned but they had to fit certain criteria before being accepted and funding being provided. Initially, the DES and HMI were bypassed and some saw this as an attempt to 'ginger up' the DES by initiating curriculum development through a different department.

So why did this approach to curriculum, staff and professional development gain any support from educationalists? The economic climate was a key factor which drew LEAs to place bids with the Manpower Services Commission (MSC). The late sevenites and early eighties were a time of unprecedented cuts and the incentive this provided for LEAs to apply for TVEI funding was widely acknowledged. There was a positive side to this new approach. LEAs, schools and the MSC worked in partnership, the TVEI objectives were broad and schemes could be matched to local needs. The early funding of LEATGS also had a local component – a mix of government and local priorities were funded. This partnership has broken down in recent years as funding for local priorities was dropped and funding is now only provided for implementation of national initiatives.

The 1988 Education Act

The variability of the results of the experiments with categoric funding were to have a profound effect on the further reforms of the education system. Change had been neither as quick nor as fundamental as the government might have hoped. For several years some LEAs avoided being involved. Legislation in the form of the 1986 and 1988 Acts forced the overhaul of the curriculum.

Decisions over the level of local funding of education were taken at national level as the mechanism of 'rate capping' or later 'charge capping' (1989 onwards) of local authority expenditure was used by central government to influence local expenditure. If local councils were thought to be overspending, they lost central funds. 'Charge capping' and the fear of it caused substantial cutbacks in education at this time.

Financial accountability and value for money

New approaches to financial accountability were extended to all the public services. The notion of 'performance indicators' was introduced by government in an attempt to ensure value for money and to provide tighter accountability structures.

Ann Wignall, a senior teacher from Haydon School, carried out research into changes in financial management and the development of performance indicators. Here she describes the economic and political background to the 'Financial Management Initiative' – a policy introduced during the late seventies and early eighties to govern the management of local government finance:

> During the 1960s and 1970s the problem, facing local and national government, was how to allocate extra resources. The recession in the 1970s changed the emphasis and a massive swing of the pendulum took place. The requirement now, not only for the United Kingdom but also for much of the developed world, became one of managing better with less financial resources (Butt and Palmer, 1985, p. 5). This change in the management of the economy meant that in the UK the public sector was required to become more accountable because their funding was carried by 'budget appropriation' (bidding for and justifying the request for funds) and not by an application of a 'direct charge' on the users. The official name for this new policy was the Financial Management Initiative (FMI) which was directed at *all* government departments. FMI aimed to devolve financial management and to curtail public expenditure through the imposition of cash limits. Also greater emphasis was given to: . . . separating out . . . – policy and planning – from the executive tasks of delivering services to the public; and, in the latter area, to defining and measuring results – 'outputs' as the jargon has it.

> (Omand, 1989, p. 20)

This also led to the development of the philosophy and practice of value for money (VFM) and the associated concepts of the 3 Es – *economy, efficiency* and *effectiveness*. Butt and Palmer (1985, p. 9–10) provide definitions of these terms. This philosophy was made explicit in the 1982 Local Government Finance Act and the 1983 National Audit Act which required local and national auditors, when reviewing the budgetary arrangements within the public sector, to ensure that arrangements had been made 'to review economy, efficiency and effectiveness in the use of resources' (*ibid.*, p. 4).

The philosophy of VFM and the related doctrine of the 3 Es are often considered to be an 'industrial influence'. However, performance measures and their related indicators are relatively unknown in industry to the extent that they are being developed within the public sector, as Butt and Palmer (*ibid.*, p. 45) state: 'In the private sector detailed performance measurement is relatively less important because profitability tends to be used as the main overriding indicator.'

Profitability, being an indication of 'client satisfaction', is an indicator which for the most part is not available to most public sector organizations. Another is 'market share', which Klein and Carter (1987–8) consider may prove 'useful as a crude negative indicator of performance' when applied to the measurement of the number of parents opting for a particular school as their first choice. Michael Fallon, when addressing the British Association for the Advancement of Science in 1990, is reported as saying that 'the discipline of the market place, the power of the customer and the engine of competition were what had been lacking from British education' (*The Independent*, 23 August 1990, p. 5).

This drive for enhanced financial accountability of institutions was just one part of the changes in procedures for accountability introduced during this period. The issue of accountability is discussed in depth in Chapter 8.

Management and governance

The 1986 Act brought particular changes to the governance of schools. These provisions coupled with those of the 1988 Education Act have had and will have for some time to come an enormous impact on the structure and functioning of the education service, but a less predictable impact on the quality of work in the classroom.

The membership of governing bodies was extended to include more parents and members of the local community. HMI (DES, 1990) voiced concern at the poor quality of education management and the DES set up a 'School Management Task Force' which drew on the expertise of industrialists and educationalists in examining the problem.

During this period, a view was prevalent that management models used in industry could usefully be transferred to education. Approaches to improving quality were also influenced by industrial models.

Further education colleges in particular adopted the approach to quality management set out in British Standard 5750 (1987) – a rather mechanized approach to quality management similar to the school-based review procedures of the mid-seventies. The concept of TQM (total quality management) with its focus on setting quality standards (Randall, 1991) also influenced 'school managers' (i.e. headteachers). The Department of Trade and Industry was encouraging efforts in this field in industry (Department of Trade and Industry, undated). TQM is similar in some ways to the approach schools use in development planning (Hargreaves *et al.*, 1989; Hargreaves and Hopkins, 1991) but as with BS 5750 the approach requires reinterpretation to fit it to the educational context.

This move from the traditional forms of management and accountability of education brought a clash of values. Much of value in educational terms cannot be measured in ways used in industry. In obtaining 'value for money' it is hard to place a monetary value on the 'quality of teaching and learning' or 'independence of thought' yet it is those areas which are the principal concern of teachers – with good reason: for they are seen as delivering quality.

Educational evaluation strategies

In accord with developing practice in educational evaluation in the late seventies, evaluation was made an integral part of the TVEI and LEATGS schemes. Although this work derived from contractual obligations, in practice it often prompted the development of sound professional accountability systems. Developmental work in evaluation techniques and 'needs analysis' continued throughout the eighties.

Strategies for self-appraisal, peer-appraisal and for appraisal systems based on professional notions of bringing about change were developed on the basis of earlier work and taken up in a national pilot scheme on appraisal. But there was concern that these professional approaches to appraisal seemed to be 'at odds' with the more contractual approach to appraisal suggested in DES Circular 12/91. It remains to be seen what impact this national approach to appraisal has on the quality of the education service.

Inspection: HMI and the role of LEA staff

In the areas of advice and inspection, the interpretation of an LEA's responsibilities after the 1988 Act changed the ways LEA teams worked. LEAs were under pressure to change their practice from support to teachers and schools through advisers to inspectorial approaches – to check that the National Curriculum was being implemented.

The implications of these changes and new funding arrangements meant that the infrastructure (advisers/advisory teachers) used for helping teachers to keep up to date and for supporting the implementation of new government policies was weakened. As teachers' centres closed and advisory teams disappeared, individual teachers lost access to other colleagues – such access had, in the past, enabled a sharing of understanding about developments in a teacher's specialist field.

Michael Fallon, Minister of State for Schools, indicated in an interview that he did not know what role 'these people' (LEA advisers and officers) played in the education service (Sharron, 1991). Changes in funding and pressures for accountability following the 1988 Act meant that the role changed. In the summer of 1989 many LEAs changed advisers' posts to inspectors' posts. Some LEAs introduced or kept a dual system of advisers and inspectors.

Throughout the eighties, audit/management consultancy firms were increasingly called upon to comment on educational management and structures and this issue is further discussed in Chapter 2.

Initial teacher training and teacher supply

'School takes on "good lad" of 18 to teach' (front-page headline in *The Observer*, 8 September 1991, p. 1). The teaching profession was nearly an all-graduate profession in the mid-eighties but since then there have been substantial attempts to bypass qualifications for entrance. The appointment of an 18-year-old who had just taken A-levels to the post of geography teacher in a school in Hertfordshire (not London where teacher shortages are usually more acute) highlighted this change in attitude.

Although the offer of the post was rescinded in the face of public criticism, a similar appointment had been made the previous term with a 19-year-old being employed to teach maths in the same area. Whilst it could be argued that these appointments were a 'flash in the pan', anecdotal evidence from a number of counties suggests that 'market forces' and shortages have led to increased numbers of unqualified people taking teaching posts.

Schemes for licensed (those over 26 years of age with two years' higher education) and articled teachers (those with degrees but no teaching qualifications) were introduced during the late eighties to cope with shortages of teachers – both groups went straight into schools. The articled teacher scheme which provides training off as well as on the job was, at the time of writing, receiving favourable reports although it was much more expensive than the traditional one-year full-time post-graduate (PGCE) course.

Proposed changes in teacher education at the time of writing bear the same hallmark as change in other areas. The proposals are poorly thought through but must be implemented in a rush. 'Successful' schools (i.e. those with good examination results) are to be designated training schools, and funds are to move from the colleges to the schools. The implications for children's learning and for their examination results in the training schools has not received a mention.

The National Curriculum

Within a short time of its introduction, there seemed to be general acceptance among teachers that the notion of a national curriculum was a step forward. But there were shortcomings. The model developed was too detailed, particularly for primary schools and, unfortunately, the curriculum was introduced piecemeal without proper piloting. This caused problems as parts had to be rewritten – the Maths and Science National Curriculum Attainment Targets were revised in the summer of 1991, within a couple of years of introduction, and the teachers who had worked hardest at changing the content of their teaching, their assessment strategies and schemes of work were faced with doing this work over again. Those who had held back in implementing the National Curriculum were seen to have gained most. This is not the message that those managing change should be giving!

The assessment strategies, too, were inadequately piloted. All primary schools were involved in Key Stage 1 assessment in the summer of 1991 and, although this was a 'pilot', results were to be reported to parents and the results for LEAs were to be published nationally.

But ambiguities in administration and inconsistencies in interpretation of the 'tests' emerged throughout the testing period. At the end of the affair, there was little certainty among teachers that a child who had been given Level 3 in English in one school would be given Level 3 in another school. These confusions were ignored when a league table of LEAs' results was published by government and used to back up statements about, for example, appropriate funding levels for education.

Local management of schools

The LMS initiative had two major prongs. One was to give governors more responsibilities for the running of schools, the other was to provide schools with a budget which was to cover all their expenditure and which was based on the number of pupils. Some weighting was also allowed for small schools, pupils with special needs and so on.

There were 'winners and losers' among schools when the formula was applied. There was little scope for funding on the basis of need established through professional judgment. At the time of writing, the full impact of these changes is yet to emerge. A number of the issues arising from the early stages of LMS are addressed in Chapter 10.

INSET

During the eighties, the INSET available to teachers underwent considerable change. There were two main areas of change which opened up new opportunities but which also closed off previous opportunities.

Firstly, the funds used for long-term secondments available for the few in the seventies were redirected into new schemes (TRIST/GRIST/LEATGS/GEST) which allowed for a variety of uses of the money. Schools were delegated money for INSET and planning INSET to fit the analysed needs of staff became widespread. A consequence of this is that few teachers now have the opportunity to gain release to study for a higher degree.

Secondly, the requirement that schools organize five 'professional training days' per year ('Baker Days') provided the time and the opportunity for teachers to discuss professional issues. In many schools, this time was used to plan the work of the school and to work on the school development plan through a collaborative process.

Teacher morale

Poor relationships between teachers and the government were a feature of the eighties. There were extended strikes in the mid-eighties and the education of many children was disrupted over a period of years. Negotiating rights for teachers were withdrawn and changes in service were imposed. The introduction of TVEI in the early eighties was accompanied by suspicion about the government's approach to curriculum development. It was widely seen as a back-door approach to change. The cutbacks and rapid pace of poorly planned curriculum change of the latter part of the decade exacerbated problems.

Some changes, such as the five professional training days or Baker Days allowed positive collaborative work to develop in schools. Others, such as the requirement for teachers to spend 1,265 hours of 'directed time' per year in school seemed to be based on a child's-eye view of teaching – that the time spent in front of the class represented the totality of the teacher's work. This issue of directed time confirmed teachers' views that the demands of the job were not widely understood.

Conclusion: preoccupation with the short term – a British problem

'In the thirties there began to be interest in the question of how long educational reforms take. Mort and Cornell . . . found that it took nearly 50 years before any particular improvement was used by 100% of schools' (Van Velzen *et al.*, 1985, p. 285). Less than twenty years ago the UK education system was 'pre-ROSLA' – only the most able were catered for through the examination system; restricted-access grammar schools provided the route to further education; the secondary curriculum was undeveloped; and further education post-16 was only available for the most able.

Change in the intervening years has been dramatic. Yet, quite rightly, aspirations continue to spiral upward. A highly developed education and training system is now required which caters for all young people up to 19 or 20 years of age and which provides services to meet a multitude of different demands, and it is wanted now – in one go!

To achieve these goals it must be accepted that change is normal – that no one has to be blamed for the necessity for updating the education system. Regular reviewing and updating of the education system is part of a natural process of renewal which enables the service to respond to the ever-changing demands of modern society. But those with a stake in education have the right to expect that such change will be handled effectively and will be the result of careful consideration. Supporting and developing the quality of teaching and learning in the classroom must be the focus of reforms, and improvement needs to be a joint venture between society, the community, teachers and students.

In Chapter 3, four phases in the development of education in England and Wales were identified:

Phase 1 (the mid-forties to the mid-sixties) was teacher focused.
Phase 2 (the mid-sixties to the mid-seventies) was curriculum focused.
Phase 3 (the mid-seventies to the mid-eighties) was school focused.

Phase 4 (the mid-eighties to the early nineties) was focused on systems of management.

At this point, development in education has had as major focuses: teachers, the curriculum, the whole school, and management systems. Each phase of this development has provided information about ways of improving quality but this information has tended to be lost as another phase is implemented.

As a result of this developmental work over the last fifty years, there is now a body of knowledge about the functioning of major aspects of the education system – although the accumulation of this knowledge might have been an unconscious process. The time is now right for a *conscious* attempt, nationally and locally, to utilize the knowledge acquired about development and to establish the conditions that will enable long-term improvement to take place.

The requirement now is to have a fully developed framework comprising all aspects of development balanced and in phase with each other. It is not a question of a new phase of curriculum development or school development or teacher development but of all aspects tuned together within a long-term arrangement that increases the capacity of the service at all levels.

We believe the case has been made for the necessity for change in the future to be planned coherently – with the long term as well as the short term in view – and for a body to be established which is responsible for overseeing the debate about education and for ensuring that what is best from each phase of previous development is considered when planning future change.

Issues for consideration

1. What balance between different types of teacher education is most appropriate given the different approaches in the past?
2. What are the most appropriate management approaches in education? What are the benefits and disadvantages of financial delegation? Is modification of the scheme needed?
3. What forms of curriculum development and adaptation of the National Curriculum will provide the best possible education for young people?

Further reading

Caldwell, B. and Spinks, J. (1988) *The Self-Managing School*, Falmer Press, Lewes.
Fullan, M. (1991) *The New Meaning of Educational Change*, Cassell, London.

Hargreaves, D. H. and Hopkins, D. (1991) *The Empowered School: The Management and Practice of Development Planning*, Cassell, London.

Leask, M. (1992) School development plans: their history and their potential, in G. Wallace (ed.) *Local Management of Schools: Research and Experience*, Multilingual Matters, Cleveland/Philadelphia, USA.

McBride, R. (1989) *The In-Service Training of Teachers*, Falmer Press, Lewes.

Simon, B. (1991) *Education and the Social Order 1940–1990*, Lawrence & Wishart, London.

PART III

IMPROVING QUALITY THROUGH UNDERSTANDING DEVELOPMENT

The purpose of this part is to examine the process of school development and improvement so that those responsible for the process have both the map and the compass.

Chapter 5 identifies the central ingredients in the development process including the context for change in the nineties and relevant concepts, processes and structures. The chapter concentrates on four aspects of the process: development, maintenance, planning and plans.

Chapter 6 examines in detail the contribution individual and institutional learning plays in the development of schools and their staffs.

Chapter 7 describes an approach to the management of multiple initiatives and the way in which schools can cope with overload.

Chapter 8 deals with the way in which evaluation and accountability play a crucial part in the development process.

The chapter also examines the contribution of systems including the place of inspection.

Chapter 9 concludes Part III by drawing together the threads through an examination of the stages of development that schools move through as they mature. Termed the 'proactive and consciously developing school', the processes of development are viewed from a holistic perspective.

5
THE DEVELOPMENT PROCESS

Introduction: the improvement process

This chapter comprises four main sections: firstly, an introduction to key issues of the change process, its context in the nineties, the relationship between improvement and development and an overview of the elements of improvement; secondly, a detailed examination of the development process including the part maintenance has to play; thirdly, the contribution of plans and planning to the development process; and, finally, there is a section by Ian Terrell on the views of teachers about school development planning.

Key issues: change and improvement

There is a need to clarify some of the terms and concepts that are being used throughout the book and in particular in this part. *Improvement* always involves *change* but change does not necessarily lead to improvement. Applying the term 'improvement' to any initiative involves a value judgment. In many walks of life it is possible to define improvement in the sense of whether a system or machine works more efficiently or effectively but, even then, there are often a wider set of considerations that require value judgments to be made. The debate over nuclear energy provides one example. Whilst the process can be seen to be efficient there are wider environmental considerations which widen the debate and involve other value judgments as to whether it is an improved form of energy or not.

One person's improvement may be another person's disaster. Take for example a suggested change in a particular teaching approach. Child A may gain from the alteration whilst child B may lose.

It is also difficult to define when a change becomes or ceases to be an improvement. Most educational alterations take time to become established and be effective. At the start of the process, it is often impossible to predict the value of an initiative. If only all of us had the gift of hindsight.

Development is taken to describe the process by which change takes place. There are many forms of development. Development processes should not be value laden but the difficulty that exists in proving that one aspect of the process works more effectively than another leaves room for assertion rather than objectivity.

Improvement of anything involves a decision about quality. What is a good school? What is a good development? These are value-based decisions. They are rooted in normative considerations about quality and are firmly located in past experience as well as in what is happening at the time. As we have pointed out in Chapter 1, agreement about quality needs to be the outcome of a debate at various levels. Improvement in quality is underpinned both by a debate about values and also by achieving success in the management of the development process.

Similarly, improvement of the development process involves judgments about whether one way is better than another. However, lessons can be and should be drawn from empirical studies.

This chapter draws on such work and the experience of the authors in the field of development. Each individual's situation is different and only the reader can judge whether the messages in this chapter and the sources it draws on are likely to result in improvement of the development process in their own context.

Ideas about development (or the process of change) do not have a long history. Nor is the process fully understood or easily explained. The previous chapter outlined the genesis of many of the practices that have improved the developmental process. Ideas have developed from the examination of practice as well as theoretical leaps into the dark. Even more work is needed if the development process is to be improved.

The current danger is that the politicization of the debate on quality and improvement has reduced the discussion to ideology, which simply means that certain theories of improvement are favoured and others are labelled as 'fashionable'. It does not help our understanding of development for it is the drawing out of a range of ideas and practices, whatever their origins, and taking the 'best' mix that provides the sound way forward.

We are reminded of a statement about Einstein that he produced more failures than anyone else but he had more brilliant ideas. The important point is that he had more ideas than anyone and he kept trying.

Development and uncertainty

Much has been published about the *management of change*. It is or was a very useful banner under which the various aspects of the change process have become better understood. Some care, though, now needs to be exercised in the use of the word 'management' in case it implies that change is a process that can be totally planned for, controlled and thoroughly organized. This is unrealistic. Also untrue is the view that by improving our understanding and practice at change, development will become easier. Greater understanding tends to fuel aspiration so quickening the pace and complexity of change as well as extending the goals, thus making development harder to achieve and the process of change more complex.

The most helpful principle about change is that development is about learning and, as with the process of learning, it can be enabled and improved upon. But like sailing, development is subject to powerful and unpredictable forces that have to be handled and that sometimes cause a change of course and plan.

The context of the nineties

Development occurs within a context. In the same way, any understanding we have about the change process has been derived from a particular context. Whatever has been learnt in the past about change will only remain valid if it still applies to the current context. People change, so do circumstances. Rates of change increase and aspirations increase. Therefore our previous understandings about development require re-examination. It is important for the reader who is undertaking development to analyse their own context, for it is within their particular setting that the strategy and processes of change have to be effective. There is no one approach that will work in every setting. It is only through the growth and analysis of understanding of the significant features of the change process that any valid set of concepts can be formed. Unfortunately the understanding of these concepts may not be transferable to other settings. In all forms of social understanding there are few absolutes.

The pressure for change in the nineties is the result of society's heightened aspirations leading to complex, far-reaching initiatives. We have observed that this is an accelerating process. The gap between reality and public/private vision increases with the extent the person and/or organization has travelled along the developmental path. The further one travels successfully, the more one is motivated to accomplish. This characteristic of development lies at the heart of the increasing rate of change. Society strives for higher goals, the school for the implementation of a better curriculum and the individual for improved achievement. It is not the ideal that necessarily shifts that much, all of us have our dreams.

What changes is the belief that the ideal can be achieved because success forces everyone on. Unfortunately, those who are less successful do not share the same belief and cynicism sets in. The developing society or school is likely to be frustrated by its own success. Handling that tension is part of the maturing process.

Development in the nineties is no longer about a few simple unconnected changes that introduce, for example, practical mathematics or an additional approach to the teaching of reading. It is about handling a whole series of previously unimplemented developments, e.g. providing a real curriculum for children still affected by the raising of the school-leaving age with a raft of new ones that stem from the need to provide a broad, balanced, education and training for all young people to the age of 19-plus within a restructured, more participatory, lower-resourced service. Everything appears to be changing at once or at least has become subject to change. The key feature of managing the change process is knowing how to rebuild the whole through a series of apparently discrete initiatives. In reality, each innovation is not separate, they are interrelated, mutually dependent and critical to the success of the whole. The solution to the problem of handling multiple initiatives lies in seeing the development process in its entirety. All aspects of education – curriculum, teacher education, management, advice and support, evaluation, etc. – have to be handled in concert.

Change in the nineties is therefore complex, multi-dimensional, value laden, participatory, simultaneous and highly organic. Whilst our previous knowledge of handling development through separate initiatives is useful, managing the development process as a whole is not the same as the sum of managing the parts.

The elements of improvement

There are two sets of components that together make up the improvement process. The first set consists of *aims, policies and goals*. These are the statements of vision and direction where values play the dominant role both in society and in any organization. True aims provide direction and are central to the process of improvement.

The second set comprises four components:

1. *Developmental process* Current understanding of the process is based

on a complex set of concepts and factors that help us understand the means by which change takes place. The process is underpinned by individual and institutional learning. The essential component in any developmental process is whether the school, college or LEA provides an effective learning environment for the students, the teachers and all other staff.

2. *Developmental structures and resources*   Attention has to be paid to the development of the organizational structures and resources that support the processes. Development structures include arrangements that identify those responsible for the development process within the formal system and the infrastructure of the organization. Each organization has to establish the management and decision-making processes that facilitate effective change. Many schools only have structures and resources that are geared to the maintenance of the status quo, which results in a lower capacity for change.

3. *Planning and plans*   The development of effective planning improves the development process but it should never be taken as a substitute for the developmental process which has more to do with the act of learning. There are a number of factors which need to be strengthened in the work of schools, especially the formation of strategy and action planning.

4. *Evaluation*   The processes of monitoring, review and evaluation are crucial to successful development. In simple terms evaluation is the critical examination of all aspects of development.

The development process: improving the institution's capacity for change

There are a number of key concepts, factors, processes, structures and useful techniques that enhance insight and can be used to develop skills in handling the developmental process. Each of these represents a piece in the successful development jigsaw. Not every aspect of development is included within this section. Those that have been selected lay the foundation for sound development.

This part of the chapter is organized into five sections:

1. The dynamic of the development process.
2. A definition of leadership qualities, skills and knowledge.
3. Key factors in the development process – stages and forms of development.
4. Improving the development process.

5. Maintenance and development.

The dynamic of the development process

Change occurs within an institutional and wider context. Whatever our general understandings about the development process, the particular circumstances of the institution or the organization have to be mapped, analysed and understood. The identification of these characteristics of the context provides the basis for understanding how to harness aspects of the change process to the development needs of the staff and the organization. The rationale behind this is the same as for any learning environment where the learning experience of the pupil has to be matched to their needs and previous experience. Development follows the same rules as for learning.

There are various labels that describe aspects of the institutional context, i.e. *the climate for change, the school's capacity for change* and *its stage of development*. They are not synonymous. The climate for change encompasses the general attitude and disposition of the staff towards change. It is a sub-set of the school's capacity for change, which is concerned with the school's ability and resource to manage the change process effectively, including its technical and physical capacity. The developments of the climate and capacity of a school are closely interwoven and relate to the simultaneous building of all of the features of the improvement process outlined in the introduction to this chapter.

The stage of a school's development is a loose term that is related to the school's progress in its management of the change process. This concept is further discussed in Chapter 9.

Recalling that development is part of the improvement process, improvement can be viewed as development plus the statement of policy. Development therefore comprises:

- The process of learning.
- The allocation and deployment of resources (for development).
- The formation of appropriate structures.
- The establishment of planning arrangements and plans.
- The operation of an evaluation system.

A particular way of illustrating the linkage between these features of the improvement process is to examine them within a model that picks out the essential characteristic of all change, namely the difference between where the school is now and where it wishes to be and its ability to devise an appropriate development process that helps the school/LEA to move towards the desired goal(s) (see Figure 5.1).

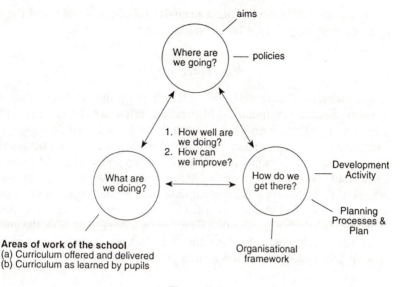

Figure 5.1

During the initiation of development planning in Enfield in 1987, a set of questions were formed into a model to identify the various components of the process and to clarify the dynamic that exists between them.

Where are we going?

This is by no means a simple question. It incorporates all the value-laden aspects of what is good, the overt aims and goals of the school and the school's definition of quality. The espoused aims though may not be the real or operational aims of the school. For covert or unintentional reasons, the school may well be acting in accord with another set of goals, the real goals, the ones that guide the everyday practice of the institution and its staff. There is ample evidence that espoused aims have limited impact on the practice of the school and its staff. The school may, for example, talk about meeting the individual needs of pupils but in practice seek conformity.

The school has to work with these realities and the various perceptions of reality staff have. The school has to ascertain, understand and analyse the full range of aims and goals and the introduction of innovations that enable their implementation. The outcomes of a process that seeks to clarify aims may result in the identification of a diverse range; however, it does provide a definition of the true goals of the school and forms the basis and one starting point for real development.

Where are we now?

If the analysis of espoused and stated aims produces variety then even more so does an examination of practice. What are the teacher and the school doing? Does it do what it says it does? How does it describe it? Are the schemes of work implemented? Total conformity may not be desirable. There will always be some tension between the aims, goals and practice of the school. This can be a positive factor, unlike many areas of our society where this characteristic is inappropriate because the organization requires strict adherence to the one form of action to ensure achievement of desired outcome. In education some divergence is necessary to provide the creative force for development. Striking the right balance is crucial and in many schools there may well be too great a divergence.

What evaluation procedures are in place?

The evaluation component works with a range of factors. Evaluation needs to examine three linked aspects:

- What is currently happening in the school.
- The identification of the needs of the pupils which helps to formulate the vision of the school and its policies.
- The provision of a constant mechanism to monitor and evaluate the effectiveness of the change process.

Not only does the evaluation process draw out what is happening but it should also provide information on how to improve the school, its policies and its practices (this is amplified in Chapter 8).

How do we get there?

This question covers all the development processes including planning and plans. An effectively developing school is one that is able to match its development work to its needs as a result of a conscious process of analysis, planning, discussion of aims, values and goals, and the construction of learning experiences for staff that are well matched to their individual needs and the needs of the school. Through the application of this model and the four key questions listed above, we are beginning to define the term 'improving the capacity of the school for change' and to describe the technical processes that have to be in place.

The development of the school's capacity for change is a development in itself and will need to be addressed explicitly in the school's development arrangements and plan. In other words, it is important for the school to have the development of its capacity for change as a major and identifiable feature of its school plan.

Educational leadership

In order to improve the development capacity of a school and underpin the general process the model illustrates, three elements of educational leadership need to be in place: vision, managing the environment, and confidence. In essence, these individually and collectively focus on the school's ability to learn and to become more effective and efficient at development.

This section examines a number of activities, concepts and ideas that, from our own experience, underpin the improvement of the school's capacity to develop. The goal is to incorporate them into the leadership responsibilities and practices of all staff, thus providing a strong climate and capacity for change in the school.

Vision

Without vision, effective development cannot happen. An image of the desired state or goal has to be articulated both in the individual's mind and stated collectively by the school. That is not to say that such an image represents the unrelenting goal that has to be implemented irrespective of the outcome of the development process which seeks to give it meaning and achieve the aim. That is an unrealistic understanding of the change process. The vision is the statement of the direction. As the school moves towards it, the experience of the developments that take place should cause the school to reassess the appropriateness of the envisaged goals and to judge their continuing value.

Modifications to the vision are essential if the change process is to command the respect and the credibility of the staff involved. The acid test that always has to be applied is whether the proposed changes work in practice. The closer the change gets to full implementation the greater the need for adaptation.

Vision is a vital part of leadership but not the prerogative of leaders. Irrespective of one's place in the structure it is possible to have vision and to fulfil a leadership role. By the same token, not all leaders have vision. Articulating the vision is the first step that has to be taken in mapping out the future. It can either be a self-generated vision or acquired through listening to someone else. The source is irrelevant.

There is a story of three stone-masons. They were asked what they were doing. One said, 'I am carving a stone.' The second said, 'I am carving a monument.' The third said, 'I am building a cathedral.' To look upwards, outwards and forwards gives one the power to be in control. It is important that we understand our own vision as well as other people's, whether we agree with them or not.

INSET activity 5.1   Perceptual analysis

> A very useful INSET activity is to explore and share vision by taking an innovation and to view it through the eyes of other groups or individuals. Perceptual analysis can be employed as an extension to many of the activities outlined in this section. It involves exploring the values, viewpoints and wishes of particular groups, e. g. parents, students, business or role types (e. g. headteachers and beginning teachers). It provides a way of exploring the different standpoints of the participants in any change scenario.

The examination by a school of its vision contributes to its management of the development process and to the school's overall management. Vision is essential to strategic planning (see the later section on plans and planning), for it helps the school to be free of surprises. Change cannot be controlled, as any proponent of contingency theory will tell you. There are too many factors outside the control of any individual or organization. All change is contextual and particular actions are formulated on the basis of an analysis of the situation. In addition, effective action has to be based on a shared understanding of the future, for that image helps in the positioning of the school in relation to its goal and thus helps it to deal with change.

Vision, though, takes time to build. In the process, those with a vision have to be patient and work with their colleagues. Acquiring and sharing visions needs to become part of the normal procedure of the school and should be encouraged, for it forms part of the process of opening up the staff and the school to other ideas.

One of the means by which vision is acquired and shared is through the conscious application of networking both outside and within the school (see Chapter 6).

Further benefits of the acquisition of useful information about the school and its aims, are that this helps with the process of adaptation to the changing environment. When an individual or a school is made aware or becomes aware of forthcoming changes and the visions of influential groups, it has the advantage of possessing a greater amount of lead time to work on the innovations that are beginning to build up externally to the school. As a result school priorities for development can be shaped in relation to externally imposed initiatives (see Chapter 7).

Managing the environment

The environment of the school and an LEA encompasses two domains: that which is within the direct boundary of the school and that which adjoins it. The definition of the boundary of the school varies from school to school. Some schools and LEAs define their boundaries quite narrowly. In some instances a school would only include the staff and the pupils; others would include the parents and governors; and in others, some form of partnership with the LEA would be included. The operational test in this is the extent to which the school enables the constituent groups to play an active and appropriate part in the development of the school. The boundary issue has considerable ramifications, for it affects the way in which a school is able to handle its external pressures and the extent to which it is able to acquire information to contribute to the formation of its vision.

Any organization has to live within its environment. A high degree of mismatch, especially in terms of the institution's goals as between itself and the wider context, ultimately leads to tension and pressure. Neither is total harmony desirable or feasible. It is a feature of the change process that states are in different conjunctures. For this reason, it is important to differentiate between what is possible in the short term, which may also be temporary, and longer-term, more substantial and permanent developments. This aspect of vision contributes to the effectiveness with which the school or organization can maintain relative harmony within itself and with the external pressure for change.

Danger occurs when significant differences become established between the school and its environment, for this often results in the school establishing a strong, somewhat impermeable boundary to protect itself. The reason for the difference may well be the result of changes the school has made that are out of step with the wider context. This may be through a misreading of the innovations the school is being asked to take on or a shift in its policies that have put it out of step with the parents and children. The danger is not in the short term for such changes may be part of the first stage of the change process. However, if this becomes a long-term gap then sooner or later the school's boundary is broken down by the outside elements.

There are also boundaries to the way in which developments and their innovations are defined and worked on. Development is the result of the identification of a particular need that requires the formulation of a response. Without a careful approach to the identification and analysis of the problem, the solution the school finds may not be correct. Some solutions can only be found by looking at the wider context, by reformulating the boundaries of the issue. The solution to the raising of attainment in a particular subject or skill may lie not in better teaching but in the construction of a better curriculum framework in which that subject or skill is taught. For example, many schools enable students to retake GCSE. Nationally, there is a very low rate of improvement but there is evidence that schools that enable students to retake exams in the context of a new course framework, e. g. the Certificate of Pre-Vocational Education, help those students to make the necessary gains in those GCSE subjects that are retaken within a different course framework. Boundaries sometimes have to be redefined to arrive at an effective solution.

The acquisition and sharing of information about internal and external developments enables individuals and the school to manage their environment. Ignorance results in a reactive approach to change. The individual and the organization remain unaware of what is happening elsewhere and cannot then read the road of change. The wider the range of information, the more able the school is to adjust its development work to meet the changing situation. A simple example illustrates the point. The motorway driver who only focuses on the car ten yards in front runs the risk of collision. Only fast reaction saves the individual and, at speed, this is a major risk. By looking ahead the driver can act positively, adjust accordingly and, given the lead time that can be built up by looking ahead, the situation can be better managed. The same applies to schools and organizations.

The skill and experience of the school and the individual lie in being able to read the road and to differentiate between the irrelevant and the relevant. This skill is built through experience. Many teachers find this difficult for there are so many messages currently facing the education service, let alone all their conflicting directions. The teacher is unsure whether some of the changes are short term, or appear to be, or are, against the general trend of improvement over the last few years. The task is to identify those changes that are substantial and long term and do need to be incorporated into the school. Increasing the capacity of the school depends on the acquisition and application of the necessary knowledge to decide direction. Chapter 7 provides further insight into this issue, as does the section on networking in Chapter 6, which suggests that the school that is well linked into the wider environment through involvement in a range of projects, LEA staff and links with other schools is well placed to manage change.

The school or organization that manages its environment in the widest sense of the term will become proactive as opposed to reactive. The school will achieve this state through the involvement of staff in local, regional and national decision-making situations where they can obtain information but are also able to influence the formation of ideas and policy. To varying degrees the value of the representative or involved person depends on their ability to manage the relationship between the outside and the inside.

Confidence

Confidence is a difficult commodity to pin down in either its individual or institutional form, yet it is a very empowering state that enhances success in the change process. Confidence is the result of an attitude of mind; for some it can be a philosophy of life. Being confident is a disposition to action that probably has its starting point in achievement, skill and knowledge, e.g. confident skiers know they have acquired a set of skills and knowledge that can carry them over virtually any terrain.

Institutional confidence has the same characteristics as individual confidence, being the result of a successful learning process. It is the collective attitude and practices of the school that enable it to acquire the skills and knowledge needed to handle change.

It has long been recognized that confidence is an important factor in learning. It contributes to the ability to keep going however difficult the daily slog can be. Confident individuals can see the light at the end of the tunnel (drawing on their vision!) and can cope with the change-dip characteristic of the development process. The concept of the change dip needs further examination (Figure 5.2). The implementation of change can often result in the temporary de-skilling and subsequent drop in confidence of the school or individual as the changes embed themselves in practice. A useful analogy to describe the process is that of the golfer who decides to improve his or her stroke and overcome years of acquired, common-sense approaches. At the start, the separating out of the various elements of the stroke in the training can well result in a temporary loss of performance until the coaching and support lift the performance to a new level.

This analogy illustrates the implementation difficulty of the National Curriculum, where the segmentation of the curriculum into subjects and other components alongside the development and implementation of new

The change dip

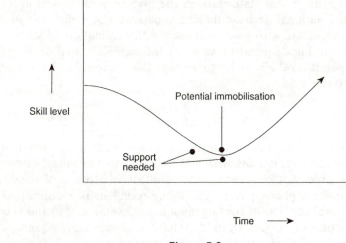

Figure 5.2

practices has caused difficulties by focusing on parts of what was previously an integrated activity in the minds of teachers. Eventually the curriculum will establish a new coherence. The only caveat, especially in the primary sector, is whether the extent and depth of the change has so deskilled teachers, and their confidence has become so lowered, that it is insufficient to bridge the dip. The danger manifests itself in immobilization, the point where the person or institution ceases to learn, has little confidence in their ability to tackle the new and finally comes to a halt. The result is that the job is done at a lower level until such time as the person leaves the school or an outside agency seeks to rebuild the situation. This is the role many LEA advisers and officers perform. It is impossible to leave the individual or the school in isolation because, as they move into this state and begin to fail, it is the children who suffer. The market-force approach is singularly dangerous in this context. The situation cannot be allowed to exist for long as a whole generation of students is then permanently affected.

The role of those developing the confidence of the individual and the school constitutes a balancing act. Too much change and the negative picture referred to above results. Confidence is one of the barometers of the school's climate for change. Institutional confidence is often referred to as the morale of the staff and it is one of the main means by which the support of individuals can be achieved through the change dip (see Figure 5.2).

Other aspects of confidence are equally important. Teachers are teachers of their colleagues as much as they are learners from colleagues. We often come across situations where teachers deny their leadership role. It is very difficult to persuade teachers to lead INSET in the area of pedagogy or to articulate their vision of the curriculum. It seems easier for them to share information in a collaborative way.

All of us have knowledge, skills and experience. Those with less experience or skill need the help of others. There are different roles in the developmental process. Some discussions in education are based on values where one person's view is as valid as another's but, in the growth of practice, those who have the necessary skill and knowledge need to be enabled to impart it to others. It is the mature leader and school that enable their members to gain and use their confidence to 'teach' colleagues. Sharing knowledge is vital to the growth of the individual and the school. Knowledge is a major part of power and people hold onto it for this reason. Lack of knowledge often causes the individual to make a wrong move, to put a foot wrong. Not only does this impede the development process but it also leads to a loss of confidence.

Key factors in the development process

This section is in three parts. Between them, they help to inform our understanding of the development process through an examination of

- the stages in the process through which innovations pass;
- the different forms of development that enable change to take place; and
- two sets of principles and concepts that underpin effective change and the development of the school's capacity for change.

Stages in the process

A general understanding of the stages in the change process has emerged over the last decade. The following is based on the work of a number of researchers but particularly Berman and McLaughlin (1978) and Fullan (1982). This identifies three stages in the change process: initiation, implementation and institutionalization. Each stage involves changes in structures, materials, practice and belief in various combinations. The general features of the process apply to national initiatives as well as school-based developments.

Initiation   This stage begins with the genesis of an idea. For that reason, it may take many years for the idea to grow within a school or LEA. Often the idea is modified in many ways before it becomes part of the work of those individuals, schools or LEAs that pioneer the ealy phase of development. Most innovations have antecedents in other developments. Take, for example, school development plans. Their origin in Enfield was the result of some development work in 1985, which drew on the work of Per Dalin.

The initiation stage is characterized by the mobilization of staff around an idea. The work is usually undertaken by an advocate (group or individual) that promotes the ideas. For this stage to be effective, the idea has to be related to the agenda of people and their perceived needs. The concept of the National Curriculum is a good example, as the idea received fairly general support. Many larger schools and LEAs support initiatives through the establishment of working groups where individuals with similar aspirations and energy can come together to tackle problems. Initiation has to be active. Change cannot be left to happen. Thus initiation in a school has to be promoted.

Implementation   Implementation is about putting the initial ideas and practices into wider use. The transition from initiation to implementation requires a change of approach in the development process. This stage involves the adaptation of original ideas in order for them to be adopted by others. Initiation is based on the creativity of a few. While those same few then become the driving force behind the implementation stage, there are important differences in the way in which this stage is handled if it is to be effective. The ideas and practices have to be transferred from the initiators to the remainder of the staff. The transition process has to be supported by a widening of the groups and individuals who are involved in the change and the development structure. The working group that comprised committed volunteers has to alter and align itself with the school's main structures if the spread of the ideas and practice is to happen. If the original group stays in power too long then the adoption process is hampered.

The implementation stage has to be managed and someone has to have responsibility for the process. This is helped by the charting of responsibilities for implementation, which should form part of the planning process. The process has to be shared and spread from the advocates in order to empower those who are taking on the ideas. Ownership of the innovation is a prerequisite to successful implementation. The modification of the initiative to suit the school's circumstances or the individual's practice is a natural part of development.

Change has to be supported. There are many aspects to the support process this section cannot cover. The list includes the need for external help, technical assistance with new pedagogy and the provision of physical resources at the right time and place. The failure to provide the necessary help for a sufficient length of time is one of the prime reasons for the disintegration of innovations.

Support, though, has to be matched with a degree of pressure, otherwise the innovation will lose its momentum. Finally there has to be some perceived gain from the perspective of the teachers who are taking on the innovation. If the initiative does not meet the agenda of the teachers' concerns, then it becomes classed as a poor solution to the problem the teacher thought it would solve.

Whether the innovation is imposed by law or not, the process of innovation rejection or acceptance has more to do with whether the change has improved the situation and met the perceived problem either in the idea itself or the skill with which it was implemented. A poor idea is a poor idea. Should an innovation imposed by law prove to be ineffective, then its legal status merely slows down the process of rejection or major adaptation. The use of law can constrain the search for improvement. Good ideas, poorly implemented, will also be rejected.

Reward is an important commodity but it should not be seen in a narrow financial sense for, although some do gain financially out of innovation, most change is taken on for professional reasons.

Institutionalization   Very little is known about this stage. Successful institutionalization occurs when the change has been well embedded into the practice of the school and its staff. For this to happen the practices have to be linked to what is currently occurring. Most curriculum change involves a change in the staff's teaching approach. Only when this has happened can institutionalization be said to have happened. Successful innovations need to have depth. Shallow changes are easily thrown off. This may involve the removal of competing practices but the development process operates more by adaptation than outright replacement. However successful the implementation stage, staff turnover can result in new staff being unaware of the changes, and previously successful innovations can fade away if there is not continuing induction and help for new staff.

The timescale for the whole process is often underestimated. There are no hard and fast rules but the period most innovations take to move through the initiation and implementation stage is between three and five years where the conditions are satisfactory. Our belief is that innovation overload may well slow the timescale down for the effective implementation of individual innovations. All organizations are handling a range of initiatives at various stages of development. Those who are responsible for the management of the change process should be able to identify the stage of development of each innovation. By so doing they can develop the appropriate strategy for each individual innovation and form an overall strategy through an understanding of the state that all the school's innovations are at. This concept is further examined in Chapter 9.

Forms of development

There are distinct but interrelated forms of development, which can be classified according to their focus:

- Staff, professional and management development (including all forms of teacher education).
- Curriculum development.
- Institutional development.

These forms of development, distinctive though they are, remain part of the management of the institution, the staff, the curriculum and the school's physical resource.

These terms require definition and elaboration. *Staff and professional development* are terms that are often taken to be synonymous. We wish to use them more precisely and to locate them within an overall framework of teacher education.

Teacher education covers all aspects of teacher development from initial training through induction to in-service. Initial teacher training is any formal course that prepares beginning teachers. Induction is a programme of systematic development organized by the school, LEA and/or college for teachers in their first year of service. In-service education is the general term that covers professional development, staff development and management development.

Professional development is concerned with meeting the individual teacher's professional needs, which may or may not align themselves with the staff development programme of the school or LEA. For example, the teacher may need subject updating which is not an LEA or subject requirement.

Staff development supports the implementation of major innovation, e.g. a new national curriculum or a new school-curriculum policy. This is often highly utilitarian, task focused and training orientated. The initiative for professional development lies with the teacher, whereas the school, LEA or the government has responsibility for the other forms.

Management development is a particular form of development that is concerned with improving the capability of all teachers to work with adults to improve the quality of the service.

There is no need to define the term *curriculum development*. In one way or another, all schools are involved in curriculum development. Curriculum development takes many forms. It may not be formalized or part of an LEA or regional project, but in classrooms and schools many teachers are involved in the development of some aspect of the curriculum. There is often a plea from teachers that change should slow down. This is as unreal as the heart wanting to stop for a while. The real problem is overload caused by constrained resources. Continual curriculum development is essential as educational change is evolutionary and central to quality and its improvement. There is no place for the big-bang approach. The school cannot shut down to re-tool as children are constantly moving through the system. Change is incremental. Each successive year group has to be treated as a new cohort in terms of its curriculum programme, especially in the secondary school where the outcome of curriculum change results in new courses that have a changed syllabus.

The involvement of staff in curriculum development is important for it provides them with direct experience of how the curriculum as a whole is constructed. There are marked differences, in our opinion, between those teachers who engage in curriculum development and those who do not. The latter are more technical in their work, the former have worked through why something has to be taught and are now more able to relate innovations to the needs of students. As a result the curriculum is handled more flexibly.

Schools that have major programmes of curriculum development are better able to work with incoming innovations and mould them as necessary. The school's ability to undertake curriculum development is a major component in the building of its capacity for change.

This chapter is unable to cover all aspects of *institutional development*. Whilst all the chapters in Part II contribute to institutional development, this section focuses on two additional and important elements: institutional structures and leadership. Both factors contribute significantly to the development of the school's capacity for change.

The formal staffing structure of the school is often hierarchical and, in larger schools, is departmentally organized. The rationale behind the arrangement is usually the need to meet the management and maintenance needs of the school in the provision and organization of the curriculum. The salary structure often reflects this. The development structure of the school is often embedded within this arrangement. In primary schools the salary structure combines both the responsibility for organizational co-ordination along with the developmental responsibility. In secondary schools there is a similar pattern but it is more complex with the additional designation of staff for the development of an aspect of the curriculum.

Whatever the extent of the formal structure to support development, each school has to consider and establish informal arrangements. In most cases this is achieved through the establishment of an infrastructure that is lateral and based on the energy and commitment of those staff who provide leadership in the development process.

Smaller schools are not in need of such structures as the staff are able to work together as a whole group, with each member playing different roles. In larger schools with more than a dozen staff, some working arrangement becomes necessary.

The most common approach to development is the establishment of a working group. This harnesses the energy of the interested and can be very effective – unless it alienates itself from the rest of the staff. Large schools may construct a strategy around long-term working groups that involve every member of staff with the major development goals of the school. The formation of academic councils or curriculum committees provides a non-departmental and lateral arrangement for the involvement of staff who would not normally be involved in the management of the school. The operation of the infrastructure of the school may well incorporate the points outlined in the section on networking in Chapter 6.

There are many ways in which a larger school can approach the task of supporting development, but the management of the infrastructure must be the responsibility of the senior management team. In many places this is delegated to a named deputy or senior teacher who may also have responsibility for INSET. There is strength in this arrangement for the skills, knowledge and operational areas have a lot in common. In secondary schools a small team may be created to co-ordinate and manage all aspects of the development work.

As the school develops its structures, a matrix approach to management becomes established. The warp and weave represent the combination of the development infrastructure with the formal system. When it is fully in place, each dimension of the overall system will have established methods of communication and co-ordination and be linked together. However, such systems will always be in a state of flux and require constant attention, for the development structures will be constantly changing as will the personnel.

Complete books have been written on the subject of leadership. We would refer the reader to those publications for a deeper discussion of the issues, but in the context of development one aspect requires examination.

Leadership has to be distinguished from formal leaders. The literature on school effectiveness and school improvement emphasizes the crucial role of the headteacher. It is clear to us that the headteacher and, for that matter, other members of senior management have important roles to play in the development process. The gatekeeper function of the headteacher will, to a stronger or lesser degree, support or constrain the leadership role played by other staff.

The issue that requires addressing is, what is effective leadership in a learning environment? We explore throughout the book the centrality of the learning process to the development of the school and its staff. Learning requires a supportive structure but the traditional role of the formal leader is the management of that structure. Structural management needs to be examined in relation to the leadership function exercised by effective curriculum leaders whose function it is to lead and teach colleagues within the learning environment of the school.

As we explore in Chapter 6, the creation of a learning infrastructure for the school and LEA (including networking) is a substantial ingredient in the development process. The relationship of the leader to colleagues both as a guide and mentor underpins the infrastructure. Those who are performing the leadership role in a learning environment have the same qualities, skills and knowledge the teacher has in relation to students.

The characteristics outlined earlier of vision, confidence and the ability to manage the environment are often recognized as the main attributes of such people. The school, and likewise the LEA, has to identify and support the leadership aspect of the service. A balance has to be struck between the managerial role and the educational leadership function. Improvement is unlikely to happen in the absence of educational leadership.

Improving the development process

Two sets of concepts and principles are examined here. The ideas in this section are illustrated in Chapter 9, The Proactive and Consciously Developing School.

Educationalists in the UK and, for that matter, in most developed countries, have built up their understanding of development through the implementation of single initiatives. Most educational and social-change programmes have been about the development of single initiatives handled somewhat separately. It is now clear both as a result of the speed and extent of change as much as the result of our understanding of it, that successful development occurs when the organization (school or LEA) understands the interconnections between various developments, their constituent events and phases, and their relationship to the individuals and institutions that are the focus of the change.

The International School Improvement Project first identified these concepts when it stated that change is multidimensional and complex. By developing this idea, the holistic characteristic of development required in the nineties can be identified as one of the keys to successful change but, at the same time, this analysis presents a vast range of new challenges. Holistic development requires the careful, concerted and simultaneous handling of all the contributing initiatives so that they can be drawn together into a complementary whole. In this way development is facilitated and each innovation effectively implemented. Such a construct requires those responsible for development to see each initiative as part of the whole, rather like the mechanic uprating the performance of a car engine. There are a number of changes that have to be made to a range of components. Each change has to be undertaken in relation to the other parts of the system.

There is a need to be conscious of the implications of any change and its impact on the rest of the system as well as a need to realize that all the changes that affect a successful outcome have to be handled simultaneously. To undertake some innovations and not others will not work. The implications of multi-dimensional change are considerable. Such an approach to change has to inform our understanding of the way in which the service (LEAs and schools/colleges) sets its priorities and handles the phasing of the change process.

To explain the concept further, an analogy might help. Whether you are learning to swim or ride a bike or drive a car, the process is similar. It is not possible to learn one skill at a time (i.e. to pedal or learn how to brake or use your legs in the water in lesson one) and then when that has been achieved, to move onto the next area. Once the bike or the car starts moving all the component skills have to be practised together. At the start, this is difficult and support is needed – the hand on the saddle, the instructor's pedals and hand near the wheel or the water-wings on the arms. The priority is to get some momentum and to keep moving, then to gain confidence, to feel supported and to learn about balance and staying afloat in all senses of the word. The priorities are of a different order and are certainly in stark contrast to the way in which the education service currently subdivides the total change process. Consider, for example, the National Curriculum, which was introduced subject by subject and key stage by key stage as opposed to an analysis of what was involved and then the formulation of a strategy that introduced the components holistically.

The planning trend in recent years has been to break up the overall goal into manageable tasks. The logic of this seems obvious. The aim is to help implement the various discrete aspects of the management process in such a way that everyone can grasp what needs to be done and complete it. Regrettably most educational change cannot be achieved in this way. The importation of production-line management has serious flaws. The context in education is very different. The components cannot be made anywhere at any time and then brought together to form the whole. The components are animate and the process organic. In trying to separate out the various tasks, the reductionist approach only succeeds in making it feel as if the task is being achieved whereas, in reality, it has broken up a holistic process, thus thwarting the achievement of the intended goal. It is only by working on the whole as it develops and the analysis of the impact of one change on another that results in the improvement of the whole.

The rush to a highly planned approach seems to stem from a need for security and false clarity; hence the construction of a rational systems model. Improvement and development are not rational. Systems and plans help but they are not a substitute for grappling with the complex nature of change. For these reasons we see problems about the general movement towards performance indicators and the focus on targets and tasks. They have a place in the action-planning process, but they certainly should not interfere with strategic development. The actions related to reductionist processes can easily become a substitute for real change and lead to the avoidance of handling the complexities.

A further reason for taking a holistic approach is that the majority of innovations currently on the agenda of change are interlinked in one way or another. Their interdependence has to be recognized and the phasing of their implementation matched in order to provide the mutual support each requires. The phasing of the stages of change can be managed by slowing down the process for some innovations and/or by concentrating resources on other developments in order to accelerate their implementation. The management of the synchronization of innovations is helped by the application of planning techniques, e.g. critical path analysis, at the development stage.

The complexity of the development process and the range of initiatives affecting education demands far more from the individual and the institution than ever before. As a result, the learning process that underpins all change has to be brought to a new level of consciousness in order to handle the higher-order processes.

The means by which development is improved has all the hallmarks of a maturation process. A lot of initial learning is responsive and unstructured, and this is generally very effective at that stage. Later on learning becomes increasingly structured and, as understanding develops, the process becomes more conscious and certain experiences are sought in order to develop further skills and understanding. When the learners are in full control, they are able to identify gaps in their knowledge and skills and, as a result, learning is undertaken to meet the challenge. For the individual or school to become conscious of the change process is a crucial stage of development, as it enables the staff to reach the necessary stage of conceptualization about the development process.

Schools appear to 'learn' in similar ways. They progress at different rates and use different approaches – for the school is the sum of the staff. It is the translation of individual practice into school knowledge and routines that constitutes institutional learning. The learning path for schools has less security about it than for individuals. Institutional learning is not permanent. The constant movement of individuals through the school may reverse the institutional learning process as new staff may not have the skills and knowledge of their predecessors unless the school has an effective induction programme to overcome these problems. This is a major issue for the education service, especially for LEAs. The ebb and flow of staff may operate to advantage in the market place where the job is very task orientated and labour can be slotted easily into the vacancy without impact on the system. The developing school has very different characteristics where each part can only operate by integrating with the school as a whole.

Maintenance and development

The concept is very simple but its application is very difficult to achieve. Within any institution there is a total resource. This is not finite but capable of being increased and redistributed in a number of ways. The physical resource for development may be increased: through the appointment of more staff allocated to the development function, i.e. to release staff; by the use of time (e.g. the five INSET days); or the deployment of cash to purchase materials.

Resource, though, has other forms. There is goodwill and energy, the result of the creation of a good climate which, if it is not abused, can help increase the developmental capacity of a school quite considerably. There is also the increased capacity that flows from enhancing the effectiveness and efficiency of the school's development process. Understanding development and being able to support it involves the acquisition of a set of skills and knowledge. Where the school possesses these skills, it rarely gets involved in dead-end projects. INSET becomes more effective and the school moves forward at a faster rate.

Even though development is important, the maintenance of a school's established goals is crucial. Whatever the capacity of the school, a balance has to be struck between the use of its resource for maintenance and development functions. This has to be a conscious process if it is to enable a school to make the most of its resources.

As developments become implemented they require maintenance and support. The reality is that most innovations do require more in the way of resources. Some innovations may displace a previous activity but only in part. A tension is created, for the school is faced with the potential choice of redeploying its development capacity into the maintenance of the recently established innovations. This becomes even more noticeable in times of reduced expenditure when there is a general pressure on the resources of the school and the first priority is often believed to be the maintenance of what is, without any regard for the future. The total removal of the development resource is counterproductive for, sooner or later, further initiatives have to be made and the resources found. A new balance has to be struck even if the level of resource for both development and maintenance is lower.

Another resource-allocation problem emerges when there are too many initiatives competing for support. As soon as the turn of one innovation is 'over' the pressure is to shift the resource to another innovation whether or not the existing innovations still require support. The consequences are substantial, for it is likely that the earlier innovation will wither as attention and resource is shifted away.

Many schools have encountered the difficulty of tackling too many developments, especially at the initiation stage, which has resulted in insufficient resource to handle them all at the implementation stage. This has negative consequences for the resourcing of the maintenance activity. The current legally imposed timetable for many innovations has serious implications as to whether the schools and the support structures have the capacity to handle the volume.

The message for schools and LEAs is to ascertain, continuously, the requirements of innovations in their various stages of development and relate these to the capacity of the school. This constant checking process is a central feature of the development planning process.

The following section on school plans and planning develops this further as it is through such procedures that the resource is managed.

Planning and plans

The planning process has a particular role to play in the life of the organization. The outcome of the various procedures is a plan that helps the users to set a course everyone is able to refer to. The planning that goes into it is the obverse side of the development process. Neither is a substitute for the other. Sound development benefits from good planning but planning of itself will not ensure development.

Three major components to planning and plans are considered:

1. The statement of aims and policies.
2. The development strategy.
3. The operational plan including the action steps and resource allocation.

Each component locks together with the others to form a comprehensive system.

Aims and policies

Each school has, or should have, a set of aims and policies. Policy can take many forms and sometimes schools are unaware of the extent of their policies, for certain documents are labelled procedures. Not all policies and procedures may be written down. It is open to question whether a school that has all its policies written down is effective. What is important is whether the staff of the school agree sufficiently about what they are trying to do to bring coherence to the work of the school. Written policies help but if they remain in the drawer then the school may well lack direction. School policy, especially curriculum policy, is very complex. For this reason the process by which the school adopts and/or develops its policy is crucial to the eventual success of policy implementation. The formal or cursory construction of policy that is disseminated to staff is often destined to remain unused unless it is accompanied by an implementation strategy. Participation in the formulation of the policy increases the chances of staff understanding and eventual changes in practice.

The development strategy

One of the most crucial yet underdeveloped aspects of development planning is the formation of a strategy. The context of change in the nineties necessitates that schools and organizations create a strategic framework to embrace all the innovations in such a way that the school and its staff are able to move forward.

The concept of strategic planning is that it is a conscious and systematic approach to the way in which the school organizes itself and its development activities in relation to the environment. This will help it to ensure that it is as free from surprises as possible, has the greatest amount of time possible to develop in relation to outside pressures and is able to locate the various activities within a coherent framework.

In education, a strategy is often applied to the development of single innovations. Whilst this has its value the central strategic task for any school is to develop a more macro-approach that deals with the multiplicity of innovations and their connections.

The formation of a strategy is built up from an understanding by key staff of the nature of individual innovations, their relationship to each other and to the aims and goals of the school and its current practice. Thus, the formation of a sound strategy is based on information and analysis (for a fuller examination of this, see Chapters 7 and 8).

The strategic framework occupies the space between the aims and policies of the school and the operational plan, thus lying above the domain of the action plan that defines specific actions but providing the structure upon which those plans can be built. We have observed that the development plans of schools often lack such a framework. The detail is there but, without a skeleton, it has little shape.

A strategy is constructed from the particular mix of the various forms of development (teacher education, management development, curriculum development and institutional development) that enables the development goals to be achieved. The framework should incorporate all the development goals of the school and the various innovations attached to them. (The process for undertaking this is outlined in Chapter 7.)

The formation of a strategic framework and its goals is highly contextual to the school/college or LEA. The success of a strategy lies in the creation of a set of particular projects that enable as many of the desired objectives as possible to be met. The projects have to be capable of

- generating wide support from the staff;
- accommodating a range of innovations at the macro- and micro-level;
- providing a framework for all activities that takes forward individual innovations and whole-school development; and
- having the potential to improve the capacity of the school for change.

Strategic projects and approaches are less likely to be single innovations, e.g. a National Curriculum subject implementation, although more complex innovations (such as assessment, appraisal and TVEI) do have the necessary characteristics. Other approaches include the identification of strategic goals alongside particular projects – for example, the building of team work amongst the staff, the raising of student achievement, increasing student numbers or the improvement of pedagogy. Such goals would remain valid for a number of years and provide a focus for all the school as well as enabling other future single innovations to be developed through this medium. Chapter 9 illustrates strategic planning.

INSET activity 5.2   *The strategic planning tree*

There are various strategic planning techniques that can be used. One method is to create a branched tree with the overall goal at the top and then to break down both what is meant by the goal and ways in which each statement can be achieved. The outcome is then analysed and a framework created (see Figure 5.3). Chapters 7 and 9 provide further techniques.

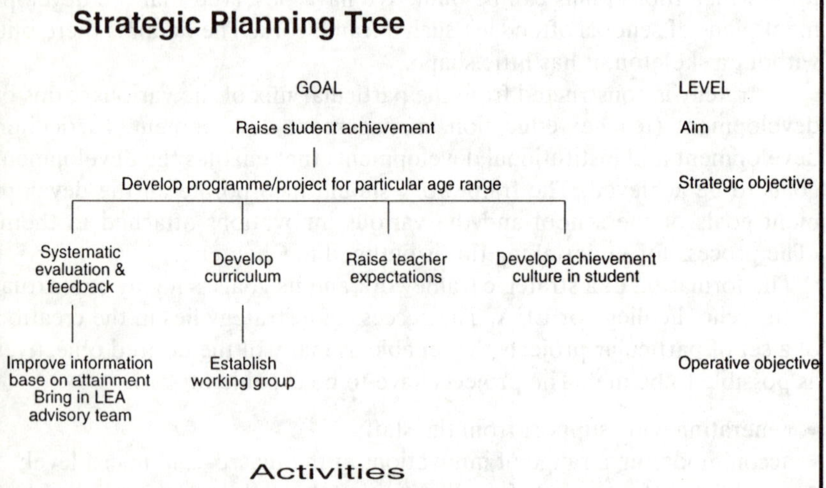

Strategic Planning Tree

	GOAL			LEVEL
	Raise student achievement			Aim
	Develop programme/project for particular age range			Strategic objective
Systematic evaluation & feedback	Develop curriculum	Raise teacher expectations	Develop achievement culture in student	
Improve information base on attainment Bring in LEA advisory team	Establish working group			Operative objective

Activities

The illustration provides an indication of the kinds of objectives and activities. The list is not exhaustive.

Figure 5.3

Strategic planning, when it involves the whole staff in various parts of the process, provides a means of bringing the school together and helping each member to locate their contribution and identify how their own or departmental action plan fits into the whole.

Useful planning techniques

Three particular techniques that aid the planning process are described: critical path analysis; responsibility charting; and the construction of planning cycles.

Critical path analysis

First introduced by the Du Pont company in 1958 as an aid to planning, critical path analysis can be profitably applied to the management of change, especially the phasing of multiple innovations. All of us use critical path analysis in our daily lives: it is the sequencing of activities to achieve a particular goal by plotting the various components on a timeline to get the optimum arrangement. It aids efficiency by helping to ensure that particular features of the process are completed on time and improves effectiveness through the opportunity it offers the planner to get everything in place at the right time, thus enabling the goal to be achieved.

A simple analogy that explains the process is the giving of a dinner party. All the components are put in sequence from the sending of the invitations to the preparation of the meal and the room. Each aspect is put into a sequence, including the cooking of the various dishes, which have to be ready at the appointed time. Managing development has many similarities to the dinner party. Things go wrong, sometimes the food is not in the shop or it has gone off, or . . .

The sequence for the work on development can be mapped out and located over the appropriate timescale. Initially each innovation should be mapped out in this way but the full benefit of the technique can only be obtained when all the projects are mapped in relation to each other and sequenced to avoid overload at particular times of the year or to ensure that they don't all come on stream in the classroom simultaneously. The exercise also enables the school to plot the optimum time for the use of its INSET days so that they can be used to maximum advantage for the development of staff as opposed to time set aside for working groups or staff meetings. The location of items for meetings and the INSET programme can then be fixed in relation to the pace of the development programme.

A simple network diagram can be constructed that locates all the events and activities in a sequence. Such a chart can be displayed to show the timetable for the development programme.

Responsibility charting

One of the key factors in the implementation of change is the identification of a key person who is given the responsibility for managing the achievement of the particular innovation or steering the overall strategy. Responsibility charting can go a lot further by identifying everyone who is involved with particular initiatives and the form of their involvement. The charting process identifies their contribution to a working group. Are they linked to the group as a supporter or a consultant but not directly involved? Are they the recipient of the minutes of the group? A simple chart can be made that is organized into rows for each development goal with various columns drawn across them to list the different roles to be undertaken (Figure 5.4).

Responsibility Charting

Area of activity	Responsible Person	Action Group	Support/ Consultants	Inform
Equal opportunities	J Brown	Names of working party	LEA advisory teacher	All staff & governors
Maths Implementation of National Curriculum	R Singh Co-ordinator for Maths			

Figure 5.4

Planning cycles

The construction of an overall planning cycle underpins the action plans. It enables the various significant points in the financial and academic years to be plotted in relation to crucial decision-making events. Whilst there is no clear development cycle there are points when curriculum decisions have to be finalized for implementation in the following year. These points can be plotted on a linear or circular diagram and provide a useful reference tool for planning.

The operational plan/the school plan

Three distinct terms have grown up over the last few years to describe the plan document. In 1985, Enfield LEA introduced the term Institutional Development Plan (IDP) to cover both a process and a document. This term was taken by Goddard from the work of Per Dalin and IMTEC (International Movement Towards Educational Change), where it stands for Institutional Development Programme. The more general national description of the document is School Development Plan, which recognizes its application to schools.

The advent of local management of schools (LMS) heralded the term School Management Plan. The confusion caused by this label stems from the managerial as opposed to the developmental aspects of the process and document. In order to overcome the unnecessary emphasis towards either development or management, we use the term School Plan.

Plans, planning and development

Plans are not a substitute for development. The school plan, i. e. the written document, is the product of a planning process which itself should be embedded in the development process of the school. There is always a danger that the plan, instead of being the means to an end, becomes an end itself. The formation of all plans (especially resource plans on finance and staffing) need to be the result of an integrated approach to school development.

The planning process is a continuous one throughout the year drawn together by the periodic production of written plans. Plans should be used, not left in drawers or produced just for the LEA. The description that is usually applied to this approach is the need for plans to be 'dog eared and coffee stained'.

A dynamic balance needs to be struck between the planning and development processes. Each facilitates the other although, at times, there are tensions in the process, particularly from the constraints of timetables. There are elements and occasions when the planning and the plan need to be specific, with accompanying timetables (e.g. the budget process) and, on other occasions, there is a need to be flexible in order to support the motivation and creativity of staff and to tackle the unpredicted. In these circumstances the development work of the school may not easily fit into prearranged systems.

The rapidly changing context of education necessitates a flexible approach to planning and plans. The document has to project far enough forward to ensure that major goals can be identified and achieved, yet it must be neither so precise in the long term nor so inflexible in the medium term to be unable to cope with any changes. Evolutionary planning is not an excuse for doing it as it happens. Hence the school plan is best constructed on a three-year rolling basis in three phases (see below), and updated annually. The work of Wallace (1991) and Hargreaves and

Hopkins (1991) draws similar conclusions, and readers may wish to examine these works for further sources of ideas.

The development process and the production of a school plan should draw on and link with the following school documents and procedures.

Aims and policies   The school plan will need to refer to the aims, policies and schemes of work. Such documents inform the context of the plan and, as such, any developments in the school's policy should be recorded.

Evaluation procedures   The evaluation and review procedures within the school and the LEA should provide important information and support substantially both the analysis of the context and the formation of the development objectives. There are three aspects to the evaluative component:

1. Evaluation of the previous plan and development programme which is normally within the document.
2. The outcomes of any formal evaluations, reviews or inspections which can be included in a summary form.
3. Proposals for the evaluation work over the forthcoming period.

School management arrangements   Effective school development is synonymous with effective school management. The structure and procedures for the management of the school have to be linked effectively to the school plan and development process. To achieve this, the school will need to define the roles, responsibilities and relationships of particular groups and individuals to each other, especially those who are directly involved in the management processes. These include the senior management team, the governors and key co-ordinators (e.g. for INSET). However, the contribution and involvement of all staff is essential if the plan is to mean something in terms of guiding their future action.

The governing body   In consultation with the headteacher, the governing body has clear responsibilities for the setting of the school's aims, policies and resource allocation. It has a particular responsibility for the direct resource implications of the development process and needs to be informed of the professional arrangements for the development of the curriculum and staff.

Practices vary, but the governors' involvement in the development work of the school may well help them to become better informed about the process and the outcome. Discussions with the curriculum sub-committee may also help prior to the plan going to the main governing body for information and discussion. Resource plans require formal adoption.

The resource cycle   The budget process has its own timetable and imperatives. It rarely fits neatly with the development process. Development and maintenance operations and the financial and academic years often fail to coincide. For this reason, the school and the LEA should construct a timeline that draws out the crucial decision-making points over the first two years of a three-year cycle. In this way the LEA and school budget process can be co-ordinated and related to the academic year.

A suggested format for school plans

Content

An optimum arrangement consists of a set of linked plans and statements that describe the following:

1. The vision of where the school is heading, including a whole-school perspective (related to school policies).
2. The context the school finds itself in and its needs, i.e. the needs of pupils, staff, curriculum and the community the school serves, as informed by the outcome of reviews. The evaluation procedures should include the school's review of previous plans and their development targets set against the needs of the pupils and staff. Evaluation that is solely based on the achievement of previously stated targets can set up a false cycle of development. This is especially the case when the goals and targets may have been poorly constructed and fail to meet the real needs of the pupils or the school. In some circumstances the school could meet the development goals but fail to meet the needs of the pupils. Evaluation has to check constantly whether the goals are related to pupil needs and to ascertain what those needs are.

   The following example illustrates this point. The school may identify the need to improve children's reading. The school turns this decision into an initiative to establish a new reading scheme. The scheme is implemented with 'success' but the children's reading remains as it was. The issue is to examine whether the scheme met the needs or whether something else was needed. More work at the stage of identification of the problem may have correctly identified the issues and shown an alternative strategy. Simple evaluation that looks only at the goals of the initiative is of limited value.
3. A clear development strategy and proposals for action that describe the goals and priorities for a three-year period and that are defined in terms of short-, mid- and long-term objectives.

   The strategy and action plans should take account of the priorities of the LEA and central government. The plan would also outline any

options or proposals that may have resource implications and that there-fore need to be agreed by the governors.
4. A separate though related resource plan that outlines the allocation for the immediate period. This should cover all staffing and financial as-pects. The longer-term resource needs should be identified and stated in the document.

Structure

Developments over the last few years have provided some evidence from a range of LEAs that

- the optimum period is three years;
- three distinct phases can be identified that roughly correspond with each year; and
- there are two distinct functions to the plan – the overall aspect and strategy and the detailed actions. The plan can, therefore, be produced in two parts that divide the overall statements of vision, context and strategy from the detailed plans.

There is a continuing debate about the length of school plans. The case for a short document is well made in terms of time spent on its production and readability. However, there are arguments for a longer total document. The first part may well be contained within ten pages. The production of the detailed plans, on the other hand, may well extend the document to over sixty pages in a secondary school by including departmental and work-ing group plans. The advantage is that the plans provide information to a wide audience so that all staff know what is happening. The LEA can also use the second plan in its detailed planning of support – with the first part supporting the LEA school link at the institutional level.

The question of length relates to purpose. The optimum arrangement appears to be the construction of a two-part document.

Phases

Phase 1   This phase should include a statement of the specific actions and plans, including resource allocations for the period up to the end of the following academic year. It is a summary of agreed action.

Phase 2   This covers the second year of the plan (commencing at the start of the financial year following the plan's publication) and includes all mid-term development objectives. In addition, this can contain proposals for future resource requirements including the budget exercise for the mid-term.

Phase 3   A brief summary of the school's long-term proposals.

Format

Part one of the plan should contain

- the vision for the school;
- the context and evaluation; and
- the strategy.

Part two of the plan should contain statements that relate to the various programmes and projects affecting the whole school and various sectional perspectives that cover aspects of the school's work, e.g. departments/ operational groups, finance and staffing plans for phases 1 and 2.

What teachers think about school development planning

This section has been contributed by Ian Terrell, Advisory Teacher for Evaluation and Assessment in the London Borough of Enfield. Ian is currently working on a project which is looking at the links between development planning and the raising of pupil achievement.

In this section he describes the context of development planning in the London Borough of Enfield and reports teachers' views on whole-school planning issues, including

- the purpose of whole-school planning;
- the usefulness of the process of whole-school planning;
- the process of writing the school development plan;
- the evolution of the planning process; and
- the culture of developing schools.

The LEA context

Much has been written about school development and school development plans (SDPs). Perhaps rather too frequently, little notice or attention has been given to the views of the teachers who write and work on them. The following comments were collected from various sources between 1989 and 1991:

- A detailed interview survey of all department heads in one secondary school.
- A study of a primary school and a secondary school for the DES School Development Plans Project.

- Various meetings in the borough and within institutions.

The London Borough of Enfield has required each school to produce an annual Institutional Development Plan since 1985. There is, therefore, a long history of their use. Each school has adopted its own approach to development planning adapted to its own needs and culture. This has led to a wide variation in the styles of plan produced and the process of production.

The purpose of the SDP

Although some teachers felt that there was 'no shared belief in its value' a large number of teachers felt that 'forward planning' was the major purpose. Other planning activities mentioned were: 'clarifying plans', 'setting priorities and targets', 'establishing a timescale' and 'establishing a structure'.

Some felt that the whole process was 'a complete waste of time' and a few saw the main purpose as 'evaluation', particularly as the means by which others might know what is going on: 'Keep those above you off your back and keep the borough happy.'

Whole-school planning

In secondary schools in particular, departments and working areas have traditionally been fairly autonomous units. In Enfield it has become reasonably common to find that secondary SDPs were collections of departmental plans. Each department would write its own plan. Usually the head of department would work with members of the department. Sometimes department members would write parts of the plan. Often, group members would be given responsibility for implementing parts of the plan.

The whole SDP can therefore be a large document. However, a number of staff found it to be one they could use to see what others were doing in the school. Learning support and library staff, for example, found areas of development they could link into. There was also some cross-fertilization of ideas.

Some teachers saw the need to develop the SDP to ensure coherence and consistency across the school. This has been achieved in a number of schools by

- identifying whole-school priorities early so that departments can address them;
- establishing cross-curricular working groups;

- outlining activities and use of INSET time prior to departments writing plans;
- establishing frameworks for departments to address priorities within plans;
- monitoring departmental submissions; and
- outlining a school management overview detailing the priorities to be addressed within departmental plans.

The usefulness of the process

One head of department said:

> I think there are enormous advantages . . . I feel very positive about it as a process. I think that it does help to review what you have done during the year. It helps to look back. It provides a useful record of what has been achieved. I think it does help you to look forward to what you are actually going to achieve over the next year and over the next three years. I think that you can provide yourself with realistic goals for your work. I think at a time when there is so much change going on, or there could be so much change, if you allowed the change to take over, rather than try to make sense of what you are doing, it's useful to have some kind of outline of where you are going and what you are doing . . . It stops those feelings of panic and makes people feel in control.

In one school, half of those interviewed said that writing the SDP had been useful and successful. Dissatisfaction was connected with lack of time to undertake development work, being too ambitious in planning and not being able to control circumstances, like key staff leaving. Uncertainty about government and local decisions made planning very difficult.

A number of department heads in two different schools have made the point that they wanted senior management to follow up what the department had planned to do. Sometimes this view was related to a need to resolve issues that were beyond the capacity of a department to resolve on their own (for example, appointing part-time staff or room allocation).

One interesting comment was that writing the SDP had made one department head realize that she was doing a professional job and not muddling through. Another had come to understand the complexities of whole-school planning.

One headteacher commented that the SDP 'helped [to] manage . . . staff knew when their initiatives were going to come up. . . . There is no pressure on staff. . . . Actually it helps you to manage the governors and the LEA.'

One member of staff reported that

> We reviewed it the other week actually . . . it was nice to see what we said we would do and what we have covered and also to see what we said we would do

and haven't. Just to know that the way we are working, it's either reassuring or it just sort of brings us up to date. . . . It's good to have one, otherwise with all the work that you are putting in you don't know where you are. . . . It makes it all worth while . . . you know that you are going to get there.

The importance of the process is summed up in the comment: 'the way that we produced guidelines, the way that we do our planning has actually affected the way that people work in their classroom.'

The usefulness of the document

There is a widespread belief that the document itself is less important than the planning and implementation process. Once the SDP had been written the writers knew what was in it and did not need to refer to it except to remind themselves of key dates or events.

Some felt that once something was in the SDP it could be used to bid for resources or to motivate people: 'Look! It's in the IDP and we haven't done anything about it yet.' A few saw the SDP as a chance to look at the work of other departments, to seek liaisons or to share good ideas and information.

The process of writing the SDP

Most schools produce a detailed timeline of how the SDP is going to be produced. Schools have started the process earlier in recent years but between Easter and July is a typical planning period. Teachers on the whole welcomed an identified period for reflection on the previous year and for planning for the future. The rest of the year could be devoted to implementing development.

Audit and review

Schools in the LEA are informed about national and local developments through an annual 'gold letter' produced by the education department. Schools organize a range of review mechanisms including staff conferences, 'GRIDS' exercises, questionnaires, professional development interviews and so on. Some schools have adapted *Curriculum in Action* (Open University, 1981) materials to support their audit. Increasingly, video and paired observation work informs the audit. A number of staff felt the need to sharpen the review process.

The SDP period gave people time to collect information from syllabuses, examination boards, the DES and so on. Meetings with INSET co-ordinators, curriculum deputies and advisers were arranged.

In larger departments it was a time for meetings to decide what had to be done and what needed to be done. Where teachers taught in more than one department this raised problems of dividing commitment between different departmental development plans.

Staff turnover made planning very difficult, particularly in small departments. However, SDPs were seen as useful documents to give to staff newly appointed to the department.

Maintenance, management and development

Several teachers have commented that the majority of work that goes on within a school is maintenance. In Enfield, the SDP does not document this.

Some activities within the SDP are activities managing new developments – for example, buying resources, looking at a new syllabus or writing a policy. In general these are easy to plan for since the staff know what ought to be done and how to do it. Development that involves a large amount of learning on the part of teachers is different. Such learning must be about new insights and new understandings. There are examples of how development involving learning has taken place.

In one school, what began as an exercise to look at record-keeping has led to a deeper understanding of the connection between assessment and planning and delivering the curriculum. Put simply, they have learned that assessing children's learning tells them a lot about their aims and plans for the curriculum and their own performance as teachers. Managing the learning of teachers, because it is not necessarily sequential or consistent in pace, is more difficult to plan for:

> It was decided to stretch the plan to three years instead of two. . . . We decided that in the summer term there would be no SDP work because we needed a break . . . there had been so many changes, it's difficult to see the results of a specific one in the classroom so therefore we needed time to look.

The SDP process itself can aid teachers' professional learning. Teachers can work collaboratively, share ideas and learn from experience. As a number of teachers commented, 'the process we've been through is far more important than the finished document'.

As schools work with new developments they learn approaches to managing change. Underlying this notion is the comment by the Chief Adviser: 'The SDP is about increasing the capacity of the school to take on board and handle change.'

The process of planning evolves

There is some evidence that schools do not settle on a planning process but learn to adapt with experience. One school started with planning and budgeting INSET as a focus for the SDP. The first year the plan was written by the senior staff. The idea of involving more staff emerged. The following year the SDP was written by department heads and collated by the senior management team. This raised issues about how whole-school issues could be addressed through thirty separate department or working-group plans. The following year school priorities were described in an overview written by the co-ordinators of priority working groups and senior staff. Each department was able to respond to the overview and submit a plan that included its own specific developments yet also addressed whole-school priorities. The following year the process was adapted to include bidding for development money under LMS.

Some general advice was offered by one senior teacher:

- Don't be too ambitious.
- Start small and allow to grow into larger areas.
- Planning for three years allows you to bring forward parts of the plan.
- The process of change takes time; people have to grow to be comfortable with it.

This kind of learning can result in changes to the SDP documentation. In several schools the documentation has become more sophisticated over time: 'There had been an increasing formality of writing and publishing the document.'

Such changes do not necessarily result in more effective development. Deciding the balance between the administrative and bureaucratic element of planning and the developmental aspect, is the key.

The culture of developing schools

The SDP process has been central to the culture of development in schools in Enfield. In some schools the process has been linked over a period of five years to new styles of managing development. These include using

- working/development groups;
- cross-curricular groups;
- staff conferences;
- collaborative research and evaluation procedures; and
- involving pupils and parents in development.

The SDP process has also contributed to the communication process between staff. At another school, the SDP process involved

- staff being interviewed about their professional development needs;
- LEA funding to support personal professional development;
- staff being encouraged to take on new responsibilities; and
- staff being encouraged to work in teams to share learning.

Increased collaboration and participation by all staff is generally central to successful planning. In one primary school where all members of staff are involved in the process, detailed work is undertaken by working groups but these report back to the whole staff. Draft work is kept by all staff in red files. All teachers can comment on the pilot implementation before the documents are finally accepted by the staff and then kept in black files.

At the school it was noticeable that the staff always talked about school development as 'we' – 'we decided that our priorities were . . .'

However, an important aspect of school development was the leadership role of the senior management. Teachers' learning and development was felt to be a normal part of school life. Often the headteacher and senior staff were seen as 'course attenders'. Yet they also had an active school role. One primary school headteacher was involved in

- collecting reports from teachers' classroom work;
- interviewing staff about development needs;
- monitoring the progress of development from the minutes of meetings; and
- supporting development projects by finding and allocating resources.

Conclusion

At any given moment, there may be many different perspectives about the SDP process. This brief summary of the views of staff drawn from some schools in Enfield illustrates the need to acknowledge the views of teachers in the planning process.

Schools need to build their own SDP process to meet their own needs and their own culture. The school development-plan process can evolve over time and the evolution needs to be managed carefully to ensure that development is not replaced by bureaucratic documentation. Building collaboration and ensuring the participation of staff requires careful leadership, management and planning in itself.

Planning and implementation can be straightforward. Where development involves teachers learning new principles or beginning to work in new areas, having a fixed notion of outcomes can be more problematic. Underlying the process, the overriding concern should be to build the capacity of the school to adapt to changing circumstances and to meet new challenges as they come along.

Conclusion

The central value of a school plan is that it helps a school to manage change more effectively through the conscious articulation of its goals and forward planning. As a common document amongst all the members of the school, it provides a focus and framework for reaching agreement about action. When the IDP was launched in Enfield, the purpose of the plan was stated as being to help the school manage the increasing complexity of change. That purpose remains valid.

Issues for consideration

1. How can the institution support staff in the acquisition of the knowledge and skills of the development process?
2. What are the most appropriate formal structures and informal arrangements for the support of development in the school/college and the LEA?
3. What is leadership in a development context and how can it be supported?
4. How can the planning process in all its forms, especially the strategic aspects, be improved, and who should take the lead responsibility in an organization?
5. What format should a school plan take?

Further reading

Dalin, P. and Rust, V. (1983) *Can Schools Learn?*, NFER/Nelson, London.
Everard, B. and Morris, G. (1990) *Effective School Management*, Paul Chapman Publishing, London.
Fullan, M. (1991) *The New Meaning of Educational Change*, Cassell, London.
Hargreaves, D. H., Hopkins, D., Leask, M., Connolly, J. and Robinson, P. (1989) *Planning for School Improvement: Advice to Governors, Headteachers and Teachers*, DES/HMSO, London.

6
LEARNING

Introduction

All development involves learning. This chapter examines aspects of learning as they apply to teachers and schools/colleges, regional and national systems and organizations. Learning, as applied to teachers and the education service, is directly enhanced by three different forms of development: inservice education (professional, staff and management development), curriculum development and institutional development. Learning is not confined to inservice training courses for teachers. It should permeate the way the service operates. The contribution of structures and supportive arrangements is discussed in Chapter 5, though the particular value of networking is discussed later. These arrangements provide the framework for the learning environment.

This chapter begins with an examination of the features and the underlying principles that support learning as they apply to and underpin all forms of development, albeit in different ways.

Learning – some general features

Learning and development

Learning is central to the development process. Real change involves doing something differently. Whether it is taking on a new idea, new values or a change in behaviour, change always involves learning. Thus all that is known about learning should be applied to the way in which individual teachers, staffs, departments, schools and colleges, LEAs and government carry out development.

Providing a learning environment is not just about the creation of effective inservice but also the creation of operational structures and processes throughout the education service. The implications of viewing the institution and the service as a collaborative whole are considerable, especially at the interface of the development activity with managerial systems and aspects of accountability which are not historically based on learning processes. Whilst it is easier to understand the notion that individuals need to learn in order to change it is essential that more is understood about how professionals and organizations learn and the context that facilitates such learning.

The term the 'Learning School' has been in use for a long time. The features of effective schools have been identified and various useful lists have been produced (Rutter *et al.*, 1979; Mortimore *et al.*, 1988), but there is a need for a deeper understanding of the learning process as it applies to the school. Ideas about school development as a learning process are in their infancy. More work has to be undertaken to help a school that is not learning to move forward. The set of operations that need to be supported in such an institution cannot be gleaned from the current literature. (Some of these issues are examined in Chapters 5 and 9 as they apply to the development of the capacity for change.)

To use an image, successful development involves working towards the creation of a completed picture. Most artists have a general idea of what they are working to. They work via a set of temporary images. Unlike the artist, education never achieves its final picture. One simple message to take from this is that it is necessary at every point to have an image in mind but to be prepared always to shift it as the picture develops.

So what are the elements of learning that contribute to effective development and how can each piece be developed so that successful change can occur?

A number of key features can be identified:

• The balance between content and process.
• The relationship of learning to experience.
• The development of a conscious, continuous process.

Content and process

Whilst this chapter is concerned primarily with the learning process, the content or substantive aspect of any change is equally important. They are two sides of the same coin. The content affects the process in terms of the kind of learning that needs to take place and determines the balance between the skills, attitudes and knowledge that are required by staff. Thus, for example, the development of primary science may have more to do with teacher knowledge and pedagogy (i.e. pupil learning) than attitudinal issues; equal opportunities may involve all three aspects.

Learning and confidence

Confidence is an essential part of learning, but how does it play its part? Vision, knowledge and sets of skills all contribute to the feeling of confidence. If change is to be effective, then schools and teachers must be helped to develop their confidence to meet their responsibilities and accountabilities. The difficulty is that in education no one can be quite sure that what is being taught is entirely valuable nor that there is a guaranteed way of teaching that enables children to learn. The profession has to work with these two fundamental uncertainties and no manner of attempted curriculum prescription, political assertion or alleged conclusive proof will resolve totally the continuing dilemma. Many of these issues are as complex as understanding the operation of the universe.

Most people feel confident about making a cup of tea. The car manufacturer is confident about the production of a vehicle. The outcome is clearer, the technology precise. The false dream of society (especially politicians) is that education can be managed into the same arrangement. At the level of teaching a simple skill, such a mechanistic approach is likely to work.

But education cannot be reduced to a series of simple elements of knowledge or skill. It depends on the creation of a weave of interrelated objectives and components that interact with the individual who is not an empty vessel to be filled or moulded in the image of the maker. The complex interaction of the curriculum with the child and their motivation and capacity to learn has to be managed holistically by the teacher and the school.

So how do teachers become confident and effective practitioners? One characteristic of quality teachers and teaching is the way in which continuing doubt, the source of all improvement, is handled. We are not referring to the confusion stemming from a lack of understanding about various innovations that do not seem to have any logic, but the internal debate about the best way to teach. Quality in terms of student attainment and achievement is the result of the interplay between learning and teaching. Thus an analysis of the work of the teacher is central to understanding how teachers learn about their jobs, the balance between different forms of accountabilities and the fostering of a climate of confidence that enables the teacher to work with the constant dilemma of not being totally sure that what they are doing will be effective.

Effective teaching requires the teacher to interact with the student in such a way that the designed learning environment facilitates the student's

growth. The creative construction of the student's learning experience requires the teacher to reflect continuously on their teaching and the student's progress. Thus quality teaching is a continuously creative activity.

Learning, interconnectedness and accountability

Two main strands can be picked out from this definition of effective teaching that relate to accountability and the way this is enshrined in professionalism. Firstly, the concept of downwards (moral) accountability to the
student flows from the central relationship of the teacher to the child. But
in most education systems there are dominant and often negative pressures
for upwards (contractual) accountability to meet curriculum (society) and
managerial goals. The tension between these two accountabilities is becoming sharper and can be seen in the operation of the National Curriculum and in schemes of evaluation, teacher appraisal and pupil assessment.

Secondly, there is the powerful concept of the interdependent learning
system as a prerequisite to educational effectiveness. This concept draws
on the belief that the facilitation of pupil learning requires the teacher to be
supported as a learner. The concept in turn sees the school as a learning
organization that provides students, teachers and parents with a learning
environment that itself is created and maintained by the LEA and various
regional and national structures and organizations. The contrary perspective views the teacher solely as a member of an institution which is seen as a
freestanding entity. Such a view fails to see learning as a social and connected activity with the result that it does not support or improve the
learning environment for teachers, thus decreasing the collective work of
the profession in the area of teaching and learning, and weakening the
support for the improvement of quality.

A further feature of effective teaching and the work and role of the
teacher is the teachers' ability to develop and synthesize their understanding and practice of the various components of the curriculum, their range
of pedagogical skills and management capabilities (in terms of their work
with adults), and their knowledge of the educational context. These abilities are important whether or not the teacher is in a leadership position or
working with students. A simple test as to the importance of these features
is to observe the absence of these elements in the work of a teacher!

Learning, teaching and the curriculum

Not only is the teacher's learning central to effective teaching but it is also
a vital component in the development and delivery of a quality curricu-

lum. There are several reasons for this. The curriculum can never be produced as a step-by-step instruction manual for the teacher. Thankfully those days appear to be behind us. There is no evidence from any part of the world that a high-quality curriculum can ever be totally prescribed nationally or even locally. Curriculum has to be reconstructed at every level of the system. This reality of the education process requires a sophisticated curriculum development process of the highest order at every level.

The curriculum has a number of facets. Curriculum policy will always signal direction. When the policy is properly constructed it provides a clear statement of the values, vision and principles of the organization, whether it is a school or an LEA. But it may not always be to everyone's agreement. Understanding the purpose of curriculum policy in the improvement process is essential for, although the detail often changes, it is crucial for every teacher to understand the curriculum framework, even though it won't tell you when, where or how to do something. Any National Curriculum framework will always need fleshing out and modifying locally and at school level.

Even if curriculum policy could remain static, the teacher constantly needs to match the policy to the needs of individual pupils and the changing needs of society. To be translated into the classroom and into student achievement, the curriculum has to be organized and designed into student experiences. This is a creative process where quality is dependent on the full understanding of what has to be done, coupled with a considerable degree of professional commitment to the adaptation process by the teacher and the school.

There are few parallels in other areas of work. The teacher is closer to the architect than the builder whilst embracing both tasks. The size and complexity of the operation requires the active mental, physical and emotional involvement of the teacher.

The development of the curriculum demands the full involvement of the teacher in its construction, especially if curriculum policy is to inform the teaching process fully. Thus professional responsibility and accountability (see Chapter 8) have to be equal partners, otherwise there is little basis for delivering an effective curriculum.

The quality of the education service and its work is dependent on effective development processes at every level and stage. The education service requires all its participants to be effective learners. Effectiveness can only be achieved if a holistic model can be developed that has learning as the key operational characteristic of the service at all levels and for all parties.

Models of learning for the profession

Quality in education can only be achieved if the teaching and learning process is underpinned by a model of learning for the service as a whole. For pupils to become better learners, the nature of the teaching process demands that teachers must continue to be learners throughout their careers, otherwise they will cease to be effective. Even if this requirement was thought to be unnecessary previously, then it is obviously unrealistic in the changing nineties to expect teachers to remain up to date, creative and fully effective without the support of a continuous programme of learning through staff and professional development. Professional development is a dynamic concept interrelating the needs of the individual teacher with the challenges of the job and the opportunities for improvement. It is also unique to each teacher as his or her profile of need is highly individual.

A major requirement in education is the maintenance and enhancement of the motivation of teachers to remain learners and engage in professional, staff, institutional and curriculum development throughout their careers. These are the features of an effective teaching force, for they underpin professional accountability through the development of understanding and skill in the ways in which children learn and teachers teach. Only through the development of such understandings can there be a professional dialogue about the effectiveness of schools and teaching. Most if not all professions have built up a knowledge and skill base in order to improve their work.

In order to help those concerned with the operation and organization of teacher education and school development, the following paragraphs bring together a number of processes that help schools and their staffs learn.

Individual development is the result of a complex set of motivational factors and learning experiences that enable the individual to move forward. Institutional learning has similar though more complex sets of factors at the heart of the improvement processes. Schools are not homogeneous institutions. They comprise a number of people with their own values, goals and motivations. Each person's contribution has to be recognized and built into the way the institution functions. However, the general state of development and the way in which a school learns is built upon similar concepts to the way in which individuals learn. The premiss of this section is that professional, staff and institutional developments operate according to similar principles but that they have different arrangements and features. This chapter deals with the main concepts and principles and Chapter 5 with the implications for practice.

INSET activity 6.1   How do we learn?

An INSET activity that a school can mount for itself is to identify the learning styles of individual members of staff alongside the ways the school learns/develops. This can then be used to check the similarities and the differences. The activity starts with a brainstorm of the ways in which individual teachers believe they learn and the ways in which staff feel the school moves forward.

The second stage is to examine the results, especially the differences between individuals, and to look subsequently at the way the school's institutionalization of learning through its management and development practices mirrors the learning differences of individuals.

The third stage is to consider how relevant the ideas in this section are to viewing teacher and school learning as being part of a continuum.

A variation of the exercise for the assessment of the learning style of the individual is to use the various training instruments that are available, especially those of Kolb.

The two models described in the next section draw out different features of the learning process.

A model of learning and conscious improvement

This model (see p. 119) draws out two essential characteristics of learning which underpin effective development. It can be applied to both the individual and the institution:

- The need to be conscious of and able to articulate the process of development.
- The constant and dynamic relationship that exists between practice and belief.

The model illustrates the individual's degree of consciousness and articulation about practice and belief, and the match or mismatch between them.

Beliefs (including individual as well as school aims and goals) and practice are two major components in the learning process. It is rare for individual and institutional belief to be matched totally. The job often requires teachers and schools to do things they don't quite believe in. This only becomes a problem if the gap between the two becomes too large. At that moment a number of possible courses of action can occur: the person leaves the school, some attempt to bridge the gap is made or the person seeks to change the institution to bring the enforced practice closer to their personal belief. The situation applies to a school when it either has changes forced upon it or it has decided to change its aims, goals or practices.

Effective in-service work and school development depend on the level of understanding the organizer of development activity has about the process of learning and the relationship between practice and belief. Equally, any inability on the part of the subject (teacher or school) to be objective about their existing practice and to be able to articulate that to others impedes the development process because it hampers the means by which the gap between belief and practice can be discussed and worked with. Learning cannot take place with any degree of security because the relationship of what is being learned in relation to what exists is unknown by all the parties concerned. The outcomes of any learning experience built around such a situation may be interesting in itself but they are likely to remain items of unconnected knowledge and skill with the result that real change and real improvement is thwarted.

INSET activity 6.2   Analysis of practice

> There are a variety of activities designed to enhance the level of individual and institutional understanding about practice. These include the work and materials on classroom action research (see the work of CARN), school evaluation (and inspection) and appraisal for professional development. All help the teacher and the school to collect and analyse evidence of practice, identify the gap with aims and goals and, crucially through the process of INSET, to increase the person's or school's consciousness of their position within a procedure that supports articulation, enhances understanding and links changed understanding to action so that change can happen.

The model provides a framework for the analysis of the institution and the support of the individual in the development process. Figure 6.1 outlines the characteristics of the model.

The model classifies four states:

1. Belief and practice are apart and the person is conscious and able to articulate the difference.
2. Belief and practice are together and the person is conscious and able to articulate this.
3. Belief and practice are together and the person is unaware or unable to articulate this.
4. Belief and practice are apart and the person is unaware.

The model does not imply that any single state represents an effective or poor teacher in terms of their current practice. Each box can contain effective and poor. What the model does reveal is that effective development can only result from conscious spiral movement (across boxes 1 and 2).

The teacher whose situation causes them to remain in any one box ceases to be a learner. Notwithstanding gross generalization, this can cause frustration or cynicism if the teacher is in box 1, happy harmony if they are in box 2 and a blissful lack of awareness in boxes 3 and 4.

Relationship of practice to belief

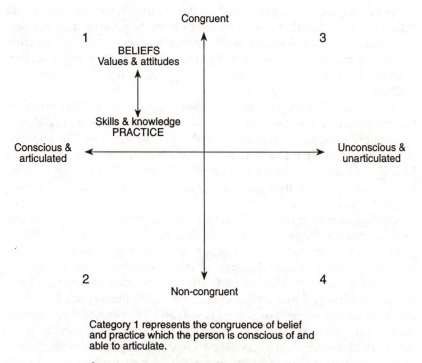

Category 1 represents the congruence of belief and practice which the person is conscious of and able to articulate.

Category 4 represents the non-congruence of belief & practice which the person is unaware of.

Figure 6.1

The movement between states 3 and 4 occurs as a result of *ad hoc* changes, often as a result of external innovations. Some learning takes place at the level of new knowledge/ideas and in the person's practice but such changes are usually temporary as they are not underpinned by understanding and rarely relate to existing practice.

The implications of the model for the improvement process are manifold. Self-motivated teachers and schools continually seek to improve practice. They are conscious of the gap between their rising aspirations both of themselves and their institution and their desire to bring practice closer to these aspirations. There is a constant oscillation between bringing practice closer to belief and the realization gained by understanding that the newly arrived-at practice is again short of a revised set of aims. Improved practice serves to heighten awareness of the possible.

One of the characteristics of self-motivated teachers is that they do not necessarily find themselves in accord with programmes of staff or institutional development. They may well be the group that seeks to change the beliefs/practices of others by all means possible (e.g. curriculum development and in-service). Whether self-motivated teachers or schools are effective or successful depends on the extent to which they improve their practice. They may remain in box 1, full of belief, but are unable or restrained from putting ideas into practice.

Neither state 3 nor 4 provides the basis for development. They represent the stable state where the practice/belief relationship is either together or apart but the teacher is unaware or unable to articulate this. The improvement goal is to help teachers to become more aware of their practice and beliefs and their relationship in order to help them move into an effective learning cycle where they can consciously handle the process of moving forward belief and practice.

All programmes of staff, professional and institutional development continually seek to alter the status quo. They seek to alter practice, values, goals or whatever part of the system is deemed most appropriate. Often such programmes utilize elements of internal and external innovations which are a source of pressure and external legitimacy for change. Those who are leaders of development seek to influence others either by instituting changed practice and/or setting new goals/aspirations that encapsulate their beliefs. To some extent the source of the change is important. If it is the result of discussion in a school or a working group then the change may well be initially accepted by other staff. If the innovation is externally imposed then some early hurdles can increase resistance even before the gap between belief and practice can be worked with.

The development implications: practice and belief

Development based on changing belief first (the value basis underlying the curriculum) is only likely to be effective for those teachers who are consciously motivated by and understand the relationship between aims and practice. Once personal or institutional aims have been altered then there is a constant in-built pressure to change practice – otherwise disenchantment may set in or the ideas embodied in the aims will be left at the level of rhetoric.

Where practice has been changed first, then it is essential that at some point the created gap with belief should be explicitly addressed in the implementation process. In changing practice there may well be a shift of belief – if beliefs do not change then sooner or later practice will revert back to its former position.

These issues pose key problems in the development process. What is the balance between seeking to change practice and the development of belief? Imposed initiatives often seek to change practice first because that may be the only way to achieve some momentum in the change process, but this results in the need to support development work on the aims and values that lay behind the innovation. This constant dilemma in the improvement process can never be easily resolved nor is there a blueprint that can be followed. Effective development involves the establishment of a learning process that addresses both practice and belief for both the individual teacher and the institution.

Explicit consciousness

The dilemma facing many leaders of change is that for the development process to become effective, each person must have a thorough grasp of how learning takes place by becoming conscious and able to articulate their beliefs and practice and the relationship between them. A prerequisite of improvement is self-development and to help the teacher become conscious of their own professional and personal learning.

In the context of the model, the teacher-education process is about helping a teacher to move from right to left, i.e. from a position where practice and belief are either apart or together to the same position but with increased awareness (Figure 6.2). Whilst the actual path travelled by individuals is unlikely to be similar to the diagrams, the process will pick up the features of spiral development between boxes 1 and 3 as conscious understanding and articulation develop.

The model can easily be applied to institutional learning. Where a school

Changing awareness of practice and belief

Initial step is to increase the teachers consciousness
of their practice and ability to articulate it

a)

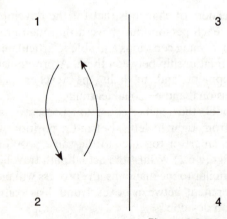

The continuing process is to develop practice/belief
through an iterative process

b)

Figure 6.2

is not collectively aware of its position and/or is unable to articulate it, then it is unable to undertake effective development. Whilst there may be teachers in the school who are effective learners, the school's procedures do not support development. This particular state describes a school that is unable to undertake self-review, articulate its practice and be clear about the gap between practice and intentions.

The leader of development in such a situation has to create a climate and establish various projects and in-service work that build up the opportunities for teachers and the school to move from right to left and then between 1 and 2. In order to do this, a development profile for each individual (personal and professional) and the school has to be drawn. From this it is possible to design the learning experiences of colleagues.

Other states can be drawn from the model – for example, the school that has a statement of aims that is well apart from its practice and has little desire or ability to develop. This school has all the characteristics of box 3, with a statement of aims that is merely a sheet of paper. Its real values may lie somewhere else and the developer has to identify the school's true position in order to establish a starting point. The final assessment may locate it in box 2, 3 or 4.

A framework for continuous teacher development

The second model builds on the first and in so doing outlines a framework of a teacher education curriculum for the teacher and, potentially, for the school. The model draws out the third essential characteristic of learning – namely, its relationship to experience. (The previous model examined how development is helped by conscious and articulated learning and the relationship between practice and belief.)

The teacher as learner

In much the same way as a child's learning is not confined to school nor to the classroom or the syllabus, much of the development of the teacher occurs outside the normal context of INSET. For this reason the model has a wide application to the development arrangements the school and the LEA provide. In addition the model has implications for all aspects of teacher education because the improvement of quality is not confined to the development of schools or to teachers who are in service. The three forms of in-service education (professional, staff and management development) overlap with each other but the distinctiveness of each must be maintained in any framework of teacher development in order to enable the organizer and the recipient to understand the source of the goals of the activity and to appreciate the motivational forces at work within the particular experience.

The model is based on an analysis of the role and work of the teacher which itself is based on the practice of teaching and an understanding of learning. It is for this reason that the model of teacher development is underpinned by the key assumptions about teaching and learning outlined in the previous section.

The framework comprises three components:

1. The purposes and principles.
2. The model.
3. Assessment, recording and accreditation.

The purposes and principles

The following set of purposes and principles embraces all forms of teacher education.

Purposes   Teachers should

- have knowledge of the curriculum and the interrelationship of its components, insight into school aims and tasks, and the place of the school in a constantly changing society;
- have knowledge of, insight into and a critical attitude towards the school as an organization;
- be capable of evaluating themselves and viewing their own role and leadership within the organization;
- have knowledge of the education system as a whole and its operation;
- be able to improve their performance in post and prepare for changes in role; and
- be able to develop themselves by accepting and acting on the need for continuous professional development.

Principles   A programme of teacher development should

- be a continuous process;
- provide coherence;
- be substantial;
- be negotiated, responsive and balanced in relation to the identified needs of the teacher, school, the LEA and society;
- provide equal opportunities including access and the removal of barriers to all forms of development;

- be evaluated and reviewed; and
- enable individuals to select from the provision to meet their needs.

The model of continuous development

The model comprises five components that have been integrated into a three-dimensional diagram for ease of representation (Figure 6.3). An optimum representation would result in a multi-dimensional diagram.

In the areas of experience (dimension 1), two components are identified:

1. Subject/curriculum knowledge (including cross-curricular aspects).
2. Professional knowledge and skills (pedagogy, psychology).

Every teacher needs to have the necessary knowledge and skill to teach.

A model for Professional Development

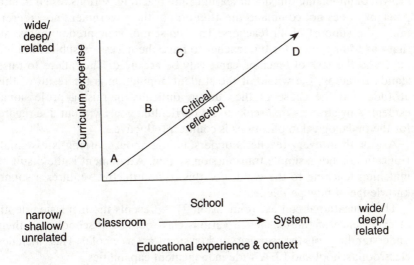

A The teacher in Initial Teacher Education

B The induction period

C Experienced teacher with a bias to subject/curriculum expertise in the classroom

D Experienced teacher with a balance of curriculum/subject and whole school management expertise

Figure 6.3

There is little that has to be added to this, although the extent of that knowledge is growing considerably. There are a number of curriculum changes that demand a broadening of the teacher's understanding and knowledge. The spread of primary science and the development of broad, balanced, science in the secondary sector are two examples in one curriculum area. The list can easily be added to. The service has traditionally relied upon the basic general education and higher education of its teachers. This has to be recognized as inadequate for the nineties. The education teachers received when they were at school and higher education twenty years ago will not suffice. There is a constant need for updating and extending the knowledge component.

The level of pedagogical skill amongst teachers is one of the most important assets the education service has. It is the profession's stock in trade and equates to the skills of any other profession. With an increasingly complex curriculum and an educational context that demands more from the service, it is becoming critical for an investment to be made in the growth of understanding about learning and teaching. Serious research into pedagogy does not command the attention of the government nor, regrettably, the support of all teachers. The old-school view predominates: all that has to happen is for the teacher to have the necessary subject knowledge and the task of teaching can easily be acquired. The failure to raise standards across the whole of the student population is the result of this attitude and the cause of the current difficulty in raising professional esteem. Any strategy that seeks to set curriculum goals without due regard for the pedagogical implications is counterproductive.

A growth in every teacher's understanding about learning is essential. Education is not a simple transmission system. Attainment is the result of matching teaching to the child. For this to be effective requires a sound knowledge of how people learn.

The educational context (dimension 2) represents the increasing depth of experience of the teacher in various classrooms and schools and their understanding of the service and system as a whole. This includes classroom/school and LEA-wide management capabilities.

Teaching has often been seen as an individual activity. The stereotype image is of the teacher who goes into the room and closes the door. Those days are over. It is not possible to deliver a whole curriculum that has progression and coherence without working with colleagues and being fully aware of and working with the wider educational setting and the community.

The third dimension is concerned with the ability to reflect critically upon practice. This ability is a major part of learning and therefore central to both this model and the previous one. There has been a steady flow of literature on the subject and, although critical reflection is a substantial goal in initial training, it is still the poor partner in the scheme of continuing teacher education. Critical reflection is the energizing and dynamic element that enables the teacher to bring together and learn from the other dimensions. The process of reflection is the means by which teachers are able to link their experiences in a meaningful way with the knowledge and skills they possess, thus providing the basis for further development.

Critical reflection is a conscious process concerned with identifying and working with the gap between practice and aspiration. The process is essentially one of evaluation that underpins learning by operating upon the ideas, actions and feelings of the individual.

At its most effective, critical reflection involves collaboration and involvement with other individuals and groups in both informal and formal systems. The benefit to critical reflection of collaborative working, peer and professional appraisal are that they lead to the collection and examination of evidence about teaching and learning and in so doing reinforce the process. The development of critical reflection enables the teacher to synthesize the various components identified in the model into their working practice.

The fourth and final component is the development of the self. Self-development embraces all the other components, though it is central to critical reflection. Teaching is a personal activity. The work of the project 'Teachers' Jobs and Lives' (University of East Anglia) provides evidence that the 'professional self' and the 'personal self' are interlinked. It is for this reason that self-development must be given greater prominence in teacher education. Narrowly focused development of the teacher ignores the nature of the teacher's role. Maturity is an important aspect of the effective teacher.

To view the teacher as a continuing learner has a number of implications for the way teachers work and the profession is managed. There are financial factors but, more significantly, the forms of teacher education have to relate, to turn the principle of continuous development into practice.

The notion of the teacher as learner has a number of implications. The teacher has to have the ability to stand back, to handle both the professional and the personal implications of the situation and to know how to handle the tensions that emerge in the development of practice. The complexity of uncertainty demands a mature response. As Henry James is believed to have said, 'Maturity is the ability to handle ambiguity'. Hence the need to help the person's development, for without the maturity to support the process, learning becomes fragile and ineffective.

Improvement of the teacher is illustrated in the model through development in each of the main components and their progressive synthesis. For dimensions 1 and 2, the goal is to increase the depth, width and interrelationship of the various elements. For example, a subject (mathematics) teacher increasingly understands the content of his or her subject in relation to the curriculum as a whole and the means by which it is taught and learned. The primary teacher successively builds up his or her knowledge of the whole curriculum, the means by which it is taught and his or her understanding of learning. The increasingly effective teacher is one who is able to bring all the dimensions together. The crucial factor that helps or hinders this is the teacher's ability to be a conscious, critical learner.

To illustrate the improvement aspect more clearly, the model can be drawn in two ways. Figure 6.3 defines the axes and components. Figure 6.4 highlights the central importance of critical reflection and the ultimate aim of achieving synthesis.

Achieving synthesis

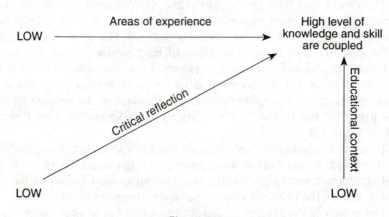

Figure 6.4

Within a continuous model it is difficult to identify clear stages in a teacher's development. Therefore, with one exception, to the first stage up to the point of initial qualification, the stages are not defined but the framework can be used to help the teacher's progression and continuity of development. This will enable those concerned with any form of teacher education as well as the individuals themselves to formulate appropriate learning experiences. In addition, the model can be applied to the professional-development aspects of appraisal and used by those concerned with the accreditation of programmes of study to identify appropriate criteria.

Assessing, recording and accrediting professional development

A comprehensive system of teacher development requires a set of procedures for assessing, recording and accrediting the professional development of teachers. The main purposes of such a system include

1. receiving feedback;
2. achieving progression and coherence in professional development;
3. career development; and
4. awards and qualification.

A firm foundation for a national system of accredited professional development exists in initial training with the work on profiling and recording the achievements of student teachers (Lancaster University, 1990) and in induction programmes for beginning teachers where there has been some early work on the accreditation of programmes within a postgraduate arrangement.

The framework also provides the basis for accrediting prior experience and learning at any stage of a teacher's career. Criteria could be established that identify the extent of the interrelationship, depth, breadth of understanding and attainment in each of the three main dimensions of the model. Evidence of the level of attainment would be ascertained through the various schemes of accreditation and courses. At present the system for appraisal comprises a mix of contractual and professional components. The latter are not sufficiently developed to be incorporated within a model of professional development but such a step could be taken if the conditions were right.

Applying the framework of continuous teacher development

The model has numerous applications and implications. It can be applied to the development of

- a coherent national, regional and local system that links all aspects of teacher education together in a fully balanced progressive form;

- a framework for initial teacher training in terms of setting goals and assessment criteria;
- a comprehensive induction programme which links initial training to INSET;
- an interlinked system in higher education that accredits professional development as part of a continuous process; and
- appraisal for professional development and needs identification.

The model can be applied to all of the above developments by informing the design, organization and level of any professional development activity and programme, thus providing the means for any individual teacher or programme organizer to design a range of experiences that

1. achieves progression, continuity and coherence;
2. matches the activity to the individual's developing needs; and
3. can be set within the level of any award or accreditation.

The way forward

Each of the identified components of the framework requires expansion to form a curriculum for teacher education in the areas of content, skill and understanding. It is not an objective of this book to tackle the formation of a teacher-education curriculum in depth. However, the establishment of a truly professional framework for teacher education brings with it professional rights and responsibilities.

The main features are

- that teachers have an entitlement to appropriate release and support throughout their career and a responsibility to maintain their own learning;
- that schools, the LEAs and the government have the responsibility to resource and support the framework and have the right to expect teachers to participate; and
- the development of a system of accreditation related to higher degrees for all teachers that rewards achievement and experience.

The implementation of these proposals is dependent on the establishment of the structures outlined here.

This chapter concludes with an examination of networking, as the authors believe that its contribution to the creation of an effective learning environment for teachers and schools has not been fully understood let alone utilized. Networking does not feature in the list of characteristics of effectiveness, yet for many effective individuals, schools/colleges and LEAs it is a significant feature of their operation and greatly contributes to the formation of a positive climate for change.

Networking

The term networking is being used and possibly misused in an increasing number of contexts. To call it a concept or a principle is probably too grand; nevertheless, it does describe the range of activities and forms of relationships that exist between individuals and between institutions.

The value of networking is often not appreciated. Over the years, staff surveys have resulted in an observation by teachers who would say that over half, even three quarters, of the staff were involved in working groups inside the school (secondary) and a very significant number were involved in activity outside the school. The implied concern seems to stem from the belief that the volume of involvement (meetings and working groups) is detrimental and overloads the individual and/or the institution. The same characteristic can exist in an LEA. Ranson (1991), in an analysis of LEA characteristics, described the extent in Enfield of the involvement of teachers in working groups to develop the curriculum, teacher expertise and to share knowledge. For various reasons, networking is not seen as an integral factor in the development of the school or the LEA. Yet in the examples we have examined, it is obvious that the institutions, the LEAs and the individual teachers were effectively developing their work by using networks as a learning mechanism. In many quarters, the amount of effort and energy put into networking is seen as negative. The direct relationship to learning is not understood and as a mechanism for change its value is untapped. So what are networks and what is their contribution to the development process?

Before we consider these questions there is a need to clarify the term. Here are two useful definitions:

> At the most abstract a network is simply a set of nodes or points connected by lines or links. . . . In social networks the nodes are persons, groups or organisations. The things that travel between the nodes are socially relevant . . . they are usually objects, labour, affect, evaluations, knowledge, prescriptions, opinion, influence and power. So a network is a connected set of social actors exchanging socially relevant material.
>
> (Miles, 1978)

> A network is an institutional model or an organisational principle consisting of several threads or relations of communication held together by knots or individuals, who learn from and help one another while they solve specific problems . . . [networks are] particularly suitable when objectives are not easily achieved by

single central institutions or groups where regional variations mean that different groups and forms are best suited to meet local needs and circumstances.

(Huczinski, 1983)

Havelock (1969) identified networks in his models of change under the heading of social interaction. Much of the literature in the UK on the function and operation of networks was generated through a series of papers on the subject by Beresford and Goddard (1978–81 – see Chambers (undated)). Goddard's work in teachers' centres in the 1980s clarified the operation of networking still further. From this experience, a further description can be offered that also outlines the benefits of networking.

Networks take a similar form and have similar purposes to the brain. A network is a series of linkages or synapses. The greater the number of linkages between people and/or organizations, the greater is their collective and individual capacity to communicate and to work at problems and issues. A school or group that utilizes networking is increasing its 'intelligence'.

Networks are not formal, overtly structural devices but operate in the infrastructure of the organization. They provide the environment for learning, for the risk-taking, the construction and abandonment of ideas. All of this is more easily undertaken outside the constraints of the mainstream structures which are predominantly designed to manage, even control the maintenance functions of the institution. Networks are to the infrastructure what formal committees and line management are to the structure. The neurological model of networking emphasizes certain key functions.

Beresford and Goddard (1981) identified six major characteristics of networking:

1. The task of a network reflects a perception of need identified by its members.
2. The membership of a network often reflects a similarity of role or function.
3. Networks are, by definition, not in control of organizations.
4. Networks link and use a variety of human and physical resources.
5. They extend the professionalism of their members.
6. Relationships within a network tend to reflect the quality of the contribution made by an individual rather than their formal status.

The purpose of networks is to improve quality and effectiveness through the generation of ideas upon which future development is based. In addition to the above characteristics, networks are based on common purposes and values. They are about partnerships and equality of status.

Networks abound in many forms and depend on the purpose and

energies of the staff that comprise them. They are about achievement and activity. There is no place in a network for a passive member; however, this does not exclude those who take knowledge from networks and use the outcomes for their own benefit but rarely contribute and therefore appear to be passive.

Networks are often about influencing change and decision-making systems. But if networks were solely defined in these terms then all groups and committees could be defined as networks, including formal and bureaucratic systems.

The key characteristic of any network and an indicator of its value is the extent to which it provides opportunities for its members to learn. The learning process involves the exchange of information, the acquisition of knowledge, the development of ideas, the creation of a vision and the development of practice.

The creation of a network comes about through the linking of those with a vision. It enables individuals to move away from the isolated position that so characterizes the education service and may, regrettably, continue to do so. Such movements are in apparent conflict with the competitive model of the eighties and nineties, but they are essential to the development of quality and to forward thinking. The attempts to starve networks through the reduction of resources ignore the level of collaboration that is necessary in order to develop knowledge, solve problems and share practice. Development is totally dependent on the creation of ideas and the drawing together of people who have the energy, insight and skill to push the boundaries forward.

The formation of 'think tanks' and policy-study units is based on the application of networking ideas. It is interesting to note how they have proliferated in the political world at the same time as they have been discouraged within the education setting (e.g. through the removal of the Schools Council and similar other bodies with networking sub-structures).

The recent trend in applying the misguided principle of market forces to the generation and sharing of knowledge by putting a price on it linked only to the obvious cost is both dangerous and counterproductive. If everyone starts to price their knowledge then development will slow down. The impact of LMS may have this effect as schools restrict the release of staff to networking activities on the grounds that the immediate benefit may not be obvious or realized. The problem is being aggravated by the financial difficulties that face LEAs, thus restricting their ability to afford this form of support. Such short-term approaches are a national problem that will ultimately result in the deterioration of quality.

Networks are crucial to development. The effective individual, school/

college or LEA establishes and supports networks in order to improve their capacity to learn and develop. Networking at an organizational level operates both inside the organization and between itself and other bodies. A conscious approach to networking by the leadership would result in the resourcing and support of various activities. From the evidence of the authors over the last twenty years, it is clear that the ability of the individual or organization to develop is directly related to the extent of its linkage.

Networks are not easy to operate. They are fragile and are based on the commitment and the altruism of individuals and organizations. We do not know of a network that doesn't rely on this rare commodity. The difficulty now facing the service is that the organizational basis that provides invaluable support for educational networks is fast disappearing. LEA advisory teams support a vast number of teacher networks that have generated a significant amount of sound developments used throughout the world. Teachers' centres do likewise. The Schools Council sponsored both major and minor projects that improved the quality of education through its 'Programme of Small-Scale Funding'. Similarly the Training Agency has adopted a networking approach to the achievement of its goals in TRIST, Flexible Learning and TVEI and, under the banner of partnership, it promotes the education–industry linkage.

Curiously, the activity of the Department of Employment, which has partnership and collaboration at the heart of its work in various schemes, appears to be at odds with the intentions of the DES, which seeks to limit collaboration and the means by which the service can work together.

One of the most serious implications of the threatened abolition of the LEA or, in the meantime, its development resource, is the removal of the infrastructure that provides the support for teachers and schools and with it the leadership of the profession in the development of quality. Schools will never have the resource to give their time and energy freely. Schools or single organizations are too small to be able to form a viable group with the necessary qualities. There are just too few people with the energy, insight, ability and commitment to lead and work in networks and it is noticeable how their energies are currently being dissipated.

To look on the bright side, the advancement of networks should and could be pursued by schools to provide support for their own development. Whilst the cash implications have to be considered there are considerable benefits to the climate of the school in terms of the goodwill and energy networks create to support staff and help development.

Within the institution, the leadership of the school should facilitate the energies of teachers to join together *across* the normal structures and divides. There is collected evidence of the value of this approach (Leask,

1988), especially in the secondary sector where school size facilitates internal networking.

The questions for the leadership are: How can the time, resource, goodwill and the encouragement of energetic staff be brought together outside the formal structures of the institution to lead future development? How can the school create its own think tank, its own development leadership?

Such groups need to be *linked* in some way to the formal structure in order to link the initiation stage to the implementation process but not so tightly that the initiative is stifled. Composition is also important. Recalling the characteristics of networks outlined above, members of groups are there to contribute; they are *not* representative bodies. That is a characteristic of the implementation stage of the change process. People are drawn in because they have something to offer and, secondly, something to take. Within any school the most appropriate person to be the facilitator of networking would be the INSET co-ordinator on behalf of the senior management team. Such a person should have been appointed because they have an understanding of the change process and the necessary interpersonal qualities.

Networks between institutions open up the creative and learning opportunities for individuals and ultimately benefit the institution. For small schools, linkage across schools is essential if any viable learning environment is to be created. The viability of networks depends on being able to bring together enough people to create the motivation, capacity and creative energy to be productive.

The partnering of schools in education is rapidly extending. Called 'cluster groups' or 'pyramids', they may have a formal structural role in the education service (link or feeder primary schools to a secondary school) and may also facilitate networks. Large schools also benefit from the opportunity to work with others, as this overcomes the institution's introspection which can be a major inhibitor to learning. To return to the example at the start of this section, schools and teachers who are developing have extensive linkages with other schools, the LEA and other organizations. Often they absorb more advisory support and contribute more to LEA networks. Their overall level of activity is altogether higher.

LEAs perform a crucial development role through their leadership, resourcing and facilitation of networks. The LEA through the work of its teachers' centres and advisory team underpins the activity of teachers and schools. The benefits of LEA networking can be illustrated easily by making contrasts with countries that are developing and those with constrained development capacity where regional and local development fails to happen and quality is impaired. Many international programmes aimed at supporting the development of education seek to establish network systems, teachers' centres, etc. The list of projects and countries is too long to specify. The work of the British Council in this area is well documented. It often highlights the absence of a funded education infrastructure as a weakness in many development programmes and provides support to countries for the development of the teachers' centre concept. The collective capacity of any district to undertake the improvement of quality through its development work is occasioned through the construction and operation of a network system. Again it is interesting to note yet another example of an innovation (teachers' centres are a UK invention) the UK has failed to capitalize on.

Conclusion

The development of quality and the effective initiation of innovation at every level (nationally, locally and in schools) is dependent on the establishment of appropriate networks. All development is based on the forward thinking activity of key individuals operating with groups of people to develop their ideas. A school that is working at the improvement of its quality will of necessity get involved in an increasing amount of development work. It will encourage its staff to find out about new ideas and practices, it will create internal opportunities for staff to meet outside the school's formal system and it will draw in professionals from the LEA and elsewhere to support the process. All of these practices are based on networking and again this demonstrates the need to have a local environment that supports the generation and dissemination of good practice both horizontally (i.e. across schools) and vertically (i.e. from the individual teacher) to the national arena.

Issues for consideration

1. What is the reader's preferred learning style and how is it helped by the institution and the LEA?
2. How can the formal and informal practices (including networking) in the institution and LEA be improved to support staff learning?
3. In what ways can the two models be applied to schools, colleges, LEAs and higher education?

Further reading

Hall, V. (1988) Networks and networking: a working paper (mimeo), National Development Centre for School Management Training, Bristol.

Joyce and Showers (1980) Improving inservice training: the messages from research. *Educational Leadership* pp. 379–85.

Kolb, D. (1974). On management and the learning process, in Rubin and McIntyre.

Open University in association with the Schools Council (1980) *Classroom in Action: an Approach to Evaluation.*

Ransom, S. (1991) *The New Management of Education: LEA Perspectives on the Implementation of the 1988 Education Reform Act*, Centre for Education Management and Policy Studies, INLOGOV, University of Birmingham.

Tomlinson and Kilner (1991) *The Flexible Learning Framework and Current Educational Theory*, Department of Employment.

7
MANAGING MULTIPLE INITIATIVES AND COPING WITH OVERLOAD

Introduction

This chapter is a practical guide to the way in which anyone concerned with innovation in education can improve the way in which they can help their organization to understand the nature of innovations and their relationship to the organization. Most of the chapter is devoted to the presentation of a framework for the analysis of innovations and organizations. This is set within a sequence of exercises that enables the reader to build up an understanding of how to manage multiple innovations.

In our consideration of the change context of the nineties, we identified the management of a range of complex initiatives as one of the major pressures on the eduation service. To examine this further we need to return to the basic principle of development, namely that the change process can be handled more effectively if there is a more systematic analysis of the gap between where the institution or staff currently is and where it wishes to be. The results of such an exercise provide essential information for the development of an effective strategy and any associated activity that is organized to move the school forwards.

Schools are no longer free to decide their goals, even if they ever were. Much of their work is imposed. The National Curriculum, LMS, TVEI and appraisal are innovations that have to be addressed. School development is therefore a mix of managing externally originated activities with internal projects. For the purpose of the exercises in this chapter the source of the innovation is irrelevant.

Effective development work depends on a satisfactory analysis both of the initiatives and the institution and its staff. There are additional forms of support for this process in the various review mechanisms of GRIDS

Planning multi-dimensional development

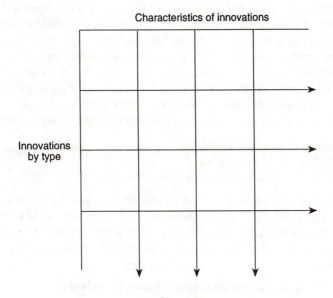

Figure 7.1

(McMahon *et al.*, 1984) and the work of the NFER/IMTEC and Hopkins (1985).

Much has been written about institutional review and priority setting. The multiplicity and complexity of current development necessitates a more systematic understanding of the innovations themselves, for two purposes: firstly, to ascertain the degree of mismatch between the innovation and the institution and its staff and, secondly, to manage the relationships between innovations.

The rationale behind each of these purposes is that the construction of any strategy for development and the creation of the learning programme for the institution and the staff requires more precise information than is usually available. Institutional review provides information about part of the process. Innovation analysis clarifies the intended goals of change and, as schools and colleges are increasingly on the receiving end of imposed change, then the description and analysis of the intended change becomes even more crucial.

A further feature of the development context of the nineties is that the interconnectedness demands that each innovation is seen as part of a whole and that successful improvement requires the simultaneous implementation of various initiatives.

The outcome of the operationalization of the concepts underpinning the management of multiple initiatives is likely to result in a more conscious development programme which recognizes both the vertical dimensions (each innovation) of the change map as well as the horizontal features (common elements across innovations), thus bringing coherence to the development process. In this way a school/college can begin to plan consciously for multi-dimensional development (see Figure 7.1).

There are two sets of components to this aspect of the change equation:

1. Innovation and institution analysis.
2. The identification of the degree of match/mismatch between the institution and the innovation for (a) the individuals and (b) the institution.

The following section sets out an approach that can be followed by individuals and institutions and organizations. Various approaches can be used to undertake what is essentially an environmental mapping or strategic planning activity and these are described throughout the chapter.

Innovation and institutional analysis

Stage one: mapping the innovations

The first stage requires those involved to increase their understanding of the range of individual innovations. At this point the source of the innovation is irrelevant to the exercise. Whether it is governmental or a goal initiated by the staff, it is still outside the institution's current set of practices.

The task is to identify and list or map on a chart all the innovations affecting a school/college or LEA, including those on the horizon. The resulting list or chart should be shared with colleagues to check that everyone has the same perception of the range of innovations affecting the school.

Stage two: the analytical framework

The second task is to analyse each innovation. One particular format is employed in the example below. In this approach, each innovation is described under a set of headings which provides the basis for examining the innovations and, at a later stage, for describing the institution in order to undertake the mismatch exercise. (A slightly different sequence of tasks is suggested below should the exercise be undertaken as an INSET event.)

The example shown in Figure 7.2 is taken from an inservice day for advisory and support staff in Coventry, organized by Goddard. The following sections help to focus on the key aspects of innovations and their implications for the school or college. The section headings of the analytical framework are best considered in conjunction with the question, what is implicitly or explicitly understood to be the main features of (insert the initiative) on the (insert the heading)? It must be remembered that not all initiatives have features under each of the headings.

INSET activity 7.1   Mapping initiatives

We have found that the best way to start an inservice activity on this exercise is for the staff group to take an initiative, e.g. appraisal, and brainstorm all its characteristics without the immediate application of the framework of headings. A diagrammatic or picture web is another approach. The rationale for deferring the use of the framework of headings has more to do with learning styles and the need to start from where people are than with providing a framework that constrains initial thinking.

The components of the framework draw out the significant characteristics of any innovation. Through a systematic approach to the analysis, it is then possible to identify the gap between the school's current position and the innovation under each of the headings. Taken together, the headings provide a comprehensive picture of the likely impact of an innovation on all aspects of a school. There are seven components to the framework: curriculum, pupil skills, resources, management, image, skills and understanding, and values.

Curriculum

There are three features to the curriculum that require separate though linked analysis: the model, structure and delivery (pedagogy). Each initiative has different curricular emphases. For the purpose of the exercise it is necessary to differentiate between required and implicit elements. This will be elaborated in the next stage of the procedure.

The model of the curriculum is best described by focusing on HMI

Analysing Innovations

	NATIONAL CURRICULUM	APPRAISAL	STUDENT-CENTRED LEARNING
CURRICULUM	Equal access and continuity	Equal value, teachers responsibility to ensure quality of learning and equal access	Individual needs process and transfer skills
CURRICULUM STRUCTURE	Cross curricular, cross phase, whole school	Cross curricular – the 'whole' teacher . . . awareness of hidden curriculum	Whole school agreement philosophy
CURRICULUM DELIVERY	Child centred learning, small group, cross age pupil. Records of Achievement	Crucial! Is it the whole teacher . . . ? Help teachers to explore together	The guts: recognizing the individual agenda without prescribing outcomes
	Working collaboratively . . . confidence/varied approaches	Reinforcing – We are all learners. More adults in the classroom	Moves from dependent to independent learning. Clear objectives . . . social roles
RESOURCES	Staff time/inservice agencies/extra staffing/ space for group work	Inservice – Needs must be met. Appraiser as part of support network	Time INSET/support services
MANAGEMENT	Different teams within the school overlapping . . .	Team units with everyone involved . . . Continuous process	Cross curricular teams that support each other
IMAGE	Making parents, governors aware, reassuring that school is already achieving. Published results	Support of governors, professional teacher bodies . . . Accountability?	Increasing awareness community of value initiative
TEACHER/ PEOPLE SKILLS	Communication, sensitivity. Positive but realistic support. Aware of pupils needs, reassurance about practice	Agreement of what is good practice? Criteria made more explicit. Confidentiality. Dealing with unexpected outcomes	Willingness to adopt change. Confidence. Sensitivity
VALUES	Individuals are valued, all children sensitive to others' needs	Equal access to all involved. Teachers are learners. Achievement recognized. Purpose– outcome–effectiveness– improvement	Commonality in teaching strategies across curriculum. Coherent package of transferable skills

Figure 7.2

RECORDS OF ACHIEVEMENT	MODULAR CURRICULUM	L.M.S
Students at centre. Available to all	Thematic, Flexible, Cross curricular	Efficiency
Whole school cross phase social and personal development	Modular, differentiated	Resources for staffing
All about this!	(Active learning. Project work – pupil centred.) Real life oriented	Resourcing. Quality of staff
Why are you learning?	Independent working. Collaborative. Open ended tasks/creative. Organizational. Appreciation of context	
Cameras etc. Material resources INSET time/clerical support	Worksheets. Exam papers. Assignments. Resources and staff resource organization	Heads time. Additional staff. Computers
Teams! Effective leadership	Timetabling. Resources and staff. Record keeping. Paperwork. Scheduling. Staff organization. Team teaching. Moderation management. Collaboration	Co-operation
Efficient child-centred schools – sell the idea employers/FE	Relevance of otherwise academic subjects. Needs 'projection'	'Market leader', value for money. Openness – where does the money go?
Partnerships in learning . . . Negotiating . . . confidentiality	Flexibility. Good organization. Collaboration. Negotiating. Pupil-centred orientation	Business skills. Finance management
Learning is ongoing. Students are able to make accurate assessments. Relevance is increased. Motivation grows	Choice, goal oriented. Cumulative?	Efficient use of resources, free market economy, business principles

Working Paper 2 (1988), which introduced breadth and balance. The inclusion of all curriculum areas for all pupils aged 5 to 16 was the focus of the initiative, which was later picked up as a feature of the National Curriculum. The HMI documents and related initiatives did not and do not prescribe the curriculum organization/structure nor how the curriculum should be taught. A further example of the way in which a curriculum model can be modified is through the accumulation of policy statements and principles in schools and LEAs which extends or modifies the existing curriculum model.

Curriculum structure relates to the way in which the curriculum is organized, for example, the decision to have a topic or subject approach or the introduction of a modular curriculum. Often this item manifests itself as a timetable matter.

Finally are the pedagogical or delivery implications: obvious current examples include the teaching of reading, flexible learning approaches and different ways of dealing with wide ability. In all of these cases the issue is how the curriculum is to be taught.

Pupil skills

Most innovations involve the presentation of new material or knowledge to students, but an increasing number of changes demand that pupils work in a different way. In many circumstances, this is not a major issue except where an innovation significantly alters the teaching and learning expectations the school has of the pupil. Whilst pupils are adaptable, innovation implementation should not ignore the possibility that some preparation of pupils may be needed. If an initiative requires the pupils to work collaboratively when they have not worked that way before, staff will need to be aware of this and the implications for pupils will need to be considered along with the implications for the staff. Many initiatives have encountered a difficult time because the pupil components have not been properly catered for. A good example of both good and bad practice in this area is with student profiling and Records of Achievement (ROA), which depend on pupil involvement and development for their success.

Resources

Resources need to be broken down into three categories: physical resources, time and capacity. The implications of innovations for the physical use and resources of the school are fairly obvious to understand although they may be difficult to detail. If a school sets out to develop a new course or introduce home reading then books are likely to be needed and resources must be allocated. We would also refer the reader back to Chapter 5, to the section dealing with development and maintenance.

The implications for time contain a number of aspects: the time the initiative requires in the curriculum, the development time it needs for implementation and the time to maintain the initiative once it is up and running (maintenance). All these need to be estimated but, whilst the total resource requirement may result in additional demands, the analysis has to be cautious in its interpretation of the time requirements. For although time is not infinite, neither is it totally fixed, and the calculation has to include other factors such as changed priorities.

The school or college's capacity to take on an innovation is the result of a complex assessment of the extent to which the institution and the individuals are able to undertake the particular initiative. It should not be taken to mean readiness for the initiative.

Whilst capacity is an item within this list it is also the outcome of a consideration of the total impact of all aspects of the innovation and an analysis of the capacity of the school and its stage of development including the levels of expertise and knowledge about the particular development and development in general. The development of a school's capacity is a crucial factor in its being able to undertake effective change. A fuller discussion of this item is found in Chapter 5.

Management

The late eighties have given rise to a number of structural initiatives that have direct management implications, i.e. LMS, but there are other curriculum developments which have requirements for the formation of working groups, course teams (e.g. CPVE) or school development planning groups which affect the management process.

Image

The perceived impact of an innovation on a school may well have considerable consequences for the internal image of the school as held by the staff or the external image as held by the community and the parents. This may be implicitly or explicitly understood. An example of this can be seen with TVEI where particular schools may not have been in favour of the industry element, or other aspects (e.g. pre-vocational courses) for they appeared to detract from the current image and emphasis. In the eyes of some, the school's image may be seriously affected by the implementation of an innovation.

Skills and understanding of all the school's partners

Recent innovations affect not only the staff but governors, parents and the community. The scope of a number of changes is far reaching, for example, the introduction of annual reports, annual parents' meetings, the assessment arrangements – the list is endless. The precise impact of any change needs to be identified in terms of new knowledge, skills or attitudes required by anyone who is affected by the innovation. The outcome of the analysis should provide the basis of any training programmes or other forms of development.

Values

Values are the most crucial characteristic on the list. *All* major innovations contain value components, be they curricular, e.g. the National Curriculum, equal opportunities, or organizational, e.g. LMS, where it may seem the innovation is value free. The actual value position of the innovation needs to be made conscious and be analysed in relation to the value position of the school, the staff (individually and collectively) governors and parents.

Stage three: institutional analysis

There is no easy way to describe or understand the position of a school, college or LEA. There are no neat formulae or instruments for assessing the state of the institution. Most of the time staff make intuitive assessments about the situation the school finds itself in. Sometimes the judgments are conscious and often they can be subjective. There are, though, some hard pieces of evidence that can be used in the exercise to describe and analyse the current state of the school – for example, the presence of documents about the curriculum policy and its organization, the staffing structure and evaluation reports/inspections.

However, there are relatively few pieces of information. The process of institutional description and analysis can be undertaken out of the context of innovation analysis. The work of Dalin and Rust (1983) in *Can Schools Learn?* describes such a process but its value lies within a fuller model of consultancy. However, we would suggest that the most effective way to build up a picture of the school is to do it in relation to the analysis of the various innovations. Over time this piecemeal approach will build into a comprehensive description of the school.

The headings used for innovation analysis could be used for school analysis. This will enable a direct comparison to be made between the innovation and the school and help it to ascertain its capacity. As each innovation is worked through, a picture of the school is also built up. The full application of this stage of the process is undertaken in stage four.

Individual development

The major purpose of the exercise is to assist in the school's development, but the development of the school is vitally dependent on the development of the individual. Chapter 6 examines the learning aspects for individuals in greater detail but these exercises benefit from a parallel set of activities undertaken by the school to ascertain the match/mismatch between the individual and the innovation and the individual and the institution. The four-way equation (the school, the teacher (and staff), the pupil and the innovation(s)) comprises the core relationship of the change process. The institution has to have some knowledge of the individual and collective position of the staff in order to ascertain the capacity of the school to meet the changes and to formulate an effective development programme, especially its INSET activity.

Stage four: the school's relationship to innovations

Before the fourth stage (which is concerned with the identification of the match/mismatch between the innovation and the school) can be under-taken, there are some additional features of the management of multiple initiatives that need examination. In summary they are as follows:

- Innovations have similar and common features.
- Schools can reduce the impact of features of innovations that are seen to be negative.
- Innovations have required and discretionary features.
- Schools need to understand innovations well before they impact on the school.
- Innovation adoption is a process of mutual adaptation by the school with the innovation.

Managing multiple initiatives or coping with overload

The actuality of overload in most if not all schools and the service cannot be ignored nor simply dealt with. The answer is unlikely to lie in reducing the number of initiatives. The context for change outlined earlier in the book explains the rationale for holistic change as the dominant characteristic of innovation in the nineties. What can be done to help everyone understand the overall task of managing change so as to make it conceptually simpler and operationally easier? The current approach to development is to identify goals and priorities in relation to separate initiatives and their sub-innovations. For example, the National Curriculum has been introduced through separate components with the intention to help teachers by a phased introduction – but in reality this approach, especially in primary schools, may well be at fault.

This section introduces the reader to a further set of features of innovations and their analysis. It draws upon the previous section and leads to the handling of overload.

The result of the previous stages should bring out identifiable features of the various innovations and their relationship to the school. If the school has not collectively undertaken an analysis of its situation then it should undertake the exercise through a form of school-based review that identifies where the school is according to the headings used in the previous section.

In order to build up a deeper analysis of innovations, let us start with the micro-position. In Figure 7.3 the key features of the innovation (as identified under the headings) are shown by the letters A, B, D, X. They might represent collaborative working, combined science and cross-curricular planning. In this example the particular innovation contains key features that already exist within the school (even though it may be necessary to enhance their quality). In this instance the school has little or no difficulty taking on the innovation. Primary schools that had already undertaken a considerable amount of work on science prior to the National Curriculum were well placed to handle that aspect.

However, innovations are not that simple. They contain a range of features of different import and with different requirements. It is necessary to differentiate between those features which are either legally required or so central to the initiative that they have to be implemented and those that are more discretionary.

Discretionary features may be pursued by political or professional influence but do not have the force of law. The value characteristics of many innovations fall into this domain. Most legal changes are concerned with content, materials and procedures. It is very difficult to legislate for a change in values and attitudes.

A concrete example is the National Curriculum. The essential change is to the model of the curriculum but it does not prescribe any curricular organization even though at one time many teachers believed otherwise

Adopting single innovations
- innovation characteristics already in place

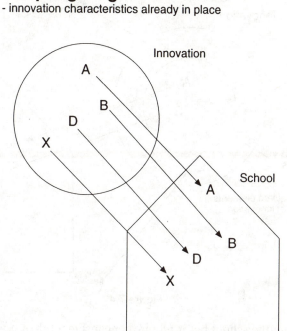

Figure 7.3

and thus confused the essential elements with other forms of pressure. Thus in Figure 7.4 the essential elements are in the centre circle and the associated features lie in the outer ring.

In this illustration, if the school has the key features of the innovation in place then it has few difficulties and it can *choose* whether it wishes to take on the other features. Making a conscious decision about the incorporation of discretionary features and the handling of essential components lies at the core of the decision-making and analysis aspects of the development process. If a school chooses to mask out features then it has to be aware of the consequences.

In cases where the school has to take on a feature that is not in place then it will form part of its long list of development goals. If the innovation

The different components of innovations

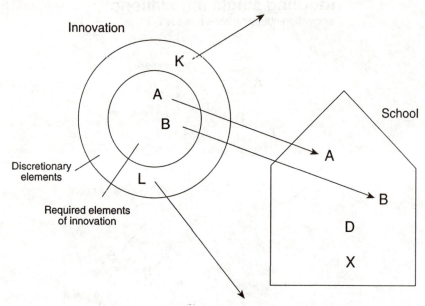

Figure 7.4

exists within the school but it requires enhancement then it will also form part of the long list of potential developments but the nature of the development process will be different.

In this context, the concept of mutual adaptation can be explored. There is a well-known phrase 'that in order to adopt (an innovation) you have to adapt' (both the innovation and the school/staff). The process of mutual adaptation is helped by the school getting as much lead time as possible in the innovation process. Lead time is the result of a number of processes, mainly strategic, that enable the school and staff to read the map of change and predict what has to be done. For example, the schools that took seriously the introduction of profiling and ROA developments and the 1984 statement of the DES were not caught out by TVEI and the subsequent pronouncements of the government.

Mutual adaptation is an active and conscious process that benefits the school in the furtherance of its development goals. Those features of innovations that help it forward can be harnessed and those that hinder development can be dealt with as necessary.

Schools, however, are not faced with single innovations. The response to multiplicity lies in the construction of a development matrix (see Figure 7.1) that can be used to draw out the common or related development features of a number of innovations which can then be related to the current context of the school. This is a strategic activity that interrelates separate initiatives into a coherent framework. It will lead to the management of the whole and to the reduction of overload through the construction of a programme of development that spans a realistic amount of work, yet at the same time tackles the important features of a range of innovations.

In Figure 7.5 the school needs to cope with a number of innovations (six is still unreal). As a result of the innovation analysis described above a

Adopting multiple innovations

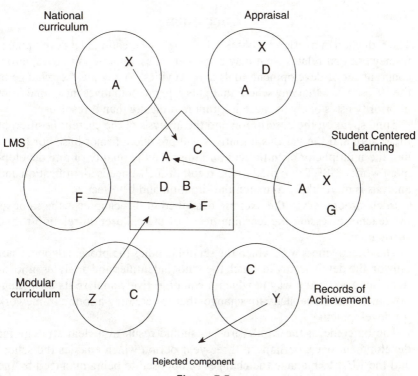

Figure 7.5

number of common and related features will be identified. Over the number of times that Goddard has done this exercise with schools and on courses, there has never been an occasion when the product of the activity has not resulted in the identification of a number of key and common features across the innovations. The outcome is the identification of a more significant set of goals which, when examined in relation to each other, form a realistic priority list.

The completion of the exercise should result in the removal, at the strategic level, of an ever-increasing list of separate innovations each jockeying for a place in the sun and with few valid criteria to differentiate them. After all, how can a school rank TVEI, appraisal, National Curriculum, etc.? The conclusion of this part of the exercise may well result in two levels of development goals: those that stem from the horizontal examination and identify items such as teamwork, improved evaluation, formation of a whole curriculum; and a second set that relates to particular developments (the vertical axis) but which supports the overall goals.

Conclusion

The reduction of overload is obtained through the creation of a development framework that relates what may be perceived as separate initiatives, into a coherent set of development goals and activities. The context of change in the 1990s means that any school that puts separate initiatives into some form of priority list is likely to cause itself more difficulty than it resolves.

Time spent on the description and the analysis of the current position of the school and the various initiatives will provide a firmer basis for handling the multiplicity of initiatives and improve the quality of any development work. INSET designed as the result of such a needs identification and analysis is more likely to match the situation and be effective.

In classroom terms, the exercise described in this chapter is the same as the teacher assessing the learning needs of the children in relation to the curriculum.

The effectiveness with which the school handles the process depends not only on the detailed way in which the school identifies and analyses innovations but also on the way in which it can objectively analyse its own situation, including its capacity for change, thereby creating a sound framework for development.

The outcome of the whole process should result in a clear strategy for development over, perhaps, a three-year period which enables the school and the LEA to manage the changes as opposed to being managed by the changes.

INSET activity 7.2   The analysis of development

There are various in-service exercises that can be used to undertake the tasks in this chapter. The sequence of suggestions in the chapter provide a framework for INSET. The descriptive element of the exercises can be undertaken through cartoon drawing, systematic grids (as in Figure 7.2) and lists that are produced either from an individual perspective or collectively.

The analysis exercise has to be undertaken by a working group or groups of teachers as part of the development process and cycle. Appraisal for professional development can be used if it moves outside of the narrow confines of the performance of the individual in relation to their job description into their needs for development in relation to forthcoming changes.

Issues for consideration

1. In what ways can schools/colleges and LEAs map and analyse their situations as part of the annual review of the development plan?
2. How can information be collected and shared between staff about the organizational context and the innovations?
3. Where in the organization can the strategic management of the exercises be undertaken?
4. How can the exercises be mounted so that they educate and involve as many staff as possible?

Further reading

Guidelines for Review and Internal Development in Schools, Primary and Secondary School Handbooks (1984), McMahon, A., Bolam, R., Abbott, R., Holly, P., Longman/Schools Council.
The Guide to Institutional Learning, IMTEC in *Can Schools Learn?*, Dalin, P. and Rust, V., NFER/Nelson, London.

8
EVALUATION AND ACCOUNTABILITY

Introduction

Teachers have power over the pupils they teach. For this basic reason it is both right and necessary that teachers and the education service are accountable to the community and society for the quality of the provision. In return society has the responsibility to know what it wants the education service to be accountable for and to know the best way to hold the service accountable so that the profession can be effective.

This chapter does not re-debate the meaning of quality in terms of the goals of the education service. Part I examined the issues, but whatever way quality is defined, the only way it can be achieved is by the development of a high-quality process of learning and teaching in schools and classrooms. Few would disagree with this statement, but how to improve teaching and the curriculum remains a contentious issue. The direction of the curriculum is the subject of a continuing debate. Regrettably there is little discussion, let alone research about how to teach and, more importantly, the way children learn.

As we have identified, there is an alliance in the UK amongst teachers and society that inhibits professional debate and development in the arena of the improvement of the educational process. It is an area of minimal activity as opposed to a state of intense research and development. Engineers, doctors and scientists all seek to improve the stock of knowledge and skill that underpins their work. This has its implications for evaluation for it is an important constituent in the process of development. In education the absence of a strong professional base of understanding about evaluation, inspection, pupil assessment and learning and teaching means that teachers are left relatively unskilled with politicians and the public (from whatever base of experience) entering into the debate. This results in assertion and counter-assertion without any recourse to a rational, empirically based consideration of the issues. Of late the education debate has almost deliberately been taken out of the professional and empirical parameters. Consider for a moment the reaction from the public and the doctors if the Secretary of State for Health was to pronounce on the best way for a doctor to treat cancer. The consequence is that teachers' confidence has been eroded along with the confidence of the community, the parents, business and the politicians in the system.

The theme of this chapter deserves a book in itself. Before we launch further into the public and professional debate about quality there is a need to stand back and consider what is meant by evaluation and accountability. Both need definition and examination separately and in conjunction with each other. Evaluation and accountability contribute to the achievement of quality but they are not the only ingredients. The improvement of quality should occupy the centre stage in the current consideration of standards. For this reason the relationship of evaluation and accountability to the improvement process will be addressed as the central theme of the chapter.

Accountability

Accountability appears to be a very precise word. As a principle it cannot be disagreed with, especially in a democratic, interdependent society. In its managerial form, everyone assumes that it is bound to deliver quality, but does it? Is it a single term or multifaceted? How does it contribute to the motivation of the profession? It is certainly the key issue of the decade, yet the very processes of accountability are so subtle, complex and central to achieving the goal of improving quality that the debate surrounding approaches to accountability should be the subject of considerably more examination than it has currently attracted.

In education, means and ends are very closely associated. Appropriate accountability methods (means) are therefore crucial to achieving quality (ends). Our continuing concern is that society, through its politicians, is pursuing a crude, simplistic and coercive form of accountability that will result in the demotivation and de-skilling of teachers, and thus result in a failure to achieve the goal of improved quality. On a good day we sense this is the result of insecure politicians being unable to find a way through the increasing complexities of education. Working collaboratively to solve a problem is not the hallmark of the current political approach.

Through a series of quotations I wish to consider the term accountability and then examine the relationship between various forms of accountability and the ways in which the improvement of quality can be helped or hindered by different mixes of the ingredients.

'Accountability must be associated with feelings of responsibility. When people feel accountable they attempt unconsciously to improve their performance. When people feel unfairly called to account they devise ways of beating the accountancy without actually improving the balance sheet' (Stenhouse, 1978). The implication is that effective methods of accountability must result in people feeling responsible. It is worth considering the value of the traditional inspection report which urges a popular school to improve its work, but the recommendations are denied by the school management, staff and governors. Not only does the report have to be professionally respected, i.e. credible, but it must also be accepted. In this scenario, is the school acting responsibly? If so, to whom: the students, parents, the LEA or society? Or does it somewhat erroneously believe it is? Improvement is the result of actions that are based on feelings of responsibility.

'Schools' accountability rests on understandings not decisions' (Nias, 1981). Action by the teacher, the school, the governor and the LEA can only stem from committed understanding. Understanding can often be so superficial or insufficient that it fails to guide real change and improvement.

The process of evaluation (including inspection or appraisal) has to be integrated with the process of improvement and learning at both the individual and institutional level. Neither can be effective without the other. Evaluation that does not increase insight and understanding is unable to inform the learning process, which is at the heart of change and the improvement of quality.

Three forms of accountability can be distinguished (see Bush, 1980):

1. *Moral accountability* – being answerable to clients/customers (students and parents).
2. *Professional accountability* – being responsible to oneself and colleagues.
3. *Contractual accountability* – being accountable to one's employers (including the financial, political components).

Within the education service there is a constant tension between these accountabilities (which the Education Reform Act has both sharpened through its legislative approach and extended by the formation of national requirements (curriculum)) and the powers of governing bodies.

A simple chart of accountability cannot be drawn. It does not range hierarchically from government to pupil even though the legislation would have us believe this. The concept of downwards (moral) accountability to the student flows from the central relationship of the teacher to the child.

Many teachers are motivated directly by this responsibility to children, even though there is a strong counterbalance caused by dominant pressures for upwards (contractual) accountability to meet curriculum (society) and managerial goals.

Professional accountability remains the weakest of the three forms of accountability, yet it probably has more to contribute to quality than the other forms. Ultimately the technical quality of the work of any teacher can only be assessed by another. Each time an aeroplane takes off, it is not some lay accountability of the engineer or the pilot that is relied on but the professional accountability their colleagues have exercised that gives confidence in the safety of the flight. The delivery of high-quality learning and subsequent teaching must be the subject of increasing professional examination. For too long this has been denied to the profession along with the means to research an understanding of the learning process. Teachers are being asked to fly to the moon with the research and development knowledge of the Napoleonic era.

This message, though, still fails to get through. The tension between these three accountabilities is becoming sharper as can be seen with the increasing prescription of the National Curriculum and in the coercive characteristics of the schemes of evaluation/inspection, teacher appraisal, pupil assessment and exam tables, which seek to create pressure without providing real information to the profession and the public about the state of education and the means of its improvement. The net result is a more difficult equation to balance.

The way changes in the balance between the three forms of accountability have taken place over the last few years merits some conjecture. Might it be that the loss of confidence within the profession and in society, for whatever reason, deliberate or otherwise, explains the shift from society's trust of moral and professional accountability to a more contractual arrangement? Whether this confidence was well placed in the past is a separate debate. The potential danger is that once contractual accountability has become prominent, it becomes a self-fuelling process that destroys the other more effective and essential forms of accountability and finally results in an unbalanced mix of accountabilities that fails to maintain or even improve quality.

Public or political security may stem temporarily from contractual accountability but when it is at odds with the teachers' feelings of responsibility to students and colleagues it results in destructive tension. Short-term and alleged gains from contractual accountability in the management of the service are unlikely to realize improvement.

Confidence and quality are more likely to be achieved when contractual accountability is the safety net, professional accountability the infrastructure of specialist responsibility and moral accountability the driving force. Together they make a full and workable structure. Together they provide the means for dealing with the unacceptable, for solving the problems and for ensuring the development of the teacher and the school and the restoration of the confidence and morale of the service and the public.

Each form of accountability on its own is inadequate. There is no lay person who has the specialist knowledge to know whether something has been properly done until it goes totally wrong. In education this is even more crucial as outcomes take several years to emerge. Education is a continuous process. It is unwise to wait for years and then find out that a pupil or school's standards of attainment have not been reached. Contractual accountability is often too crude and too late. Continuous accountability is essential if the quality of pupil attainment is to be maintained let alone improved.

A further consideration in the construction of the final balance of accountabilities is to recognize which elements of the process have to remain confidential and which have to be made public. This is not to hide problems but it is a genuine aspect of the need to achieve effectiveness. Make everything public and the service will opt for safety and standards will ultimately fall. Reduce the information flow and society will lose trust and confidence and the means to enter into the process of agreeing what needs to be done. Society and the profession need to arrive at a solution to this dilemma. Confidence needs to be built in order that the profession can work within clear boundaries where ideas can be tried out and doubts and differences discussed. Without that confidential arena educational advancement will cease. You cannot trial test the product before it enters the classroom.

Recalling that the means (the process of learning) are crucial to the end (quality), the current danger is that the present balance and methods of accountability are too crude and simplistic and, given their centrality to the process of learning and improvement, are likely to result in a system that will fail the UK. This means a thorough re-examination of the roles of teachers, governors, parents, communities, LEAs and government in the key areas of evaluation, appraisal, inspection and professional development. The focus would include the form, extent and means of agreeing the national/local/school curriculum and assessment in order to arrive at a working partnership that restores confidence and enhances quality.

Society has to work out how to strengthen all three forms of accountability and to create an effective balance between them.

Evaluation

I use the term evaluation in its widest sense. It thus includes all forms of inspection. The following quotation is particularly helpful:

> Evaluation is a general term used to describe any activity where the quality of the provision is subject to systematic study. It involves the collection, analysis, interpretation and reporting of evidence about the nature, impact and value of the entity. Thus monitoring, review and assessment are aspects of evaluation if systematic analysis of data is used to provide information for decisions.
>
> (Eraut, 1984)

The definitions of monitoring and review amplify the above:

> Reviews [of policy, performance and procedure] are periodic and semi-formal and used for questioning assumptions.
>
> Review is retrospective involving the collection and examining of evidence and information. It goes beyond monitoring to ask fundamental questions, e.g. programme aims, rationales, impact and value, reassessment of priorities and alternative policies. . . .
>
> Monitoring is to check what has happened and the extent to which things have gone according to plan. Procedures that are concerned with 'customer satisfaction' and with the qualitative aspects would be evaluative.
>
> (*Ibid.*)

The validity and the reliability of the evaluation process require careful probing. The production of information that does not meet these two objectives is dangerous. False information leads to incorrect analysis and to the construction of inappropriate solutions and action plans. To take a simple example: an unreliable or invalid thermometer will provide poor data for the doctor. The debate in the early nineties on pupil testing and school inspection illustrates the concerns many have about the use of data. All evaluation arrangements must be located within a set of valid and reliable procedures, otherwise improvement will suffer, false accountabilities will be imposed and irrelevant action plans will be established.

Principles

The first step in securing valid and reliable procedures is to establish the principles that inform practice. The following are offered as a basis for discussion:

1. Evaluation (including inspection procedures) must be part of a broader process of improvement which embraces all aspects of development (curriculum, staff and school development).
2. Judgment and reporting are related to an agreed action plan.

3. All parties to the operation of the education service (the LEA, schools, teachers and governors) have a shared responsibility to maintain and improve the quality of their work.
4. The collection and presentation of evidence, the establishment of criteria, the making of judgments and reporting are distinct though interrelated parts of the overall process and should be subject to agreed ethical and technical procedures.
5. The form of evaluation shall be related to the purpose.
6. The procedures shall be rigorous, explicit and laid down in such a way that they command the respect and confidence of all those who have a legitimate interest in the service.
7. The system shall be effective, i.e. produce action that improves the quality of education including the satisfactory reporting of evidence to those who require it.
8. Decisions about ownership have to be agreed in advance.
9. The boundary between confidentiality and openness has to be understood carefully in order to ensure effectiveness. A system that is too open can result in the production of very shallow information as a result of cautiousness, whilst a system that is closed is not likely to command the respect of the wider community. Confidentiality and openness have to relate to purpose.

Ethical and technical issues are not covered in this book, and the reader may well wish to look at Hopkins (1989) and Simons (1987). A further insight into evaluation can be gained from the work of Holly and Hopkins (1988). These authors set out three aspects of evaluation which need to be part of the improvement process. Evaluation can be seen in one of three states:

1. Evaluation *of* improvement – where it provides information about something that has happened or is happening but may not lead to action.
2. Evaluation *for* improvement – where it stimulates further development.
3. Evaluation *as* improvement – where the principles and practices of evaluation are integrated into the everyday working approach of the institution and its staff. In other words the professional operation of the staff and the school/college is constantly evaluating and improving the quality of its work.

The trend in evaluation has been to move towards evaluation for and very recently to evaluation as. An effective national approach has to strike an overall balance but within the context of education. The timeline of education, i.e. the number of years a pupil is at school, makes it almost impossible to demonstrate the value of any change in the short term. Add to that the complex interplay of a variety of contributing factors in any change and it becomes impossible to identify whether one change has had the desired effect or another. Set all this in the current period of multiple innovation and the contribution of evaluation *of* exercises has to be very carefully assessed. Evaluation *for* has much to commend itself as part of the developmental cycle.

The development of evaluation *as* should be the goal of the profession, for it forms part of professional accountability. The explicit integration of evaluation practices into the routines of schools and individual staff provides the necessary self-monitoring system that keeps everything on the course of improvement. Good teachers are constantly evaluating their work but there is always a need to build in the process of reflection and make the implicit evaluation more explicit.

The purpose of evaluation

Various terms are used in the debate on evaluation, especially on the inspection of schools to describe its purpose. Three terms can be identified:

1. Quality control, which is simply a policing function.
2. Quality assurance, which is concerned with the achievement of quality.
3. Quality development, which we take to mean the improvement of the standard.

A considerable amount of educational evaluation is about quality assurance and quality development. The need for quality control will always be with us. As with the appraisal of teachers, it is undesirable to construct a system that is predicated on the need to deal with the 1 per cent failures rather than the improvement of the 99 per cent.

The current debate and proposals on the inspection of schools suffer from a lack of clarity about purposes and the ways in which these various purposes of evaluation can be brought together into a coherent scheme. The current debate on the inspection of schools should seek to strike the balance between quality control, assurance and development. The evidence suggests that the balance is being swung too far towards control, thus starving out quality assurance and development. This will ultimately lead to a well-informed decline in quality as has been seen in the USA. Thus, evaluation systems have two sets of demands placed on them which do not easily fit together.

The main purpose of evaluation has always been to provide feedback to the subject of the evaluation for the purpose of improvement – evaluation for improvement. The second purpose is to provide information to others.

The balance in education between these two sets of purposes has been moved towards information for others as a result of the desire for choice: choices that parents can make about schools and choices under the 1991 Schools Bill about which group of inspectors should undertake the inspection of a school. Evaluation in this form is about evaluation *of* quality. It is about the provision of information for others to make decisions.

The debate has been further confused by a failure to distinguish between data and information. To give an example, the fact that the car is travelling at 50 mph is data. Until it is put with other material, often contextual, it does not become information as it does not guide action.

The provision of information and the construction of a feedback system is clearly consistent with the rationale of the current educational reforms. Without going into an exhaustive debate about all the aspects of the Education Reform Act (ERA), especially those concerned with LMS, the key element in the ERA model is the notion that it is both desirable and feasible to specify the curriculum nationally and in considerable detail and then to assess attainment against it. Quality has become defined by the national specification and the quality of schools is defined by their ability to deliver it. Whether it is sound to evaluate the effectiveness of schools by the effectiveness of students is highly debatable. Assessing hospital quality on the basis of patient recovery has the same problems. Unless the school controls its intake (i.e. selection), then it cannot be held to account for the differences in outcome.

The ERA model of improvement utilizes a form of motivation that relies on the poor school losing its numbers or on an inspection where it is told what needs to be done. When this is coupled with the free-market model where parents have choice of school then it is assumed that the model has been built.

Such models abound in the manufacturing sector. But the universal application of this model across all areas of society, rather like the universal application of anything, has its problems in that it does not consider the particular features of the service it is being applied to. It is rather like saying that management is management is *management* irrespective of the process it is managing.

Proving and improving quality in education requires its own variation on the theme of evaluation, accountability and improvement with models of management and evaluation that recognize the dynamic of the process. How does the education service's understanding of learning, improvement and accountability square with the current approaches to evaluation? The vision appears clouded. As with accountability, evaluation is not a single entity. It is a mix of elements.

The two main features of evaluation for information and improvement have been identified but the purpose of evaluation for improvement requires further examination. Evaluation as a process and in its outcomes both supports and motivates the teacher, the school or whatever to develop their practice. Even quality control has the ultimate goal of providing information for the benefit of improving the system even if it is through the means of supplying information to the user to make a choice about the state of the particular provision. Evaluation has to be seen as part of the learning or developmental process of the individual or school. If the outcome of any evaluation does not lead to improvement then it has failed. Effective evaluation for improvement can only be defined and judged in these terms.

Our confidence in the model of evaluation we propose below stems from a wide examination of the field of evaluation together with an understanding of the application of learning to the improvement process. Evaluation principles should inform the various processes of inspection, appraisal and pupil assessment and lead to the implementation of interrelated schemes for inspection, appraisal and assessment within a coherent model that has consistent principles related to learning and achievement (Goddard, 1988). The construction of a more holistic approach to evaluation helps to improve the quality of the process for each aspect reinforces the operation of the others. Any school that establishes systems of student assessment, teacher appraisal or evaluation that operate by different principles will encounter inherent tensions in the ethos and functioning of the school that sooner or later cause a deterioration in quality and development through the divergence in practice and message the different approaches use.

Let us offer the following purposes for educational evaluation:

1. To provide information that leads to a process of improvement and quality development.
2. To enable the school and the LEA to receive feedback on its policy implementation and work for the purpose of quality assurance.
3. To enable the service to obtain information about schools that are encountering major difficulties.
4. To provide information to parents about schools and their child's school in particular.

These four purposes can be accommodated within a single model but there are two issues that require initial examination: firstly, the relationship between evaluation and improvement and, secondly, the balance between quality control and other forms of evaluation.

Evaluation, accountability and improvement

It was through a Norwegian colleague that we had cause to reflect on various models of quality control/assurance and their effectiveness as found in the UK. He commented that he found the different ways in which Norway and the UK undertook their health and safety arrangements very illuminating. He characterized the UK approach as the inspectorate visit that was used to check, on a particular date, if everything was satisfactory. It either was or was not. The comparative approach, he argued, is to check whether the organization took its responsibilities seriously and had evaluation in all its forms in place in the operation of the organization. The role of the outsider was to work with the organization to provide an external validation and to enhance and examine the ways in which it maintained its safety procedures – a very stark contrast to current UK developments. The example given was the oil industry, where the location and context are similar.

Transferring this illustration to the education service raises two sets of considerations. Firstly, there is the importance of securing the responsibility for quality and the improvement process within a collaborative arrangement that is managed and operated by the appropriate involvement of all the parties (teachers, schools, colleges, governors – including parents and lay people – the education department – the wider professional group – and the LEA – on behalf of the community).

The balance of accountabilities should be distributed, understood and agreed by all concerned within an arrangement which requires all parties to be involved if quality is to be agreed upon, sought and maintained. If partnership provides the basis for quality and its improvement then partnership has to lie at the heart of the evaluation system.

The second point is that evaluation for improvement is a continuous process, coupling pressure and support in order to create the right conditions for motivation and learning – the prerequisite for effective improvement.

Evaluation, when viewed within an improvement process, becomes a significant tool for the learning of individuals and the school. How it informs the learning process and the extent to which it is able to do this task differentiates between effective and ineffective evaluation. Even when evaluation is coupled to accountability, however well balanced the different forms may be, it does not ensure that quality can be achieved let alone improved. The process of achieving and improving quality in education is a learning process for every member of the service, *not just the student*. The continuous professional development of teachers is the fuel that makes the system work, yet its contribution to quality is barely recognized. This is a singularly English failure that can be seen throughout society in the way it resources and values all forms of education and training. Helping the education service to become a sound learning environment should be society's goal.

Quality in terms of student attainment and achievement is the result of the interplay between learning and teaching. Thus an analysis of the teacher's work is central to understanding how to achieve the proper balance between accountabilities that will result in the motivation of teachers and support their continued learning within a climate of confidence that enables the teacher to work with the constant dilemmas of education.

The core of teaching and learning takes place in the classroom, but we would assert that its success depends on the implementation of a powerful concept that recognizes the interdependence of each part of the education system as a prerequisite to educational effectiveness. The concept draws on the belief that the effective facilitation of pupil learning is dependent on the way in which the teacher is supported as a learner by the service as a whole. The concept sees the school as a learning organization that provides students, teachers and parents with a learning environment that itself is created and maintained by the LEA and various regional and national structures and organizations. Evaluation processes are similarly linked: national to local to school to teacher.

Not only is evaluation central to effective teaching but it is also a vital component in the development and delivery of a quality curriculum. Curriculum is not a static commodity – it is for ever changing and constantly in need of being matched to the needs of individual pupils and the changing needs of society.

To be translated into the classroom and student achievement, the curriculum has to be organized and designed into student experiences. This is a creative process where quality is dependent on the ability of the teacher and the school to build and rebuild the curriculum to match the needs of the child and fulfil the requirements of society. The process by which this is done involves the evaluation of student needs and curriculum goals in relation to current practice. There are few parallels in other areas of society. The curriculum is not like a ready-made meal that can be packaged at some distant factory and, other than the need for a microwave, remain untouched until it is consumed – though we are fairly convinced that this is the model many still have in their minds. The teacher-proof curriculum designed by a grand architect and technically delivered in the classroom still lives on, but the teacher is both the architect and the builder. Curriculum design, teaching and learning is a dynamic process dependent on evaluation, the size and complexity of which requires the active mental, physical and emotional involvement of the teacher.

Confidence: a vital ingredient in evaluation and accountability

Confidence has many dimensions. To take just a few: there is the personal dimension, the professional aspect, the collective belief of the public, the state of the institution and the organization and the confidence that others have of someone or something else.

As the last decade evolved, confidence in all of these domains in the education service seemed to be at rock bottom. Each fed off the other to produce a spiralling decline. Society's confidence in the education service is dependent on the perception it has of the quality of the students' attainment. That perception has been shaken, not least by politicians and others. There is no evidence to support the argument about standards one way or the other. There never can be an objective debate in a system that will not support educational research and that has a normative base to educational assessment. If 10 per cent are to be graded at the bottom then there will always be 10 per cent at the bottom even if the standard of the 10 per cent improves. Standards are something else and there are few if any current measures of educational standards within countries let alone across countries that hold up to exhaustive examination regarding their reliability and validity. The current testing arrangements bear testimony to the difficulties. For this reason we will not enter the debate in anything like the degree of detail it deserves. The only statement that should command attention is that whatever the current level of students' attainment, it needs to rise if they are to live and work in the society of tomorrow. Apportioning blame for the past is also counterproductive. An analysis is necessary from the point of view that the service needs to learn from its past – but constructively.

Public, professional and individual confidence will only improve through a restoration of the means by which teachers develop their understanding of how to improve teaching and learning. This will need to be complemented by a society that learns how to work together, with each other and the profession at every level, to decide what has to be taught.

A number of changes have to be put in place to enable any restoration of confidence and the consequent improvement of quality. The idea that evaluation is central to learning and teacher effectiveness immediately demonstrates the importance of confidence, for it is a key feature of the learning process. How can schools and teachers be helped to develop their confidence to enable their responsibilities and accountabilities to be met?

The consequence of the failure to invest in educational research, teacher education and in the debate on the direction education should take has left the teacher and the service unsure that what is being taught is entirely valuable, wanted by the students or the local community, or confident that there is any guiding evidence about teaching that enables children to learn.

Many of these issues are as complex as understanding nuclear physics. It is not the failure of previous educational research to solve the problems surrounding teaching and learning, but its infancy.

Even where the profession does have some evidence, it is unable to compete with the prejudices of society that make everyone an expert in the field. Such views have been further legitimized by a government that has little regard for the development of knowledge in these matters and singularly disregards any objectivity in its quest for change. The profession is left to work with these fundamental problems.

Maintaining teacher confidence at the practical level will always be difficult. At the simple, instructional level anyone can feel confident. The battery manufacturer can be confident about the production of a battery. The outcome is clearer, the technology precise and the materials can be chosen for quality and purpose. The dream of society, especially politicians (and it is probably a false dream) is that education can be managed into the same arrangement. At the level of teaching a simple skill, there can be some confidence in the relationship between the teaching and the outcome. But the majority of education is far more complex, interrelated and individual. The complex interaction of the curriculum with children and their motivation and capacity to learn has to be managed holistically by the teacher and the school.

So how do teachers become confident and effective practitioners? How can evaluation help or hinder that process? One characteristic of quality teachers and teaching is the way in which continuing doubt, the source of all improvement, is handled. We are not referring to the confusion that stems from a lack of understanding about various innovations that do not seem to have any logic but to the internal debate about the best way to teach.

Let us examine confidence a little further in order to provide a basis for a consideration of the purpose of evaluation and the motivation of teachers. Confidence does not bear rational examination, for it often has the personal characteristics of enthusiasm and energy. It is also bound up with understanding, but what is understanding? Does it have any absolute meaning? What we thought we understood yesterday may only be part of the story today, yet it is the basis of all our actions and working lives.

To comprehend understanding is difficult. A significant component is the considerable amount of knowledge that has to be accumulated in order to make sense of the world. Viewed from the perspective of the outsider to education it is easy to understand how the parent or the lay person feels. Education is complex, information sparse and very difficult to obtain. Data abounds, but it is hard to turn it into information. To take an example: the patient has a certain level of blood pressure. This remains useless data until it is put into a meaningful context (i.e. age, gender and situation), when some interpretation can be made that is based on agreed criteria. The data is useful but only as a result of gaining an understanding about the context.

Confidence is also built on the construction of a vision of the future. Vision is not made of myths. Much of it is based on the analysis of information that is rarely communicated. The picture of the future needs to be drawn and the rhetoric of that image created in order to discuss and build the confidence and understanding that is central to learning. There is a difficult balance to maintain between the reality (whatever that is) and the image. I have a notion that the gap between reality, stated vision and private vision increases with the extent the person and/or organization has travelled along the developmental path. Ponder for a moment on how a teacher or parent builds the confidence of a 5-year-old child. The rhetoric ('that was good', whether it was or was not), the encouragement ('you can do it'), building knowledge and skill, are not founded on the destructive comment whether one is 5 or 35. Developing motivation is central to learning. Yet there are very conflicting ideas about how to do this. These range from threats of failure to positive and constructive attempts to build confidence.

The steady state where aspiration and practice are together does not provide the impetus for change. The developing person, school, college or LEA increasingly accelerate their vision beyond achievement. The trick, both personally and institutionally, is to bridge the ensuing and widening gap and to work with and tolerate the ambiguity, tension and frustration that stem from this essential component of improvement. Confidence lies in a belief of the vision: that it can be achieved and that there is capacity and capability to work with the ensuing tensions.

The development of that understanding is one of the foundation stones for the improvement of quality.

A model for evaluation in the nineties

Evaluation is not solely about the evaluation *of* schools, but about using it as an improvement process *within*. The challenge in the debate on quality lies in the creation of a balance between quality control and improvement. There appears to be overall agreement that standards need to rise. This should provide the rationale behind an emphasis for quality assurance and development. The purposes of quality control and information to parents can easily take their place within sub-arrangements designed for these purposes. To create a system built around quality control and informing choice will lead at best to a standstill and at worst to a deterioration of quality.

The events and innovations of the eighties and nineties leave us convinced that the real improvement of quality is the result of an integrated approach that combines the agreement and achievement of curriculum goals with development procedures and sound evaluation.

Effective learning is the underpinning concept in the operational process that brings together all aspects of the work of the education service, especially the work of schools, teachers, governors and the education department/LEA (perhaps in time the government itself). The touchstone of any arrangement for achieving quality is whether it enables all the parties to learn and to develop their understanding of the part of the education provision or system they are concerned with. Improving and achieving quality in education and raising standards is a change process and change is a process of learning.

In Chapter 5, a framework for improvement was introduced (see Figure 5.1) which combines three questions regarding the state of the school with an evaluation of both the state of the school and the means of improvement.

The state of the school is defined as follows:

- Where are we going? The vision and policy direction of the school which should be based on the needs of the pupils and the requirements of society.
- Where are we now? An assessment of the practice of the institution.
- How do we get there? The creation of a development strategy and plan for moving towards the school's goals.

Evaluation activity is directed at each state and to the various combinations. Thus the two questions, 'How well are we doing?' (which provides an evaluation *of* improvement) and 'How can we improve?' (which provides an evaluation *for* improvement) combine to provide a comprehensive system of evaluation.

Questions directed at the state of the school pick out, for example, how sound the policies of the school are or the effectiveness of the development procedure, or present a clear picture of practice.

Various permutations of questions in relation to the combinations of the states deepen the evaluation:

1. How well are we doing in relation to policy?
2. How can we improve what we are doing in relation to policy?
3. How can we improve the development of practice?

Evaluation and inspection

The current debate on inspection has all the hallmarks of dusting off traditional models of inspection and evaluation and placing them within the ERA model of market forces. It is rather like going to the scrap yard for a part for the car that is not working well enough to find something that looks as if it will remotely work.

Education needs and deserves something better, especially if the ERA is to be believed. Its main clause seeks to heighten the responsibilities of the DES, the LEA and the schools *to ensure* (the operative verb in the Act) that all pupils are being educated satisfactorily – not just passively monitored or inspected.

The predominant view is to locate the roles of inspectors, LEAs and governors within a framework of contractual accountability and to use traditional models of evaluation (e.g. testing and inspection) to reinforce this – set the target, appropriate or not, and check to see if it has been achieved. It is very unclear where this leaves the service and the profession in its understanding of the achievement of quality. It may control quality but does it assure or improve it? The current confusion needs deeper examination.

The central question is whether an evaluation system designed and predominantly resourced for quality control is capable of enabling quality assurance and development. To answer the question the reader has to consider whether the procedures for quality control create the right conditions for the motivation of the service to improve practice.

The assumptions behind traditional models of inspection lay in a coercive model of improvement and motivation that requires challenging. Whilst inspection practice has changed a lot in the last few years the mainstream approach rarely conforms to the principles of improvement. The principles behind the traditional model work on the basis that teachers have to be controlled and sanctioned if quality is to be improved. The periodic inspection in education is similar to the health and safety check. It checks if everything is satisfactory on the day. But does it work? Whilst the current education inspection system is changing, we have serious reservations about the value of the traditional inspection component if it operates in isolation from a total model of improvement. Evidence on the ground supports this. Those directly involved, especially headteachers, teachers and inspectors, will state in private rather than in public that traditional inspection reports rarely have the desired effect on the improvement of the subject concerned. It is worth asking why many years of traditional forms of inspection have not had the desired effect. One benefit of the focus on the evaluation process in the last few years has been to improve the process on the ground. Such changes are still working their way into the service with obvious impact in the work of schools, colleges and the LEAs. Unfortunately the time it takes to demonstrate the improvement does not fit with the political imperative and that old ideas form the centre of the debate.

We do not take the view that the profession responds constructively to contractual coercion. Sound industrial practice, especially outside the UK, supports a similar position. For example, quality circles are procedures based on the principles that evaluation, responsibility and improvement need to be linked. Most teachers are driven by their concern for the pupil. That is why many became teachers in the first place. Moral accountability needs reinforcing through evaluation procedures that teachers can build into their work: watching children, looking at how they learn and changing practice accordingly. Quality of attainment remains the product of the teaching–learning relationship. Evaluation not only has to focus on this relationship as the important factor but it has to do so in a way that is going to cause the teacher to open up and learn from the information the evaluation procedure produces.

The failure to locate inspection within sound evaluative procedures and a framework for improvement lies at the heart of the current weakness of the inspection and assessment system. For this reason any model of inspection should lie within an evaluation procedure which itself should be a continuous, integral, conscious and systematic part of the improvement process. Viewed from this perspective all aspects of the school's work, including its approach to development, are brought within one interlinked system.

Evaluation procedures have to meet the needs of the service and its users. Within a compatible framework for accountability, inspection systems should reinforce both moral and professional responsibility especially when they have the characteristics we have described. The picture we have needs defining.

The holistic model of an interlinked education service that has been described in this section is based on the principle that the student is provided with teaching and support from the teacher and the school, with the LEA supporting both. The objective of such a model is to emphasize moral accountability to the pupil and to the parents and the community within a professional framework. Contractual accountability is held both by the profession and the employer as necessary.

The evaluative procedures that flow from this model are built upon four components. First is the establishment of sound institutional self-evaluation that is located firmly within a professional framework that provides integral support and external moderation/validation. This links with professional accountability and, by its very operation, should enhance responsibility and understanding.

The second component is the opening out of parts of the evaluation procedure to include the parents, the governors and the public in a way that examines the school as a whole and brings together professional and contractual accountability. This would lead to a furtherance of the understanding and responsibility for all the parties involved, be they parents, governors or the LEA. The third component is the need to deal satisfactorily with the unacceptable either within a confidential or public arena depending on the nature of the issue.

The fourth and final component is the need for information about the quality of the school/service. Producing data without any context is often dangerous. We know the argument – people should not be treated as stupid. But technical ignorance is not stupidity. Presented with all the surveyor's facts and figures, the lay person cannot tell from the data alone whether the house can have a loft conversion without the walls giving way until the conclusions are drawn. Information has to be presented for a purpose and with an audience in mind. Information for parents is one purpose. Information for professionals to use for the purposes of improvement is quite another thing. All that is required in the evaluation arrangements proposed below is for the data that is collected in any procedure to be written up according to the purpose and audience concerned.

It is not possible to build a system of effective evaluation on the provision of information for comparative purposes and then use the same limited system for a more substantial evaluation for improvement. The establishment of a valid, reliable and useful evaluation system can only be achieved by a system designed for improvement and then extended to meet other sets of purposes, especially the provision of information for parents and the public.

The argument can be tested by using the assumption put forward by Stenhouse (1977) that accountability is concerned with the generation of the feeling and the operation of responsibility. Evaluation that is primarily concerned with information to parents and the system is likely to be cautious and incomplete.

A precondition for responsibility and effective learning is confidence. This usually stems from a mix of skill, knowledge and understanding coupled with a genuine belief that the processes will not be damaging. Within the parameters of this chapter it means that the accountability process (including evaluation/inspection and improvement) must be a sound learning process. That is not to say that learning is not sometimes painful but the balance must not be destructive. If it is, then either there is a rejection of the external or the subject is harmed depending on the reaction of the individual or school. (Let us say that these points do not relate to totally unacceptable practice when the procedures require an intervention and contractual response.)

Watching a good teacher work with children to improve their attainment and achievement usually shows a good degree of match between challenge and current performance. Get it wrong and the child's confidence and motivation is harmed. Everyone wants the child to take learning risks, to open up to comment and criticism. Effective learners do it all the time. If a school or a teacher is to be an effective learner then help is needed to develop the necessary confidence and to help the person to open up to the views of others and to act appropriately in response. Strong impermeable boundaries and resistance are often signs of a lack of confidence. How can the boundaries be opened up? How does a school help the teacher? How does the governing body help a school? How does the LEA do likewise? How can all the forms of accountability be welded together into an operation that fuses evaluation with improvement?

We believe that an evaluation system should be established that comprises four types of review, which together meet the various purposes for evaluation:

1. School self-evaluation.
2. Specific review.
3. Whole-school review/inspection.
4. LEA review/survey.

School self-review

The purpose of school self-review is to enable the school to build its capacity for school improvement through the foundation of its own rigorous procedures for internal scrutiny. The procedures should be integral to the school's development and planning arrangements. School review should comprise a number of facets. It should complement and appropriately link the work on teacher appraisal for professional development, thus providing the institution with an individual dimension to school evaluation. The safeguard needed in this proposal is that the scheme for appraisal conforms to the principles outlined in this section.

The next layer is to foster collaborative projects amongst staff that focus on the evaluation and development of practice. Materials such as the Open University *Classroom in Action* pack (1980) provide sound starting points for schools and staffs. Departmental and course review provides a curriculum and organizational perspective that is rooted in the direct provision of the work to students. This can link with specific review where an outside perspective is sought, but the school should establish its own continuous procedures at this level.

The cycle attached to the production of the development plan provides the school with the means to create a whole-school perspective. Overall evaluation is built from the accumulation of all forms of review.

The creation of a firm foundation is essential if the school is to use evaluation for improvement. One of the ways to structure this into the school's working is to create the school's own quality-assurance arrangements. Drawing on the developments in higher education, there is much to be gained by the designation of a deputy headteacher in a secondary school and the identification of a similar person in a primary school to take responsibility for the evaluation process. Such a person should be responsible for the integrity of the school's evaluation procedures and the management of the arrangements. In larger schools (including primary), a review committee or evaluation group representing the staff should be established to undertake the work. It would also have as one of its main functions the power to conduct internal evaluation, including, for example, the review of course programmes and departments in secondary schools. Most if not all schools require help with the processes for self-evaluation. The role of the LEA is to support the school in the development of its evaluative capacity as well as to provide the external perspective. An indicator of a mature school is one that has developed the capacity to evaluate its work rigorously and that has the appropriate arrangements in place for all forms of review and can relate such processes to its development programme.

This stage provides the foundation for the framework for specific and whole-school review. Without it the school is unlikely to derive the full benefit of the evaluation system.

Specific review

The purpose of this component is to provide the school with external feedback and the LEA with evidence of what is happening in specific areas of schools' work – for example, the mathematics in a school or the administration of its budgets. Specific review should be linked to school self-review and arise out of its development programme. The significant features of specific review are that

- it takes place at the point in time the school determines;
- it is an integral part of its development programme;
- it contains an external professional report;
- it would operate on a rolling programme and include such items as internal self-evaluation reports, moderators' reports (secondary-school courses, e.g. CPVE) and advisers' reports on aspects of the school's work, including those of HMI.

Evidence could also be obtained from staff from other schools who would visit the school. Such teachers could be accredited by the LEA.

Whole-school review/inspection

This should be a periodic, preferably three-year review that involves all the main partners (school staff, governors, parents, pupils and the LEA) in an evaluation of the school as a whole. It would draw on the other forms of review and be concerned with all aspects of the school's work. The agenda for the evaluation would be drawn up following the expression of views of all the parties concerned. There would be a professional report and a report for the governors and the parents.

LEA survey/review

The purpose of this form of review is to provide the LEA with essential information about the state of the service in order that it can undertake its statutory functions regarding resource management, policy and teacher development. Survey information may well be drawn from the other forms of review but specific visits by the inspectorate are likely to be needed to obtain a sound enough cross-section of schools' work to inform its judgement. Information would also be passed back to the school, thus providing another form of feedback.

Conclusion

This pattern of review meets all the purposes and principles of evaluation stated earlier. Evaluation grounded in an improvement process and undertaken according to sound evaluation procedures should enable the goals of improvement and information for others to be combined.

The difference between sound processes and ineffective inspection lies in the way that LEAs, schools, governors and the government develop their understandings, attitudes and skills about school evaluation and improvement.

The formation of an integrated approach to evaluation and improvement rather than the current vogue to separate them is the hallmark of an effective school, LEA and governing body. It assumes that at any point in time or procedure, each contributor to the process is both a teacher and a learner.

For the whole operation to function effectively, the LEA has to establish a positive local climate, for it is only the LEA that has the continuing relationship with the school and the pupils. The establishment of a continuing relationship is not a professional cover for a cosy arrangement but constitutes the main characteristic of sound learning, especially when the learner (school or teacher) may be inexperienced or not fully motivated. Neither can the governing body nor market-force model hold staff to professional account. The student is powerless and the contractual accountability is only one-third of the picture. A new head, a high staff turnover, a changed governing body, immediately changes the context for improvement and effective accountability.

Quality in education, and especially its improvement, can only be achieved through the creation of an LEA-wide learning environment that locates evaluation/inspection within a model of improvement. Such a model demands a holistic approach where all the contributory processes become complementary. The energy in people and the system can then be released. Efficiency and effectiveness manifest themselves (as with any system) in harmony. Confidence stems from seeing the arrangement fitting together, like the mechanic who knows the gearbox only works well with the gears in synchronization.

Issues for consideration

1. What are the most effective ways in which schools/colleges and LEAs can establish an integrated approach to evaluation and improvement?
2. What are the appropriate evaluation structures and processes for schools and colleges which would enable them to validate and evaluate the institution's curriculum?
3. What does a balance of accountabilities look like in practice at national, local and institutional levels?
4. What steps need to be taken to help the development of the profession and society towards a more open, confident and effective approach to evaluation?

Further reading

McCormick, R. and James, M. (1988) *Curriculum Evaluation in Schools,* Croom Helm, London (2nd edn).

Bush, T. (ed.) (1980) *Approaches to School Management*, Paul Chapman, London.

9
THE PROACTIVE AND CONSCIOUSLY DEVELOPING SCHOOL

Introduction

This chapter examines the way in which schools improve their capacity for change by moving into a more conscious and systematic approach to development. The first section discusses the main issues and factors that support improved development. The second section draws out the process by which schools and organizations move towards a more effective state, concluding with a particular illustration of a school in transition.

A number of general terms are used to describe the internal characteristics of a school in relation to the management of change. There is the readiness for change, the climate for change and the school's capacity for change. These are very general statements which may convey little to the reader and may not provide much support in terms of helping a school develop its improvement process. We would wish to set aside the concept of readiness for change. All schools are involved in change. There isn't a choice about coping with change. What is important is the state of the school's ability to handle innovation. Thus the general concept of readiness is unhelpful; it only has meaning when applied to the specific state of a school in relation to the demands of a particular innovation.

The development of a climate for change is the result of putting in place a number of processes concerned with the development of a disposition towards change. These were outlined in Chapter 5 when the features of vision, confidence and the management of the environment were discussed.

The third term, the school's capacity for change, deserves a deeper examination for it both gives meaning to the term 'capacity' and illustrates what a school has to do in order to improve its development process.

Issues and factors

The following section (on the characteristics of a consciously developing school) draws on the literature about school effectiveness and school improvement (see Mortimore *et al.*, 1985; Van Velzen *et al.*, 1985; Holly and Hopkins, 1988; Hopkins, 1987; 1989) but sets the factors within a different framework. In so doing it gives particular emphasis to features that appear to the authors to be critical to effective improvement, and it simultaneously describes the process by which a school improves its effectiveness.

The key features are as follows:

- The school has in place the capacity to learn as an institution and to enable its staff, as individuals, to do likewise. This involves the creation of sound development processes (INSET, etc.) and a constructive approach to all forms of evaluation (inspection, appraisal of staff and assessment of pupils).
- The school, through its staff, has become collectively conscious about the development process to the point where sufficient staff understand how to handle the components of the change process proactively. The establishment of a key group of staff in the school with these abilities is a central aspect of this feature.
- There is a realization that change is a holistic process where each change has to be seen in context and its impact on other innovations and parts of the school understood as fully as possible and managed.

From our observations of the change process, these three interrelated features develop symbiotically within the school as a result of a series of reactive developments coupled with fortuitous or planned staff appointments. As a result, the school and the staff undergo a set of experiences that creates an initial climate which enables the school to achieve a significant shift in its practices in each of the key features. This enhances the school's ability to implement change. The process of maturing (as we wish to name it) facilitates the school being able to switch into a different, more conscious and strategic mode of working. The change in state is both quantitative in terms of the amount of change the institution can handle and qualitative in terms of the degree of improvement that takes place.

Institutional development

Institutional development is the result of the development of the curriculum, management practices and the staff. It is a learning process for the staff and the institution which becomes effective when the school and the teacher translate the outcomes of their learning into ways of working.

The process is difficult and the relationship of the features imprecise. However, through our examination of a number of schools that have been tackling change through multiple initiatives, it has become possible to identify the way in which various sets of initiatives have been handled and the extent of their contribution to the school's overall capacity for change. In such institutions, the use of innovation has matured the development process by raising the level of consciousness amongst the staff about the process, especially in relation to the interconnections between previously discrete innovations.

The work of the International School Improvement Project (1986) drew out the relationship between the implementation of specific innovations and the school's general capacity for change. Figure 9.1 illustrates the relationship. The figure identifies the necessary linkage between the effective implementation of innovations (the top sequence within the school frame) and the building of the school's capacity for change (the bottom sequence).

The impact of innovations can be short lived and relatively minor if the school is unable to build a learning link between the innovation and the development of the school's capacity for change. The result is that the

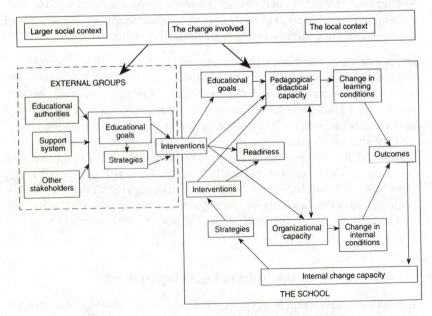

Figure 9.1 Reproduced with permission of FICSI.

school is unable to harness the opportunities and experiences available to it. Development and improvement remain *ad hoc* and individual.

The development of consciousness

The different ways in which schools and LEAs handle change in relation to the learning process have identified for us a crucial transition phase in the development process which occurs when a number of strongly related innovations are at the implementation stage. It is difficult to describe all the characteristics of the transition but it appears that the school, on the back of these innovations, is able to move from a period of collective unconsciousness about its development process – especially the holistic characteristic of change – to a state of consciousness.

In essence the school (the senior management and the leadership together with a critical number of staff) has arrived at a state where it understands consciously and can articulate the development process, the interrelationships of all the major developments and the resulting complexities, tensions and ambiguities that stem from this. This may well be a tall order but we believe it helps us to understand why effective development is so difficult. If the school is to manage change then it has to develop practices that support the staff through the change process. It is our belief that the transition is enabled by two sets of factors: the strength of the learning process and the utilization of a range of innovations that support that process. It may well be that certain sets of innovations or development goals have the 'correct' ingredients to facilitate the general development of the school's capacity.

Consciousness as a concept has been examined partially in Chapter 6. The stages of a school's conscious development can be related to children's learning. Very young children learn intuitively and somewhat unconsciously; they are generally reactive to the environment. This stage of development is effective and, as with a school's development, it should not be denigrated. However, the child's learning process matures. The child becomes proactive; he or she experiments and becomes conscious of what he or she needs to learn in relation to particular goals. The young person therefore sets about acquiring the necessary knowledge and skills that either society has decided on or the child has formulated for him- or herself. The learning process becomes a mix of the reactive and the proactive, the conscious and the unconscious. The same process applies to both the school and the individual members of staff. The conscious state finally manifests itself in the school as the establishment of a set of school procedures and infrastructures for supporting development, which includes evaluation procedures and the development of each individual member of staff to take on the changes.

Only when sufficient staff in the school have a conscious understanding about the major features of the development process (as outlined in Chapter 5) can the school be said to have developed a major component of its capacity for change.

So far we have spoken about sufficient staff and essential components. Whilst it is impossible to give precision to them, it is possible to identify certain key factors of the development process. They are as follows:

- The operationalization of an understanding about the three stages of development, namely initiation, implementation and institutionalization (see Chapter 5).
- The management of multiple initiatives and the identification of an overall strategy that clarifies longer-term goals (see Chapter 7).
- A thorough grasp of the interdependence of the four distinct operations of development, maintenance, planning and plans (see Chapter 5).
- The skill and understanding to be able to establish the structure and infrastructures, which helps to manage the process and brings staff together in various ways to work on the various developments. The need to network and to work collaboratively is a prerequisite to effective change (see Chapter 6).
- The creation of learning opportunities for the staff (see Chapter 6).

The growth of these features appears to take a varied form at the *ad hoc* stage but they have a general relationship and sequence at the transition stage.

The context for all schools is similar. Schools are handling a number of separate innovations, each of which is at various stages of development. Some are at the initiation stage, either through forced introduction which results in a slow first stage or the result of new developments. Other developments are moving out of the initiation stage or are well into the stage of implementation. As we have identified, a feature of major change is the interdependence of various innovations in the achievement of the overall goal of improving quality.

The concept that change needs to be handled holistically operates at various levels. There is the micro-level where each innovation, e. g. National Curriculum, topic work, TVEI, assessment, LMS, contains a number of smaller or sub-innovations that need to be handled together if effective implementation is to take place. However, the context of development in the 1990s means that all of the micro-innovations also need to be handled simultaneously in the context of macro- or overall change.

At the macro-level, it is possible to show the interdependence of a range of major initiatives that collectively have to be implemented in order to improve the overall quality of education. Broadly, macro-innovations fall into the three categories of development, namely, curriculum, staff and institutional/organizational innovations.

Examples of failed innovations illustrate the concept of the interrelationship of the parts. Such projects withered because either the full range of contributing components was not fully appreciated and therefore not initiated, or the school or initiator did not manage to achieve the necessary quality in the development process. For this reason, it is possible to conject that the objectives of failed innovations were not necessarily wrong. What was lacking was the understanding of how to put them into practice. The analysis of such innovations shows how various factors were missing or underdeveloped and so the innovation either failed to occur or was implemented so poorly that sooner or later its quality suffered and the change became discredited and disregarded.

Take, for example, the development of language across the curriculum. As an initiative following the Bullock Report (1975), this comprised a set of changes that required all teachers to have a sound knowledge of language and its acquisition and for teachers to understand how to apply it to their work in all fields. Not all teachers possessed the necessary level of knowledge and skill. It required increased teacher skill in their understanding of learning and teaching in order to put the goals into practice. It needed a whole curriculum. In schools the notion of a whole-school approach was rare and the idea of a whole curriculum, especially in the secondary sector, was new. Further, it necessitated a change in the way in which pupils behaved in the arena of talk. Given the considerable pedagogical implications that were rarely given classroom support at the level needed (see Joyce and Showers, 1980), then it is no wonder that the development of language across the curriculum has been relatively unsuccessful and children's language abilities have hardly moved forward.

The premiss that education is only now becoming conversant with all the factors that enable change to occur can be used to analyse critically the implementation of a number of reforms, past and present. The UK has a considerable stock of very sound ideas that have failed to be implemented properly. The difficulty lies in their half implementation which leaves both the teacher and the school in neither one place nor the other and therefore in the worst of all worlds. Many of the innovations of the seventies and eighties suffered from the lack of development of the school's capacity for handling change and the failure to understand the change process, especially in the area of effective INSET and evaluation.

The example of a current innovation, the development of cross-curricular features, illustrates the challenge and begins to demonstrate the interrelationship of initiatives and the growth of consciousness amongst staff about change. The achievement of an overall curriculum with such features continues to present problems. Whilst there are lots of contributing reasons for this, one obvious difficulty is the lack in many schools of a whole curriculum framework or at least the recognition and vision of one that facilitates the incorporation of the cross-curricular features.

Development work is begun as a result of either TVEI and/or the National Curriculum. The initiation stage is usually marked by the development of each cross-curricular feature as a separate initiative. In most schools this is the only starting point as the staff's commitment may be variable and headway can only be made where there is some support. This particular approach does improve the situation.

As each cross-curricular feature is developed, the experience can cause staff to become aware that cross-curricular features are not discrete and that each feature on its own has insufficient impact on the structure of the curriculum, pedagogy or the management of the school to have a long-lasting effect. If, as a result, the school has built up a foundation of understanding about development and is moving towards the transition stage, then it is in a position to realize that an *ad hoc*, piecemeal approach has its limitations. If the school is subsequently able to utilize the experience and learn from the process then the school and the staff reach a stage in the development process that leads to the critical realization that change has to be handled holistically.

The shift to conscious development occurs when the school, through key staff and its management, becomes aware of the development process and, in particular, that the effective implementation of one innovation is dependent on the implementation of another and that all innovations are dependent on the growth of the school's capacity to handle the changes. The increase in capacity is assisted by the ability to create an overall strategy that relates innovations to curriculum and staff development in the context of institutional development. A further feature of the development process in the transition phase is the knowledge and skill to be able to relate and phase innovations so that they are properly integrated with each other and the school.

Thus, effective development necessitates the school operating consciously with the full range of initiatives in order to bring the various facets of each development to the required level of development at the critical point in the implementation process. Handling development is complex. It is essential that all the components of particular innovations are in place at the right moment in time.

The process we have outlined is very complicated and not entirely predictable because of the dynamic process of education. It is not surprising, we contend, that only a small minority of schools have moved to this conscious state and that they find it very difficult to maintain that position.

Stages of the process

The reactive stage

The characteristics of this approach to change can be summarized as reactions to external innovations coupled with internal initiatives handled in *ad hoc* and unrelated ways with little impact on (nor development of) the school's general capacity. The net result is usually short-term changes that wither, with the staff of the school becoming overloaded by the range of initiatives that is outside their capacity to handle.

Movement from this position is often a result of outside pressure and assistance from the LEA, which develops key staff or staff appointments at a senior level that bring new understandings to the school. The absence of either of these interventions is likely to leave the school permanently in such a state.

The appointment tactic has long been used but with limited effect, as a single individual has limited impact. A more promising route may lie in the creation of school improvement programmes across the LEA. Such projects exist in the USA and Canada and are worthy of consideration as a complement to the current innovation strategies, nationally and locally. Schools can also formulate similar projects under various banners, e.g. raising achievement, whereby they tackle the change issue holistically. However, any institution or LEA that takes this approach is already at the transition stage.

The transition stage

The transition stage builds imperceptibly out of the previous phase. The timescale is impossible to determine. It is possible to identify the elements of practice and operational factors that need to be in existence for the school to move into and through the transition to conscious development.

A significant level of development work

The school has to be involved in a substantial range of development work with a significant amount of it at the implementation stage. As a result, the school is experiencing a range of curriculum and staff development which affects both the constituent parts of the school (departments and individual teachers) and the school as a whole, either in curriculum terms or in the management of the school. The presence of both kinds of development work is central to the development of the range of learning experiences the staff receive and need, for it is through these experiences that learning about the process of change takes place. Innovations that are solely about sections of the work of the school or that only affect a number of staff do not have the necessary impact. Schools that consciously manage change need to identify and/or build innovations that together have these two sets of properties.

Collaborative practices

The school has established a range of internal and external contact with other agencies, the LEA and its advisory team, other schools and teachers. Schools that are at this stage of development are well networked (see Chapter 6). Development is more likely to be successful when the school has built up strong working relations amongst staff. It is through its infrastructure and climate that the school accompanies its holistic approach to change in the curriculum and the institution, with a holistic approach to the staff, their development and teaching.

The establishment of collaborative working is often brought about through the involvement of outsiders in the school through the LEA's advisory team. In this way, the school is nudged towards maturity as well as arriving at it through its own direct experience.

Collaboration is underpinned by the establishment of a significant (not necessarily numerical) number of critically placed staff whose individual professional development enables them to understand the processes outlined in Part III of this book. Such staff are usually in a range of leadership positions in the school and are thus able to influence the change process. They would have a major presence in the senior management, but it does not follow that successful change leadership only lies with the headteacher. The formation of a critical mass of staff is crucial to any change process, for the group provides the opportunity for discussions about the management of the changes and is also a reference group for support. In addition, the group is central to the establishment of a positive climate for change through its disposition and handling of the development process.

Evaluation

The school has developed mechanisms for internal evaluation that are well linked to the development system and to the external environment. These are central to the learning process and to the raising of the staff's level of consciousness. Not only do the evaluative procedures operate at the individual level but they also have to become part of the school's infrastructure of meetings and routines.

Strategic planning

At the transition stage, the school moves into a fully strategic mode of operation concerning its development work. Until this point is reached, the characteristic of the school's development work and its plan has been piecemeal with a series of separate action plans, each with its own well-thought-out timetable and operation but nevertheless not part of an overall framework.

The strategy that carries the school forward has to be articulated in a section of the school's plan. It is not sufficient for the school's strategy to concern only the various innovations and priorities. A plan that states how the school's capacity is to be developed is itself an indicator of the transition and the school's growing consciousness about the management of change.

The transition stage can rarely be imposed. The process of conscious maturing is partly organic. The groundwork for the transition can be laid but, as with all learning processes, it has to be built from where the institution is. All the factors described above have to be in place. A strong leader may be clear about the process and, over time, build up the necessary conditions, but it is not until a significant number of staff share the same understanding that the transition can occur.

A school in transition

Figure 9.2 shows the path schools are likely to take in arriving at and passing through the transition to effective (i.e. conscious) development stage. The example draws on the concept of the three stages of innovation development: initiation, implementation and institutionalization. (These terms are described more fully in Chapter 5.)

The figure portrays a number of initiatives at various stages of development. Sets of examples are at the base of the figure. These have been chosen to cover the sectors and to show the various aspects of the process.

The school in transition

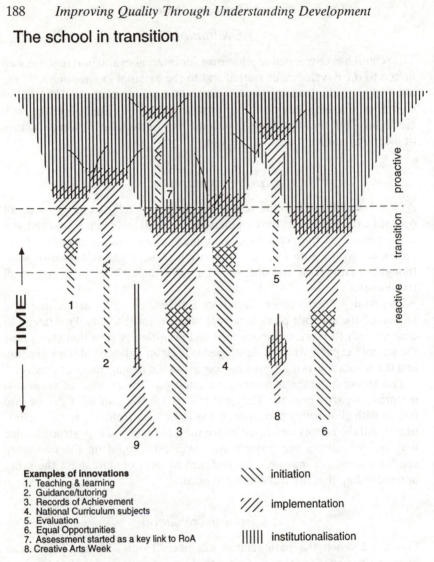

Examples of innovations
1. Teaching & learning
2. Guidance/tutoring
3. Records of Achievement
4. National Curriculum subjects
5. Evaluation
6. Equal Opportunities
7. Assessment started as a key link to RoA
8. Creative Arts Week

8 & 9 represent failed innovations

\\\ initiation

/// implementation

||||| institutionalisation

Figure 9.2

The school may have a number of projects/innovations at the stage of initiation. Some may have been started by the school either because it is required to take on the innovations or because it has identified particular projects for itself. The school's disposition to the initiative is an important

The reactive school

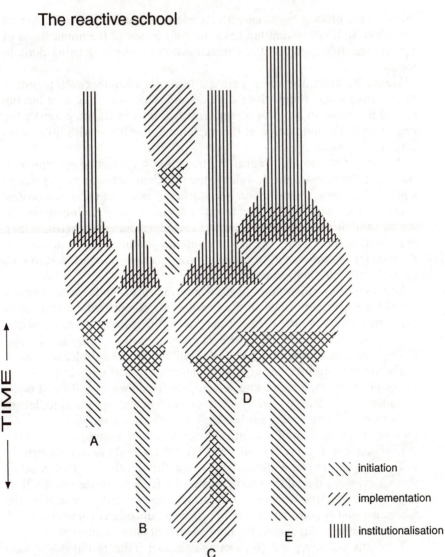

A. An innovation that develops but has little long term effect
B. An unrelated innovation that dies out
C. An innovation that contributes to the development of another initiative and merges totally with it
D. Two innovations that relate at implementation but separate at institutionalisation
E. A significant innovation that the school continues to institutionalise

nb The extent of the innovation's impact on the school is represented by the width of the column

Figure 9.3

factor in the process but even with an internal initiative it is unlikely that the whole staff are committed to or are fully aware of the implications of the change. Initiation has the characteristic of something being done to someone.

Figure 9.3 illustrates the general pattern of a school's development in the reactive stage. Innovations develop and sometimes take root but the school is unable to build on them. This is shown in the diagram by the reduction in the innovation at the implementation stage with little or no institutionalization.

A school's movement towards the transition stage can be prompted by combinations of innovations which cause sufficient attention to be given to whole-school issues. In addition, the staff (as a result of their own professional development) begin to address the development of their understanding and skill in the change process. As each development progresses then more staff become aware of each innovation's potential and its difficulties. As each innovation begins to command support then the staff start to take the initiative into their practice.

Successful implementation of each innovation depends on a managed transition stage that brings all the contributing components to fruition at the same time. A failure to do so can result in the collapse of the particular innovation and in damage to the school's capacity to manage change through the loss of confidence and credibility in the school's leadership.

The need to ensure that aspects of innovations and innovations themselves are properly phased and related can be shown as follows. For an aeroplane to lift off the runway, the factors of weight, speed, wind, length of runway and positioning of the flaps, etc., all contribute to a successful take-off, but only if all of the critical factors are in the right position at the crucial moment. If there is insufficient lift, the take-off has to be aborted.

Through the implementation stage and the development of practice there is evidence that, if the teachers can learn from the process as it affects implementation, they become increasingly aware that innovations the school previously considered as being discrete (and often managed as such) are now mutually dependent for their successful implementation.

Take any starting point (for example, school–industry links) – it soon becomes clear that this affects teacher attitudes, learning and teaching styles and curriculum organization. In the example of flexible learning, a number of contributory innovations have to come into play in order for the initiative as a whole to be realized successfully.

As the school continues to work with the innovations two outcomes emerge. Firstly, the innovations become merged as they are integrated into the staff's work. Secondly, the experience of the implementation and institutionalization phase contributes to the school's capacity for change. The conscious management of the process can result in a number of actions that draw on the ideas in Chapter 7. One example of the kind of decision that may need to be made relates to the introduction and/or phasing of particular programmes/objectives/innovations. From an analysis of the school's situation, the staff and the group responsible for the formation of the strategy may recognize the need to accelerate the introduction of a particular objective in order to support other work in the school. A particular example may be to focus on learning and teaching as a way to integrate the implementation of the National Curriculum. A programme of curriculum and staff development built around the production of guidelines may contain the necessary mix of activity. The programme would help the staff to look at whole-school aspects and individual practice and to integrate these into the various elements of the National Curriculum and assessment that had priority.

It is through these examples that the complexity of the change process is illustrated. Key staff have a need for a substantial level of skills and understanding, especially at the transition point. We suggest that moving through and out of transition is underpinned by the operation of the three key factors outlined at the start of the chapter, namely, that the school and its staff have the ability to

- learn and evaluate;
- be consciously proactive; and
- view development holistically and manage change effectively.

Issues for consideration

1. How can the leadership of a school work together to develop the school's capacity?
2. In what ways can sufficient staff develop their understanding of the change process?
3. What are the most effective combinations of innovations to form an effective strategy to take a school into and through the transition stage?
4. What are the most effective school arrangements for the management of the process and the development of the strategy?

PART IV

PROPOSALS FOR THE FUTURE

10
LEARNING FROM EXPERIENCE

Introduction

There were vital elements missing in the attempts at reform in the late eighties and early nineties – a period which in the future some may categorize as a Dark Age for education in the UK whilst others of different philosophical persuasion may see it as an Age of Enlightenment. Whichever viewpoint one takes, it is time to stand back and examine objectively the reforms and identify their strengths and weaknesses in order to plan for the future.

In this chapter we draw on the work of earlier chapters in order to identify the major problems facing education and to offer possible solutions. We focus particularly on the following components of the education service and system:

1. The framework of the system.
2. Curriculum and assessment, teaching and learning.
3. Teacher education.
4. Teacher quality and qualifications.
5. Management development for education.
6. Evaluation, accountability and motivation.
7. Resources.

Table 10.1 provides a summary of our proposals. The arguments underlying these proposals form the rest of this chapter.

In the final chapter we summarize the key points raised in the book, list the flawed assumptions behind the push for changes in education in the nineties and discuss principles which could usefully guide action in the future.

Table 10.1   A strategy for the improvement of quality: a summary of proposals

---

1. The framework of the system
Proposal A
That the improvement of understanding and links between different parts of the system be given priority. Progress will be more certain if there is partnership.
Proposal B
That a coherent framework for the development and operation of the service be established so that strategic planning can be effective. The principle of decentralization should be turned into a reality through the apportionment of responsibility for curriculum, resources and teacher education between the government, LEAs and the schools.
Proposal C
That the necessity for the management and career structure to support development in all its forms (including teacher learning) be recognized and that the development of effective practice in teaching and learning be considered as central to such structures.

2. Curriculum and assessment, teaching and learning
Proposal D
That change in approaches to curriculum and assessment and teaching and learning be based on evidence rather than prejudice and that the professional judgment of teachers should have an influence equal to that of political views in any debate about change.

3. Teacher education
Proposal E
That a national policy on teacher education be developed which ensures that the foundation provided by initial teacher training is built on by the provision of a programme for the continuing professional development of teachers.

4. Teacher quality and qualifications
Proposal F
That the following questions be addressed at national level and that recommendations for future practice are then made:

- What minimum qualifications should teachers have?
- How can teacher-supply problems best be solved?
- Is there a case for setting up a publicly available register of teachers and their qualifications (for England and Wales)?

Table 10.1 *continued*

---

5. Management development for education
Proposal G
That a coherent programme for management development be designed which can cater for the needs of teachers and other members of the service at different stages of their careers.
Proposal H
That the changes introduced under the local management of schools initiative be evaluated and that the scheme be adjusted in the light of the findings.

6. Evaluation, accountability and motivation
Proposal I
All teachers should be equipped with the professional tools of educational evaluation so that intuitive professional judgments can be backed up by informed professional judgments.
Proposal J
Accountability systems within education should be reviewed and based on a balanced model of accountability, i.e. with a balance between moral, professional and contractual elements.

7. Resources
Proposal K
That the quality of the educational experience for the individual child be a key factor in influencing decisions about class size and school size.

The framework of the system

The framework of the education system lacks coherence. It has evolved rather than been planned and systematically developed. But the time is nigh for the education framework to be reviewed with consideration being given to the needs of the education service as a whole in the context of the nineties. Issues requiring particular attention include

- decision-making procedures: the balance between centralization and decentralization;
- the lack of coherence in the infrastructure; and
- management structures for development.

Decision-making: the balance between centralization and decentralization

Partnership between community and schools has been claimed to be a central plank of education policy, certainly since the 1986 Act with provisions being strengthened in the 1988 Act. But what is the reality?

Whilst it is true that governors of schools now have considerable powers and responsibilities, it is questionable whether most governing bodies have the knowledge or expertise to carry out these responsibilities. The reality is that there is increasing centralization and politicization of education in England and Wales and decision-making powers are increasingly concentrated in the DES. Centralizing such power over the work of professionals is not a recipe for quality and no other professions have faced the same level of ministerial interference in their professional practices.

The restriction of the role of teachers and LEAs in decision-making in the service means that good practices are often neither recognized nor shared nor built upon. This flies in the face of effective decentralization. The pleas of Brian Sams, the Conservative Chair of Education in the London Borough of Bexley, for the return of trust and partnership to the relationships between government and the education service indicate the poverty of this crucial relationship. Sams (1991, p. 14) comments that

> The isolation of central government from the service is reaching crisis proportions with many reforms being out of touch with what those involved see as essential to the achievement of a high quality service. The isolation of ministers was emphasized in July 1991 with the unexpected removals (some might say 'resignations') of government appointees Philip Halsey, chair and chief executive of the School Examinations and Assessment Council, and Duncan Graham who held the equivalent post at the National Curriculum Council.

A balance is clearly needed if partnership is to have any meaning.

The rejection by the DES during 1991 of the 'Language in the National Curriculum' (LINC) project indicates the extent of political control exercised over the curriculum in the early nineties and the low ebb of respect by government for the professional judgment of teachers. A report of the project in *The Times Educational Supplement* (12 July 1991, p. 6) suggested that the project had received twenty-six million pounds in funding from the DES. Trials of the materials involved many experienced teachers across the country – between them they had the experience of educating many thousands of children. Yet the findings of this work have been able to be discounted at ministerial level. The question must be asked: Will the cause of high-quality education be advanced by such exercise of power? We make the following proposal: *That the improvement of understanding and links between different parts of the system be a priority* (proposal A). Progress will be more certain if there is partnership. (Work shadowing, e.g. between heads, DES officials, LEA advisers/inspectors, would provide one easily manageable way of enhancing understanding.)

Incoherence in the infrastructure

Strategic planning has not been evident in the reforms of the eighties. Changes such as the introduction of grant-maintained status (which lead to schools being directly managed by the DES in London rather than locally), City Technology Colleges, open enrolment, pupil-based funding, the dismantling of LEA advisory servcies (with the loss of support for schools and teachers) seem to have had more to do with ideology than with improving quality.

At a time of supposed concern about value for money, LEAs have been effectively prevented from rationalizing the numbers of school places available (as in the London Borough of Hillingdon). Schools have been able to 'opt-out' of local control to prevent closure, and opted-out schools are able to change their character and develop their own sixth forms regardless of local provision.

Changes are based on the principle of the market without considering the implications of what it means in practice for the children. Often decisions have been taken which are apparently not based on any understanding of interrelationships within the system and service nor do they appear to have been based on any firm foundation such as those provided by research findings.

The danger with ideologically based change is that wave after wave of policy initiatives are made without any grasp of the implementation problems. The assumption that change automatically follows policy decisions is flawed.

The lack of any implementation strategy means that some aspects of the reforms of the eighties will probably never become fully effective as the necessary support systems for change are being eroded. The approach could be likened to that of a car manufacturing firm where the management have ordered the building of a new car but left the detail to the production line to sort out. Just one example of the loss of support systems is in the case of training for the implementation of the assessment of the National Curriculum. In 1991, LEAs across the country organized and carried out the training for the teachers of 7-year-olds. In future years, as this training is required for teachers of the older age groups, the training will, in at least some LEAs, not be available as the money funding the development of the expertise of advisory teams has been switched to inspection. The theory is that schools can buy what they need – but from whom? Although short-term funding may be made available by government, the expertise to train teachers, built up over time, may not.

LEAs still retain an obligation to see that government policy is implemented and they provide INSET for teachers to support policy implementation. If, as is proposed, the role of LEAs is curtailed, who will ensure that such INSET is made available so that change can be implemented? The result of such a change will be that policy and policy implementation will become separated. There is a flawed assumption that law and inspection are appropriate means for effecting improvement rather than improving the process of development itself.

Proposals in the 1991 Schools Bill mean that schools will be inspected every four years. Where will schools obtain the training to enable recommended changes to take place? Higher education institutions now run on tight budgets. They are unlikely to provide as wide a range of courses as was available at teachers' centres through LEAs. In any case, for many teachers, institutions of higher education are inaccessible. We suggest the following: *That a coherent framework for the development and operation of the service be established so that policy development and implementation and strategic planning can be effective* (proposal B). The principle of decentralization should be turned into a reality through the apportionment of responsibility for curriculum, resources and teacher education between the government, LEAs and the schools.

Management structures for development

Current management structures in many schools do not take account of the development needs of the school nor of the centrality of the role of teaching and learning.

To obtain higher salaries, teachers take on responsibilities which take them away from the classrooms, culminating in the position of non-teaching head, or adviser. Classroom teachers are the people who are actually teaching yet they seem to have the least say in what happens in education! Although, in theory, good classroom teachers can now be paid more in recognition of this fact, promotion away from the classroom is likely to continue unless a promoted post is created – probably at deputy-head level. This step would allow recognition of the importance of developing classroom practice as well as recognition of the extra responsibilities of the headteacher.

In Queensland in Australia, such a post has been recently introduced – that of 'advanced skills teacher' – but it is not at deputy-head level and so there could well be financial pressure on teachers to follow the administrative route (Queensland Education Department, 1991).

An additional problem with promotional structures is that teachers who are seconded to become advisory teachers often find that their expertise is not accepted as relevant when they apply to return to schools. Similarly, inspectors, advisers and lecturers in higher education do not have sufficient opportunity to develop their teaching further.

Proposal C: *That the necessity for the management and career structure to support development in all its forms (including teacher learning) be recognized and that the development of effective practice in teaching and learning be considered as central to such structures.*

Curriculum and assessment, teaching and learning

The curriculum and its accompanying assessment provide the body of educational provision – methods of teaching and approaches to maximizing the learning of the young people give the body life. Curriculum goals are crucial – they must be flexible enough to cope with constant change. Yet the nature of the curriculum and the possibilities of different forms of assessment are poorly understood by a number of decision-makers in education. In this section, the following aspects of curriculum and assessment are discussed:

- Misunderstandings about the curriculum.
- Curriculum content as a political issue.
- Assessment: the province of the teachers or the politicians?
- The implementation of the National Curriculum and the implementation of change.

We make the following proposal (proposal D): *That change in approaches to curriculum and assessment and teaching and learning be based on evidence rather than prejudice and that the professional judgment of teachers should have an influence equal to that of political views in any debate about change.*

Misunderstandings about the curriculum

The National Curriculum is only one part of the whole curriculum – it provides an outline of the educational provision to which each pupil in the state sector is entitled (some might say restricted). HMI (1988) and the National Curriculum Council (1990) provide descriptions of the broader curriculum.

But all of this advice and guidance just provides a framework for learning. Teachers have to juggle with conflicting aims in interpreting these curricular frameworks. They have to satisfy the needs of individual students as well as those of society and they have to focus on short-term goals at the same time as long-term goals. Some local flexibility about interpretation will always be required so that learning can be made relevant to the children in their own context. For instance, a teacher covering aspects of 'My Body' – a common topic in primary school – will structure the content and approach according to the children's particular experiences of health and life and death. There will, for example, be children with individual health problems in any class, e.g. a terminally ill child. This experience will affect children's understanding and so influence the method of teaching. And the teacher's approach will change the next year with a different group of children who have different experiences.

There seems to be general agreement among teachers that all young people should have similar curriculum entitlement and that a national framework is a positive step towards this. But there is a concern that what is an entitlement could become prescription. The education of children with specific abilities (for instance in languages or the arts) is being constrained in the state sector (because of the National Curriculum) in ways which many adults would have found unacceptable in their own education.

The attempt to reach excellence through the imposition of a national curriculum can be likened to an attempt to produce a Rembrandt following the painting-by-numbers approach.

The concept of the curriculum is not widely understood by lay people. Misunderstandings about the nature of the curriculum among lay governors prompted the DES to write a leaflet explaining its nature (1991a). They had pinpointed a problem with public understanding of the term. Understanding the nature of the whole curriculum is linked with understanding the purpose of education. The best schools acknowledge the importance of the hidden curriculum – that part of a child's education which enables them to develop confidence in themselves alongside the ability to argue, reason and debate the issues of the day. It is this part of the curriculum (which relates to the fourth 'r' – the need to be articulate) which has suffered most in the conflict between teachers and government over the last decade and with the 'innovation overload' suffered by the service.

Curriculum content as a political issue

Decisions about the curriculum are political decisions as what is taught can fundamentally alter the nature of our society. In the words of Eric Hoyle (1975, p. 375), 'Curriculum change is a variety of educational change which in turn is one form of social change'. Curricular decisions affect the attitudes, skills and abilities of all members of society and, consequently, the functioning of society as a whole. Williams (1961, p. 125) puts the point this way:

The way in which education is organized can be seen to express consciously and unconsciously, the wider organization of a culture and a society, so that what has been thought of as simple distribution is in fact an active shaping to particular social ends. It is also that the content of education, which is subject to great historical variation, again expresses, again both consciously and unconsciously, certain basic elements in the culture, what is thought of as 'an education' being in fact a particular selection, a particular set of emphases and omissions.

Assessment – the province of the professional or the politicians?

Assessment is a two-edged sword. It can be used positively, to diagnose an individual's weaknesses (formative assessment) and so plan a programme of future work or it can be used negatively to filter out a certain percentage of students (i.e. norm-referenced assessment systems such as A-level). The form of assessment individuals experience can crucially affect their motivation to go on to learn more. This issue has been tackled in the service and various forms of assessment have been gradually introduced particularly at GCSE and in higher education. However, recent ministerial pronouncements have challenged and rejected professional opinions.

An example is in the limiting of assessed coursework at GCSE and the rejection of current assessment arrangements for modular schemes – widely used schemes such as Nuffield Modular Science and Suffolk Science and other popular graduated assessment schemes in maths are affected. These schemes were the result of years of work by professionals with vast experience of educating children. These restrictions on school assessment are being imposed at the same time that universities are moving to modular degrees, with end-of-module assessment and with students able to move between universities for different modules. This inconsistency over assessment strategies is yet another example of the flawed assumptions bedevilling attempts at improvement.

The implementation of the National Curriculum and the management of change

The centre–periphery model of curriculum development which had been used in the sixties was the model used for the development and delivery of the National Curriculum. It was centrally devised but locally delivered.

However, the lessons which had been gained from the sixties were clearly not understood by those responsible for devising the implementation of the National Curriculum. Good practice in terms of management of change did not seem to have been considered. A tremendous opportunity to build on the commitment of teachers for a national curriculum was not realized because the implementation phase had been poorly thought through. The problems faced in the implementation stage of curricular change were already well known to educationalists with the work of Fullan (1982) and others providing detailed advice on appropriate strategies.

It is well known that where schools have no established processes for implementing and supporting improvement then any proposed changes are doomed to failure. Curriculum changes which are 'bolted on' to the existing system rather than integrated into the system wither and die once particular individuals leave (or, in the case of targeted funding, it ceases). Experiences with the impact of the Technical Vocational Education Initiative in the early eighties provided examples of this problem. The assumption that resorting to the law is an effective alternative to gaining professional commitment to change is flawed.

Teacher education

High-quality training and regular updating of teachers is essential if standards are to be improved. Even if no other aspect of teaching changed, subject content changes continually. Just take the example of foreign languages – teachers of these need to keep up with modern idiom. The regular opportunity of a term's secondment suggested in the James Report seems logical and necessary. In this section, two aspects of teacher education are considered:

- The role of inservice training in improving quality.
- Professional development and staff development: maintaining the balance.

In this part, we make one main proposal (proposal E): *That a national policy on teacher education be developed which ensures that the foundation provided by initial teacher training is built on by the provision of a programme for the continuing professional development of teachers.*

Initial teacher training (ITT) is now being subjected to the haphazard poorly co-ordinated change that schools have suffered and we comment on ITT in the section on teacher quality and qualifications.

The role of inservice training in improving quality

'Educational change involves *learning* how to do something new. It is for this reason that if any single factor is crucial to change, it is professional development' (Fullan, 1982, p. 257). Fullan makes the point that opportunities for teachers to continue learning are essential if the quality of education is to be sustained and improved. Teaching is a continuously creative and emotionally demanding profession and a range of opportunities is needed to support the continuing learning of teachers. A balance needs to be maintained between staff and professional development as they are for different purposes. There has been an about-turn of policy which has meant that the long-term individual secondments in the fifties, sixties and seventies were almost completely replaced by LEA-based INSET in the eighties. In the nineties, long-term secondments are virtually unobtainable. Funds for staff development have also been drastically cut.

There appears to be an assumption in government policy that once the National Curriculum is in place, no further development will be needed. The most superficial consideration of what the future might hold reveals this to be a damaging invalid assumption. The gains in INSET planning and delivery which were made during the eighties will be lost unless radical steps are taken to recover the ground lost in the years 1990 and 1991. Without the change to school and LEA-based INSET, the reforms of the eighties could not have been speedily implemented. TRIST in 1984 followed by GRIST in 1986 together with the introduction of five professional development days for staff provided a framework and resources for the effective development and implementation of ideas. LEAs were enabled to build up expertise in the form of their advisory service and their work with schools and teachers.

The need for professional development and inservice training is ever with the teaching profession. Even if, at the beginning of their careers, teachers could be fully *au fait* with everything they need to know in order to teach well, the pace of change in education means that regular updating would be essential. Teachers may practise their profession for more than forty years and at secondary level may well teach five to ten thousand children during that time.

A few moments spent thinking of the changes in the curriculum over the last forty years and the changes of content and approach in, for instance, science and technology should convince the most reluctant of the importance of the substantial funding of inservice training. In the mid-seventies, the Advisory Committee on the Supply and Training of Teachers (ACSTT) recommended that 3 per cent of the salary bill be allocated to training but in the nineties this funding is still at a level of about 1 per cent.

Another dimension is that curriculum reform is often deskilling – teachers have to change practice with which they are familiar and become familiar with new methods, content and resources. Thus an essential stimulus to curriculum change is compatible inservice training. The availability of such training is linked to who provides the training. Without a doubt, the move in the early nineties to a consultancy model for training, where schools buy in trainers as they need them, cannot deliver what is required. The range of expertise which a school may want to draw on over a year cannot be sustained on a random *ad hoc* basis. The assumption that the consultancy model works for a statutory system and will ensure effective policy implementation for all schools is flawed. Freelance consultants become quickly out of date – their continuing training, previously provided as part of their work in the LEA, will no longer happen. The loss of savings of scale as funding is devolved to schools means that, unless there is co-ordination at a very detailed level of planning between tens of schools, even a limited version of the service they previously had cannot be available.

Professional development and staff development: maintaining the balance

Whilst there are clearly good arguments for strengthening school-based INSET there is still a case for long-term individual secondments. These provide opportunity for reflection, the development of new skills and the acquisition of knowledge about the education system and its management. Such work provides a sound background for those pursuing posts of responsibility in education whether at senior management level, with the LEA or in departments of higher education. McBride (1989) gives the figures for full-time, one-year secondments as 2,112 in 1986–7 dropping to 439 in 1988–9 (p. 177) with the advent of GRIST funding. On average this is fewer than four teachers in each education authority. In a time of massive change, eliminating a group whose role is to investigate issues and to reflect objectively on what is happening must have the effect of limiting the amount of knowledge about current practice in the profession as a whole.

But schools and LEAs have been poor in the past at using the skills of those who have been on secondment. McBride (*ibid.*) found that teachers who had been on secondments usually return to find their expertise is not utilized and even that their promotion or employment prospects are restricted because they've been out of the classroom. What other employer operates their training scheme in this manner? The problem is linked with promotional structures, which were discussed earlier.

Teacher quality and qualifications

The *Parent's Charter* (DES, 1991b) provides detail about what schools will do and must do to ensure a good education for the individual child. But it is silent on the obligation of government to ensure the supply of teachers who are appropriately qualified. Why? Is the problem so intractable that they dare not comment on it or do they really believe that anyone can teach? In this part, three aspects of this issue are explored:

- Teacher supply and quality.
- What qualifications should teachers have? Is a non-educational degree enough?
- Learning on the job.

We put forward the proposal that the following questions be addressed at national level and that recommendations for future practice are then made (proposal F):

- *What minimum qualifications should teachers have?*
- *How can teacher-supply problems best be solved?*
- *Is there a case for setting up a publicly available register of teachers and their qualifications (for England and Wales)?*

Teacher supply and quality

'Every newspaper and every other White Paper proclaims a national shortage of scientists and technologists.' This shortage has been universally acknowledged throughout the eighties and into the nineties. This quotation, however, comes from the Newsom Report published thirty years ago in 1963 (p. 177).

The supply of appropriately qualified teachers is still an issue which requires concerted effort in England and Wales. There were shortages and special recruitment packages in the seventies and there were shortages and special recruitment packages in the eighties. In the nineties there are licensed and articled teacher schemes and initial teacher-education providers are blamed for not doing their job properly. The programme *Public Eye* (Thames Television, Friday 7 June 1991) provides an example of such public criticism. In the view of the Conservative Research Department (1991, p. 16) 'it is clear that the Teacher Training College monopoly has to be broken, in order that students can pursue a variety of ways into the profession' – but clear to whom? Is this response not just an easy way out of a difficult problem – an attempt to solve the problems of teacher shortages by reducing entry qualifications? At the time of writing, changes in ITT are being mooted but are not at a sufficiently advanced stage for us to comment.

The mismatch of teacher qualifications with curriculum requirements is a problem hidden from parents, children and governors and it does neither the government nor the teaching profession any credit that this has been allowed to happen. This mismatch, this problem with quality of training, was earlier highlighted in the Newsom Report where the concerns voiced were about the quality of humanities teachers as well as scientists. The points made are just as valid today:

> By quality we are not of course referring to personal inadequacies of character but to professional deficiencies in knowledge of the subjects and of insight into the problems of teaching. These come from the kind of specialized higher education which many incoming teachers have received and from the lack of any professional training from which many of them suffer. The gravity of the present situation . . . because its effects are to be detected only by a clinical judgment . . . is largely concealed from administrators and statisticians.
>
> (Newsom Report, 1963, p. 177)

This comment highlights the point that knowledge of content provides only part of a teacher's professional equipment – pedagogic skills play an equally important part.

In the nineties, at a time when teachers need to be more educated themselves in order to deliver the breadth of content in the National Curriculum, the pressure is on to drop standards relating to teacher qualifications. One anomaly is that students who fail B.Ed. degree courses can be taken on as licensed teachers if they have completed two years' higher education.

Teacher quality is crucial at a time of massive curriculum change and improving the knowledge and skills of the teaching force must be an integral part of this change if it is to be successful. Rarely will anyone educated in England and Wales have the broad educational background now required of the primary teacher. Experienced teachers are able to build on their understanding of the curriculum and of the learning of children and are in a better position to develop their knowledge in new areas than the licensed teacher or the instructor who has no relevant training.

The thinking at government level about teacher qualifications in England and Wales is inconsistent. Stringent criteria for the accreditation of teacher training courses (the 'CATE' criteria) were devised in 1986 to improve the standard of teacher training but these are too easily watered down to suit new approaches.

But what qualifications and further training are appropriate for teachers? To compromise in the area of training and qualifications is surely to undermine attempts to improve the quality of the education provided.

Parents do not usually know the qualifications of those who are teaching their children. If a professional register of teachers and their qualifications were available to parents – as is the case for medical professionals, dentists, solicitors, the clergy – then parents would be able to be assured about appropriate qualifications for those teaching their children. Such a register is available to parents in Scotland. It is compiled by the General Teaching Council for Scotland.

HMI identified the mismatch between qualifications and area of teaching as a key factor influencing quality (DES, 1985b). In Scotland the match between qualifications and teaching area is said to be 90 per cent, in England and Wales, 50 per cent (*The Times Educational Supplement*, 13 September 1991). Yet in the Schools Bill (1991), which is supposed to give parents access to the information they need to choose schools for their children, this vital right is missing.

What qualifications should teachers have? Is a non-educational degree enough?

Teaching requires skills which are specific to the age of the children being taught and which non-educational degrees do not normally cover – how children learn to read, the formation of letters and handwriting, understanding mathematical and scientific concepts, the diagnosis of particular educational needs of children – to mention just a few areas of pedagogy. Similarly, the education of children in special schools should be in the hands of staff with specialist knowledge in methods for helping these children develop their potential.

Possessing a degree in the subject should provide an excellent base from which to start teaching but it will not, unless it includes an education component, provide an understanding of and practice in any of the areas of knowledge and skill which enable a teacher to support the learning of the individual child. The National Curriculum Council (1990) defines a number of factors essential to sound teaching, which include

- effective teaching methods,
- management of the curriculum,
- assessment strategies,
- motivation,
- pastoral care,
- health education,
- information technology,
- study skills,
- problem-solving,
- equal opportunities,

- special educational needs,
- multicultural perspectives,
- economic and industrial understanding,
- careers education and guidance,
- education for citizenship, and
- environmental education.

Neither is the concept of the curriculum and the need for 'breadth, balance, relevance, differentiation and progression and continuity' (HMI, 1988, p. 3) likely to be covered in a non-educational degree. Of course, educational qualifications cannot provide all the understanding and skills a teacher needs – some of these are learned with experience but qualifications provide stepping stones on the path to effective teaching.

It is often assumed that the teaching profession is well trained. That the reality may well be far from this was shown by recent research on science teachers' qualifications (Association for Science Education, 1991).

Learning on the job

Learning on the job is proposed by one group of educationalists as a more effective form of training than college-based training, but the balance between the college and the school parts of the course must be carefully worked out and there are a number of existing successful models on which to draw.

Discussion about the pros and cons of concentrating training in schools always avoids the real issue: What would this mean from the children's point of view? This issue of balance (of the amount of time a child is taught by experienced and by inexperienced teachers) must be seriously debated. If the balance is wrong the children's education could suffer. A question those devising these programmes should ask is: Would what is proposed be acceptable if it meant learning on your child? In primary terms, it might mean a student practising for a year of your child's life and learning – opportunities for learning which can never be retrieved. There is no guarantee that it wouldn't happen the next year . . . and the next. For your sixth former, might being practised on mean a grade or two less (i.e. the difference between getting a university place and not) as the inexperienced teacher comes to grips with the demands of the job and the expectations hidden in the shorthand of syllabuses?

The probationary year (the abolition of which was announced in 1991) at least ensured that trained teachers had continuing support during their early teaching and that they had induction training. Removing this safety net and with it the entitlement to support is a retrograde step in terms of improving quality.

Management development for education

School management has been the focus of major change in England and Wales during the eighties but the system now in place has brought its own problems.

Two aspects of management which seem to be particularly problematic are discussed in this section:

- Management in education: an industrial or an agricultural model?
- Poor-quality mangement in schools.

The foundations of a high-quality training programme for management in education have been laid with the work of the School Management Task Force and through the use of LEATGS funding. We propose that this work be developed further as a priority. Proposal G: *That a coherent programme for management development be designed which can cater for the needs of teachers and other members of the service at different stages of their careers.*

A third aspect of management – the local management of schools innovation (LMS) – requires thorough evaluation to establish the scheme's success and problems so we limit our discussion of this initiative to a proposal that it be reviewed: *That the changes introduced under the LMS initiative be evaluated and the scheme be adjusted in the light of the findings* (proposal H).

Management in education: an industrial model or an agricultural model?

The notion of applying industrial models to education was given a high profile during the eighties but the idea had been around for a long time. But whilst there is always something to be learned from the way others manage their work, models of management drawn from factories do not necessarily work in education where the inputs, processes and outputs are all concerned with the intangible (i.e. thought processes) and affected by the intangible (i.e. motivation). Stephens (in Weick, 1988, p. 57) summed up the argument twenty-five years ago:

> we should be making a great mistake in regarding the management of schools as similar to the process of constructing a building or operating a factory. In these latter processes deliberate decisions play a crucial part and the enterprise

advances or stands still in proportion to the amount of deliberate effort exerted. If we must use a metaphor or model in seeking to understand the process of schooling, we should look to agriculture rather than to the factory. In agriculture, we do not start from scratch, and we do not direct our efforts to inert and passive materials. We start, on the contrary, with a complex and ancient process, and we organize our efforts around what seeds, plants, and insects are likely to do anyway. . . . The crop, once planted, may undergo some development even while the farmer sleeps or loafs. No matter what he does, some aspects of the outcome will remain constant.

The agricultural model of development does seem to have more similarities to the process of education than the industrial model.

Poor-quality management in schools

HMI (DES, 1990) and the School Management Task Force (1990) have highlighted the poor quality of much senior and middle management of schools:

> More generally the mangement of schools leaves much to be desired. In only about a third of those inspected was senior management judged to be particularly effective. The proportion of middle management so assessed was lower still. Effective senior management is characterized by clear objectives; sound planning; effective implementation and review and evaluation. Such management is rare. Much more common is senior management communicating effectively but being much less successful in setting objectives; planning strategically; reviewing; evaluating; consulting staff, and providing clear remits for middle management.
>
> (DES, 1990, para. 63, p. 10)

Clearly work must be done to improve this situation. There appears to be a case for the provision of a programme of inservice training to take account of the need for management development.

Evaluation, accountability and motivation

Government approaches to accountability in education are based on extrinsic motivation as the key motivating factor – inspection, appraisal and allowing governors flexibility over pay scales so that 'good' teachers, heads and deputies can supposedly be rewarded. But in times of recession when money is particularly tight such supposed flexibility is not realistic. Public (i.e. private) schools sometimes pay higher rates than schools in the maintained sector – but they have the freedom to alter their fees to increase their income. State schools are given a fixed allocation related to pupil numbers rather than 'what the market will stand'.

The restructuring of HMI and LEA advisory services so that every school is inspected every four years is a key plank of government plans to improve quality in education. But this presupposes that teachers are chiefly motivated by external pressure. It may be that the proposed model of inspection is based on inappropriate assumptions. In service industries, a key motivator is the knowledge that service has been given and has been valued.

In this part, two key aspects of the debate over accountability structures are considered:

1. Evaluating teaching.
2. Developing professional judgment.

We make two proposals in this area: *All teachers should be equipped with the professional tools of educational evaluation so that intuitive professional judgments can be backed up by informed professional judgments (proposal I); accountability systems within education should be reviewed and based on a balanced model of accountability, i.e. with a balance between moral, professional and contractual elements* (proposal J).

Evaluating teaching

Strategies for checking the quality of the educational process are an essential professional tool for teachers if it is accepted that it is inappropriate to focus on final outcomes (e.g. examination results at 16 or 18) to judge the quality of education.

Methods of educational evaluation, action research and critical reflection have become well established since Stenhouse (1975) put the case for teachers to research what was happening in their own classrooms. There is now a substantial body of practice and theory on which to draw so that intuitive judgements can be backed up by hard evidence.

These methods are complementary to developing practice in appraisal methods where such systems are designed on the 'teacher as learner' model rather than the 'teacher as inefficient and ineffective' model.

Knowledge about educational evaluation stratregies is widespread in some areas of the service but much work remains to be done. Many student teachers on B.Ed. (Hons) courses carry out action research and/or in-depth research into educational practice as part of their training and, as a result, they go into schools equipped with some of the tools necessary for appraising their work. Many colleagues who have studied for higher degrees or who have been involved in centrally funded projects (TVEI, ESG schemes) have been trained in and practised these skills.

However, there are many members of the profession who, for a range of reasons, have not yet acquired these professional tools. If teachers do not reflect on their work in any formally recognized way, then the basis for professional accountability is shaky.

As a starting point, a common language is needed, and Chapter 9 covers this issue. It is not uncommon for evaluation to be thought of as confined to providing information of the 'how many' and 'what percentage' variety. Whilst there are times when this is exactly the type of information required to inform decision-makers, there are other times when teachers need to know about the 'feel' or 'impact' of a particular curricular initiative or change in school organization. (The former approach is that of 'quantitative evaluation'; the latter is that of 'qualitative evaluation'.)

Developing professional judgment

When Marilyn Leask was investigating planning practices across the country for the SDP Project (1989–90), she found that many teachers were tentative about the value of their own professional judgments. This finding is backed up by her experience as a Key Stage 1 moderator (1991–2). Many teachers have yet to make the step from relying on intuitive judgments to basing their professional judgments on evidence.

The unpredictability of an individual's abilities and potential and the variation in individuals' levels of motivation will always mean that teachers will exercise caution in making statements about an individual's capability, but no one is better placed than teachers to make judgments about an individual's learning and the appropriate teaching methods to apply. The practice and experience gained with hundreds and thousands of children during a teaching career, coupled with a knowledge of the teaching and learning process, is not widely recognized as providing a professional base of knowledge and skill. Moderation processes such as those for GCSE and those being used with National Curriculum assessment at Key Stage 1 are useful in developing teachers' professional judgment and their ability to exercise it but more needs to be done.

Thus a higher level of skill and improved confidence in educational evaluation is required if critical reflection is to become part of a teacher's practice and part of the school's planning processes. A word of warning is needed here. Models of evaluation should be based on what can be managed within the normal classroom context by the teacher and new models of evaluation are required which fit with school and classroom constraints. The model of evaluation used by outsiders working in the school cannot be satisfactorily transferred to the classroom teacher's work. Groundwork has been laid through the work of the Classroom Action Research Network and the work which has been done on this issue at a number of institutions of higher education (such as the Cambridge Institute of Education, the University of East Anglia, the Institute of Education (University of London) and Warwick University). Some national initiatives have also provided advice in this area: TVEI and the School Development Plans Project (Hargreaves *et al.*, 1989). Schools developing work on performance indicators use the basic methods of educational evaluation to collect data.

A challenge for educationalists in the nineties is to develop teachers' understanding and confidence in this area of exercising professional judgment. The tentativeness of the profession in this area in the past has been misinterpreted by public and government to mean that the judgment of lay people is therefore equivalent to that of professionals.

Resources

There will always be a demand for more funds for education. The frontiers of knowledge are continually being extended. The real question is concerned with what level of support is appropriate within current constraints. The impact on the quality of education received as a result of two central resource issues is discussed in this section. These issues are

- class size; and
- school size.

We make one proposal (proposal K): *That the quality of the educational experience for the individual child be a key factor in influencing decisions about class size and school size.*

Class size

Class size is a crucial issue for teachers. Although there are researchers who claim class size has little impact on cognitive learning, these researchers have taken the child's eye view of the teacher's work, i.e. that it only happens when the teacher and the child are together. They also ignore certain factors which seriously affect the learning milieu and which can be more easily contained in small groups (such as emotional and behavioural problems).

The marking of work, a significant part of a teacher's workload, is directly related to class size. Take the situation in a secondary school. How much time might a parent reasonably expect a teacher to spend marking their child's work every week? Does five minutes seem too little? A secondary colleague teaching 200 children a week calculated that she would have to spend about seventeen hours a week marking at this level. In fact, the sixth-form essays she was marking were taking her about half an hour each. A primary colleague, who recently 'retired', reports spending on average three hours a night marking. These figures are not unusual.

When the National Union of Teachers carried out a survey into class size and found that 25% of classes contained over thirty-five children, the Secretary of State for Education (Kenneth Clark) commented that class size was not a major factor in pupil achievement (BBC Radio 4, *Today*, 18 November 1991). Yet public schools make a virtue out of providing smaller classes. Indeed, within weeks, the Secretary of State was advocating the reading programme developed in New Zealand by Professor Clay which depends on the provision of one-to-one tuition for a short intensive period.

Class size clearly does matter.

Williams (1961, p. 147) draws an interesting comparison between class size in state and public (private) schools:

> The continued existence of a network of private education, in the preparatory and public schools, may or may not be socially desirable, but in any case it shows the kind of education, and the necessary level of investment in it, which a particular social group accepts as adequate for itself. The large class has haunted public education from the beginning. . . . In the private network, very much smaller classes, and the necessary investment to ensure them, have been accepted as a private duty, in quite a different way from the interpretation of public duty in the national system.

The difference in the accepted class size for young children (with thirty-five not uncommon) and that accepted at GCSE, in the sixth form and in higher education, is a puzzle. Some say it has historical roots – that elementary schools were traditionally organized in large classes; others say it has to do with power relationships between males and females. Females traditionally have less power than males and they comprise the vast majority of those working in primary schools. Hence they end up with fewer resources and larger classes.

Whatever the reason, the discrepancy has continued for too long. Where children are learning the basic skills of reading, writing and maths on which all future work depends, it seems essential that they are in small enough classes so that their individual needs can be addressed. In the long run, an investment in small class size at the primary level could be expected to be cost-effective as children are better able to come to grips with the curriculum in later years. Better use will be made of the subsequent years of schooling.

School size

School size too does not appear to be considered as influencing the quality of education. Some authorities have merged schools so that there are thousands of pupils. Isn't the main gain in this the anonymity of the miscreant? In a school small enough for all children to be known by the teachers, standards of behaviour are easier to enforce (wrong-doers can be recognized even at considerable distance) and a positive ethos easier to establish than in larger establishments. Some would argue that gains in choice of subjects are at the expense of a sense of community and a sense for the individual child of being important. Handy asks the question: 'Why would anyone want a school so big that it can only meet in a cathedral?' (1984, p. 38).

Conclusion

In spite of the intense focus on educational reform over the past years, much energy has been wasted and much still needs to be done if quality is to improve. Reform in the service should be managed in a coherent way. Piecemeal reform which has affected key aspects of the service in recent times contributes as much to increasing confusion and disillusionment as increasing quality.

This lack of coherent planning coupled with a dismissive approach to professional knowledge and experience is potentially dangerous and damaging to children's education. The concerns expressed by primary teachers that the breadth of the primary curriculum enshrined in the National Curriculum will result in less time spent on the 3 Rs and consequently a drop in pupils' learning of these basic skills must be taken seriously. There is no room for complacency if quality is to be improved.

11
PRINCIPLES OF CHANGE

Introduction

The state of the education system is quite rightly of concern to all in society. Everyone is affected by the quality of the education of young people whether they have children or not. Moreover, the material well-being enjoyed in a society is dependent on the education of succeeding generations but although the quality of the work of each individual teacher is at the heart of quality education, the responsibility is not theirs alone. The health of the education system is central to and indicative of the health of society as a whole.

It is too easy in changing education to concentrate on structural changes whether of the management of the service or the content of the curriculum or in the allocation of resources. Such a narrow focus excludes consideration of the value of the individual's enthusiasm, motivation and self-belief in influencing the quality of the education provided. Seeing quality as proven through test or examination results ignores the fact that such outcomes are the product of many, many years of education and that continuing quality lies in ensuring the quality of the educational process throughout those earlier years.

Three of the key problems to be faced in improving quality in the education system are that

1. different visions of quality are held by those who are partners in education (e.g. parents, students, employers, teachers, governors);
2. any consensus about quality can only be temporary because the needs of society are always changing; and
3. quality outcomes depend on a long-term process which is not easily measured or inspected.

Some national agreement about quality is required if change in education is to be set in a clear context with defined aims and objectives. Otherwise any change will run the risk of being directionless or counterproductive.

The current practice of developing aspects of education in isolation does not work. Each component of the system and service needs to be functioning well if high-quality education is to be provided.

The way forward

There needs to be an open professional debate about the principles, processes and structures supporting effective learning and high quality in education so that agreement can be reached about sound working practices throughout the service. Whilst the goals for education are open to public debate, how to achieve these goals is a matter for professional debate. In any public debate about what constitutes quality in education, the description of achievement produced in the Hargreaves Report (ILEA, 1984) *Improving Secondary Schools*, provides a sound starting point (Table 11.1).

The notion that achievement is anything more than examination outcomes has been lost over the last decade. That change is an ongoing and incremental process is also not widely understood.

Politicians seem only too keen to keep changing education so that another change is made before the first is properly implemented. Why? Fullan (1982, p. 251) gives an interesting explanation: 'Policy making is both more compelling and more exciting than policy implementation.' Policy implementation also takes a long time and ensuring that implementation occurs is a much more complex activity than producing legislation.

Tawney (1952, p. 1) makes an interesting suggestion that the tendency to change for the sake of change is quintessentially English: 'It is a commonplace that the characteristic virtue of Englishmen is their power of sustained practical activity and their characteristic vice a reluctance to test the quality of that activity by reference to principles.' Perhaps this goes some way to explaining the reluctance of the Scottish and Welsh Departments of Education to follow the rapid change proposed/imposed in England.

A central aim of this book is to stimulate debate about the principles, processes and structures which (if in place nationally, at regional level and in schools) support the provision of a flexible, high-quality learning environment for young people in which new initiatives are carefully planned and managed in such a way that established good practice is developed and not discarded.

Table 11.1 Aspects of achievement

Achievement aspect i . . . is strongly represented in the current 16-plus public examinations. It involves most of all the capacity to express oneself in a written form. It requires the capacity to retain propositional knowledge, to select from such knowledge appropriately in response to a specified request, and to do so quickly without reference to possible sources of information. The capacity to memorize and organize material is particularly important. Public examinations measure such achievement in that they are mainly written tests, set with strict time limits and with the requirement that pupils have few or no additional resources available to them. The examinations emphasize knowledge rather than skill; memorization more than problem-solving or investigational capacities; writing rather than speaking or other forms of communication; speed rather than reflection; individual rather than group achievement.

Achievement aspect ii . . . is concerned with the capacity to apply knowledge rather than knowledge itself, with the practical rather than the theoretical, with the oral rather than the written. Problem-solving and investigational skills are more important than the retention of knowledge. This aspect is to some degree measured in public examinations, but it is often seen as secondary and less important than aspect i. It tends to be more difficult, as well as more time-consuming and more expensive, to assess than aspect i.

Achievement aspect iii . . . is concerned with personal and social skills; the capacity to communicate with others, in face-to-face relationships; the ability to co-operate with others in the interests of the group as well as of the individual; initiative, self-reliance and the ability to work alone without close supervision; and the skills of leadership. This aspect of achievement remains virtually untapped by the 16-plus examinations.

Achievement aspect iv . . . involves motivation and commitment; the willingness to accept failure without destructive consequences; the readiness to persevere; the self-confidence to learn in spite of the difficulty of the task. Such motivation is often regarded as a prerequisite to achievement, rather than as an achievement in itself. We do not deny that motivation is a prerequisite to the other three aspects of achievement, but we also believe that it can be regarded as an achievement in its own right. For some pupils come to their schools without such motivation, yet the school succeeds in generating it in them and in such circumstances, both the school and the pupils have made an important achievement. By contrast, some schools actively reduce the motivation and commitment of pupils, thereby causing further underachievement in aspects i–iii. In one sense, aspect iv is the most important of all, since without it, achievement in the other three aspects is likely to be very limited, both at school and in the future . . .

(From the Hargreaves Report, ILEA, 1984, p. 2.)

Those participating in any debate need to be well informed. For this reason, we included a brief outline of the history of education in Part II. The past needs to be understood so that we can move forward. Change since the war has largely been on a piecemeal approach with bits of the quality jigsaw being worked on in isolation. But over the last decade we have reached a position where all the bits of this jigsaw look as though they are present. The problem is that the government has not grasped the holistic model of change and we are now losing ground as resources are cut and diverted and experienced staff leave through disillusionment.

In Part III we discussed aspects of the *processes* which support improvement in quality. At the beginning of this part, in Chapter 10, we have looked principally at *structural problems* and possible solutions. In this section we draw out the lessons from this work and suggest some *principles* which should guide development in education into the twenty-first century.

Flawed assumptions

In England the philosophical base from which decision-makers at national level work seems to be founded on a number of flawed assumptions. Unless these are recognized as such, the potential gains of current reforms will not be fully realized and indeed the quality of education provided may well fall. Table 11.2 provides examples of these assumptions. The list is not intended to be comprehensive but simply to highlight beliefs which currently influence the chosen path of development.

Table 11.2 Examples of flawed assumptions about education which hinder improvement of quality

---

- That effective teaching depends on choosing one particular method rather than another.
- That anyone can teach.
- That children are impervious to the values expressed through the media.
- That comprehensive education is to blame for shortcomings in the system.
- That research and evaluation have nothing to tell decision-makers and that there is nothing to be learned from the past.
- That those with professional expertise do not have the qualification to manage the areas in which they acquired this expertise.
- That legislation is an effective mechanism for change.
- That improvement is only dependent on structural alterations and processes can look after themselves.
- That the detail of the curriculum can be centrally determined.

Neglected components in the process of improving quality

These assumptions led to the neglect of five of the key components in the process of improving quality which were identified in Chapter 1 and which provided themes running through this book (Table 11.3).

Table 11.3   Neglected components in the process of improving quality

1. The influence of society's views and beliefs, actions and priorities.
2. The necessity for consultation and reaching consensus about improvement.
3. The need for a coherent and improved approach to change.
4. The motivation of those involved.
5. The need for increased understanding of the learning process for pupils and teachers and its implications for teaching.

This neglect has given rise to fundamental problems which have lessened the capacity of the education service to improve quality. One particular problem is the neglect of the improvement process.

Understanding the improvement process

Understanding the improvement process is crucial if quality in education is to be improved. The various facets of the improvement process identified in Part III are summarized in Table 11.4.

Table 11.4   Facets of the improvement process

1. The analysis and identification of pupils' needs.
2. Creating a balanced curricular framework that is progressively fleshed out from the national statement of aims and policies through local determination of goals to school action.
3. Continuous curriculum development.
4. Increased research into and development of learning, teaching and the improvement process.
5. Establishing a sound evaluation system at all levels that is firmly located within an improvement process.
6. Complementary high-quality action through staff and curriculum and institutional development programmes within improved planning and plans to support changes.

Proposals for improvement

The problems facing the education service and the possible solutions discussed in Chapter 10 come from our analysis of the current situation. These proposals are summarized in Table 11.5.

Table 11.5   A summary of proposals for improving aspects of the system and service

---

1. The framework of the system
- That the improvement of understanding and links between different parts of the system be a priority.
- That a coherent framework for the operation of the service be established.
- That a comprehensive management and career structure which supports development be established.

2. Curriculum and assessment, teaching and learning
- That change in approaches to curriculum and assessment and teaching and learning methods be based on evidence rather than prejudice and that the professional judgment of teachers be recognized.

3. Teacher education
- That a national policy on teacher education be developed which ensures the continuing professional development of teachers.

4. Teacher quality and qualifications
- That the issues of minimum qualifications, teacher-supply problems and the drawing up of a teachers' register be addressed.

5. Management development
- That a coherent programme for management development be designed which can cater for the needs of teachers and other members of the service at different stages of their careers.
- That the operation of the LMS innovation be evaluated and that findings be acted upon.

6. Evaluation, accountability and motivation
- That the tools of educational evaluation be recognized as essential professional skills.
- That accountability systems should be balanced.

7. Resources
- That the quality of the educational experience for the individual child be a key factor in decisions about class size and school size.

Principles for the operation of the service

It is from all this earlier work that we derive a set of basic principles for the operation of the service (Table 11.6).

Table 11.6 Principles on which the work of the education service could be built

---

1. The central function of the education system is supporting and promoting high-quality teaching and learning in the classroom.
2. All partners in education have duties and responsibilities as well as rights.
3. Accountability structures should be broadly based and balanced.
4. Pluralism and flexibility within a national framework is a strength not a weakness.
5. Improving quality depends on investment in people. Motivation is central to improving quality.
6. Management styles should be chosen for their appropriateness to the management of the education service.
7. The need to change is normal but agreement should be reached through consultation and debate based on professional judgements and evidence gained through research.
8. A holistic approach is required for change to be coherent.
9. Long-term approaches to achieving improvement are essential for success. Short-term actions cannot be accommodated in educational provision which for any child is an eleven-year-long process.

Whilst the need for continuous change might be accepted, those with the power for change must avoid lurching from one change to another. It is important to learn how to build on what has gone before. But on what foundations should education in the UK be built? Is there a case, at national level, for agreement to be sought on a set of principles which would provide foundations for the development of the service?

To gain widespread acceptance, such a redefinition of educational goals would require widespread support and perhaps be the product of national debate – not just consultation – but real debate. The debate that followed the Green Paper, *Education in Schools: A Consultative Document* (DES, 1977) involved conferences and discussions and drew on papers from a wide variety of people. Might this earlier work provide a basis for the way to conduct future debate? It must be remembered that the quality of national debate will improve over time as people become familiar with the approach. The debate on the Green Paper may not have been very effective at that time but if the approach had been pursued it could have led to real consultation.

Conclusion

After a decade of radical change in education, what has happened? What is apparent is that there has been no overall conscious plan for education – political expedience and crisis management have been the national approach to improving education.

The trend to seek short-term solutions to educational problems must be challenged. There needs to be a recognition that without the consideration of the individual's and the school's ability to implement change, desired changes in the quality of the education service will not occur and that without a conscious attempt to define the processes, structures and principles providing a quality framework, quality outcomes will be random.

It is time to take stock of education. The implementation of the 1988 Education Act will continue well into the nineties and unless this is properly managed the interests of the children will be damaged. Many schools have developed sound systems for managing change. It is time this good practice – of planning and managing development coherently – was adopted at national level.

Government attitudes to the professionalism of teachers need to change. There is no such thing as a teacher-proof innovation. If change is to be successful, teachers must be fully involved in decision-making, as well as being properly trained and qualified. Teacher involvement and confidence is crucial:

> A weakened teaching force will only result in the deterioration of educational standards. Confidence is an essential commodity for the successful management of schools and for the introduction and management of the national curriculum. Also the creativity of teachers is a necessary feature if all major changes are to be satisfactorily implemented. Without a sense of professional power, teachers will be unable to make their contribution to the partnership of pupils, parents and policy makers (professional and lay).
>
> (Goddard, 1989c, p. 2)

There is a desperate need for *vision* at national level. Those who make decisions need to communicate a clear vision for the future based on an acceptance that the world is fast changing and that risk taking and occasional failure will be features of change as educationalists strive to prepare young people for the unknown.

Quality in education depends on investment in the people involved (and not just cash but emotional capital investment). Without the recognition of

the necessity for such crucial investment or of the need to constantly up-
date the National Curriculum, there is a very real danger that educational
practice will become ossified to the detriment of the education of young
people who need to be prepared to face the challenges of the twenty-first
century.

So how is this coherent planned approach we see as so essential to be
managed? Some form of professional council with this specific brief seems
to be essential. Senior officials and politicians by the very nature of their
careers have only a passing influence in education. The education service
needs to operate within a stable, planned framework if quality is to be
improved and the resources available not wasted through *ad hoc* approaches. The nation's future depends on the quality of education our
children obtain and nothing less than the best we can provide is good
enough.

Improvement in education will not happen as a result of massive swings
in direction. It will only occur through a long-term programme of renewal.

REFERENCES

Advisory Committee on the Supply and Training of Teachers: Subcommittee on Induction and In-Service Training (ACSTT) (1975) Discussion paper on INSET provision (mimeo), DES, London, 13 August.

Advisory Committee on the Supply and Training of Teachers (1976) *Towards a National Policy for Induction and Inservice Training of Teachers in Schools:* A report by the Induction and Inservice sub-committee, DES, London, May.

Advisory Committee on the Supply and Training of Teachers (1978a) Paper 1st 16: priorities for long courses (paper presented at the National Conference on In-Service Training, 17–19 January), DES, London, January.

Advisory Committee on the Supply and Training of Teachers (1978b) Paper 1st 17: towards a national policy for the induction and in-service training of teachers in schools (paper presented at the National Conference on In-Service Training, 17–19 January), DES, London, January.

Advisory Committee on the Supply and Training of Teachers (1978c) *Making INSET Work: In-Service Education and Training for Teachers: A Basis for Discussion*, DES, London, November.

Ahier, J. and Flude, M. (eds.) (1983) *Contemporary Education Policy,* Croom Helm, London.

Association for Science Education (1991) *Only a Teacher . . .? An Enquiry into Science Teacher Provision,* Association for Science Education in conjunction with the British Association for the Advancement of Science and the Royal Society, Hatfield.

Audit Commission (1989) *Assuring Quality in Education: The Role of Local Education Authority Inspectors and Advisers,* HMSO, London.

Becher, T. (1984) The political and organisational context of curriculum evaluation, in M. Skilbeck (ed.) *Evaluating the Curriculum in the Eighties,* Hodder & Stoughton, Sevenoaks.

Berman, P. and McLaughlin, M. (1978) Implementation of educational innovation, *Education Forum* (40)(3).

Beresford, C. and Goddard, D. (1981) Networking: some contexts and characteristics, *Insight*, Vol. 4, no. 3, Summer.

Bolam, R. (1982) *School Focused Inservice Training*, Heinemann, London.

Brighouse, T. (1991) The uncertain future of local education authorities, *Local Government Policy Making*, Vol. 18, no. 1, July.

British Standards Institute (1987) *BS 5750/ISO 9000: A Positive Contribution to Better Business*, British Standards Institute Quality Assurance, Milton Keynes.

Bullock, A. (1975) *A Language for Life,* HMSO, London.

Bush, T. (ed.) (1980) *Approaches to School Management,* Paul Chapman, London.

Butt, H. and Palmer, B. (1985) *Value for Money in the Public Sector: The Decision-Makers' Guide*, Blackwell, Oxford.

Caldwell, B. and Spinks, J. (1988) *The Self-Managing School,* Falmer Press, Lewes.

Chambers, P. (ed.) (undated) *Making INSET Work: Myth or Reality?*, CUED-IN, Faculty of Contemporary Studies, Bradford College, Bradford.

Clark, D. *et al.* (1984) Effective schools and school improvement, *Educational Administration Quarterly*, Vol. 20, no. 3, Summer, pp. 41–68.

Clift, P. S., Nuttal, D. L. and McCormick, R. (eds.) (1987) *Studies in School Self-Evaluation*, Falmer Press, Lewes.

Conservative Central Office (undated) *Local Government Brief No. 38: Citizen's Charter*, London.

Conservative Research Department (1991) The priorities, structure and content of education (mimeo), London, 30 April.

Coopers and Lybrand (1988) *Local Management of Schools: A Report to the DES,* HMSO, London.

Crowther Report (1959, 1960) *Report of the Central Advisory Council for Education (England): '15 to 19'*, HMSO, London.

Dalin, P. and Rust, V. (1983) *Can Schools Learn?* NFER/Nelson, London.

Davies, H. (1991) In search of a new role, *The Times Educational Supplement*, 15 March.

Deem, R. and Brehony, K. (1990) *The Long and the Short of it*, The Times Educational Supplement, 13 July.

DES (1963) Higher Education: the report of the committee appointed by the prime minister under the chairmanship of Lord Robbins (the Robbins Report) (Cmnd 2154), HMSO, London.

DES (1972) *Teacher Education and Training* (The James Report), HMSO, London.

DES (1977) *Education in Schools: A Consultative Document* (Cmnd 6869), HMSO, London.

DES (1980) *The Education System of England and Wales*, HMSO, London.

DES (1985a) *Quality in Schools: Evaluation and Appraisal: An HMI Study*, HMSO, London.

DES (1985b) *Better Schools* (Cmnd 9469), HMSO, London.

DES (1988) Performance indicators for secondary schools: some practical consider-ations (mimeo), circulated Autumn.

DES (1990) *Standards in Education 1988–1989: The Annual Report of HM Senior Chief Inspector of Schools*, HMSO, London, January.

DES (1991a) *School Governors: The School Curriculum – Briefing Booklet 1,* DES/Central Office of Information, London.

DES (1991b) *The Parent's Charter: You and Your Child's Education,* London.

Department of Trade and Industry (undated) *Total Quality Management – A Prac-tical Approach*, DTI Enterprise Initiative, London.

Education Reform Act (1988) HMSO, London.

Elliott (1981) *School Accountability*, Blackwell, Oxford.

Eraut, M. (1984) Institution-based curriculum evaluation, in M. Skilbeck op. cit.

Everard, B. and Morris, G. (1990) *Effective School Management,* Paul Chapman Publishing, London.

Fullan, M. (1982) *The Meaning of Educational Change,* Teachers College Press, New York, NY.

Fullan, M. (1991) *The New Meaning of Educational Change,* Cassell, London.

Fullan, M., Bennett, B. and Rolheiser-Bennett, C. (1989) Linking classroom and school improvement (invited address, American Educational Research Association).

Glatter, R., Preedy, M., Riches, C. and Masterton, M. (eds.) (1988) *Understanding School Management,* Open University Press, Milton Keynes.

Goddard, D. (1988) *Evaluation and Inspection,* discussion paper for London Borough of Enfield (mimeo).

Goddard, D. (1989a) GRIST: the development of the design, in R. McBride, op. cit.

Goddard, D. (1989b) Institutional development plans (mimeo), London Borough of Enfield.

Goddard, D. (1989c) INSET: a support service (mimeo), London Borough of Enfield.

Goddard, D. (1989d) *Initiative Overload: A Report on a One Day Seminar Delivered to Coventry Support Teachers,* Centre Post, City of Coventry and National Council for Teacher-Centred Professional Development, 22 May.

Granheim, M., Kogan, M. and Lundgren, U. (eds.) (1990) *Evaluation as Policymaking: Introducing Evaluation into a National Decentralised Educational System,* Jessica Kingsley, London.

Gray, H. (1990) Objectives and Values, *Management in Education,* Vol. 4, no. 4, Winter.

Grubb Institute (1989) Technical and Vocational Education Extension: towards a paradigm for total learning (mimeo), London.

Hall, V. (1988) Networks and networking: a working paper (mimeo), National Development Centre for School Management Training, Bristol.

Handy, C. (1984) *Taken for Granted: Understanding Schools as Organisations,* Longman for the Schools Council, York.

Hargreaves, D. H. and Hopkins, D. (1991) *The Empowered School: The Management and Practice of Development Planning,* Cassell, London.

Hargreaves, D. H., Hopkins, D., Leask, M., Connolly, J. and Robinson, P. (1989) *Planning for School Improvement: Advice to Governors, Headteachers and Teachers,* DES/HMSO, London.

Havelock, R. G. (1969) *Planning for Innovation through Dissemination and Utilization of Knowledge,* University of Michigan, Institute of Social Research.

HMI (1977) *Ten Good Schools: A Secondary School Enquiry,* HMSO, London.

HMI (1988) *The Curriculum from 5 to 16: Curriculum Matters No. 2,* DES, London.

Holly, P. and Hopkins, D. (1988) Evaluation and school improvement, *Cambridge Journal of Education,* Vol. 18, no. 2, pp. 221–45.

Holmes, E. (1911) *What Is and What Might Be: A Study of Education in General and Elementary Education in Particular,* Constable, London.

Hopkins, D. (1985) *Doing School-Based Review: Instruments and Guidelines,* ISIP (International School Improvement Project) Technical Report, ACCO, Leuven Amersfoort.

Hopkins, D. (1987) *Improving the Quality of Schooling,* Falmer Press, Lewes.

Hopkins, D. (1989) *Evaluation for School Improvement,* Open University Press, Milton Keynes.

Hopkins, D. and Leask, M. (1989) Performance indicators and school development, *School Organisation,* Vol. 9, no. 1, pp. 3–20.

Hoyle, E. (1975) How does the curriculum change?, in R. Hooper (ed.) *The Curriculum Context, Design and Development,* Oliver Boyd and the Open University Press, London/Milton Keynes.

Hoyle, E. (1988) Leadership and mission, in R. Glatter *et al.* (eds.) op. cit.

Huczinski, A. (1983) *Encyclopaedia of Management Development Methods,* Gower, Aldershot.

Hughes, M. (1988) Leadership in professionally staffed organisations, in R. Glatter *et al.* (eds.) op. cit.

ILEA (1977) *Keeping the School under Review,* London.

ILEA (1984) *Improving Secondary Schools* (the Hargreaves Report), London.

Joyce and Showers (1980) Improving Inservice Training: the messages from research, *Educational Leadership.*

Klein, R. and Carter, N. (1987–8) Performance measurement in the public sector, *Journal of Policy and Politics,* Vol. 14, no. 3, pp. 389–404.

Kolb, D. (1974) On management and the learning process, in I.M. Rubin and J.M. McIntyre.

Lancaster University (1990) Building the bridge: profiling the student teacher – a new approach to assessment, Conference Report 26/27, 1990.

Lake, M. (1991) Surveying all the factors: reading research, *Language and Learning,* no. 6.

Leask, M. (1988) Teachers as curriculum evaluators (unpublished M. Phil. thesis), Cambridge Institute of Education.

Leask, M. (1990a) Making connections: school development plans – LMS – governors (paper presented at British Educational Research Association Conference, Roehampton), 1 September.

Leask, M. (1990b) Planning for the future, *School Governor,* March.

Leask, M. (1992) School development plans: their history and their potential, in G. Wallace (ed.) *Local Management of Schools: Research and Experience,* Multilingual Matters, Cleveland/Philadelphia.

Lengrand, P. (1975) *An Introduction to Lifelong Education,* Croom Helm, London/ UNESCO Press, Paris.

Litt, E. and Parkinson, M. (1979) *US and UK Educational Policy – A Decade of Reform,* Praeger, New York, NY.

Maclaine, A. G. (undated) *Australian Education,* Ian Novak, Sydney.

Maclure, J. S. (1986) *Educational Documents: England and Wales,* Methuen, London (5th edn).

Major, J. (1991) Education – all our futures (speech by the Prime Minister, the Rt Hon. John Major, to the Centre for Policy Studies), London, 3 July.

Markwell, D. J. (1991) Unhealthy side of Norrington (letter to the Editor), *The Daily Telegraph,* 5 June.

McBride, R. (1989) *The In-Service Training of Teachers,* Falmer Press, Lewes.

McCormick, R. and James, M. (1988) *Curriculum Evaluation in Schools,* Croom Helm, London (2nd edn).

McGregor, D. (1960) *The Human Side of Enterprise,* McGraw-Hill, New York, NY.

McKernan, J. (1991) *Curriculum Action Research – A Handbook of Methods and Resources for the Reflective Practitioner,* Kogan Page, London.

McMahon, A. and Bolam, R. (1990a) *A Handbook for Primary Schools,* Paul Chapman Publishing, London.

McMahon, A. and Bolam, R. (1990b) *A Handbook for Secondary Schools,* Paul Chapman Publishing, London.

McMahon, A., Bolam, R., Abbott, R. and Holly, P. (1984) *Guidelines for Review and Internal Development in Schools: Secondary School Handbook,* Longman for the Schools Council, York.

McNamara, D. R. and Ross, A. M. (1982) *The B. Ed. Degree and its Future,* School of Education, University of Lancaster.

McNiff, J. (1988) *Action Research – Principles and Practice,* Macmillan, London.

Merrick, N. and Manuel, G. (1991) Authorities want end to exclusion loophole, *The Times Educational Supplement,* p. 1, 25 October.

Metz, M. (1988) Some missing elements in the educational reform movement, *Educational Administration Quarterly,* Vol. 24, no. 4, pp. 446–60.

Miles, M. (1978) *Networking* (mimeo), prepared for the National Institute of Education, Washington DC.

Miles, M. and Ekholm, M. (1985) What is school improvement?, in W. Van Velzen *et al.,* op. cit.

Mitchell, A., Puxty, A., Sikka, P. and Willmott, H. (1991) Accounting for change: a proposal for reform of audit and accounting (mimeo), to be published by the Fabian Society, London.

Mortimore, P. *et al.* (1985) *The Junior School Project,* ILEA, London.

National Commission on Excellence in Education (1983) *A Nation at Risk,* Washington Government Printing Office, Washington DC.

National Curriculum Council (1990) *3 The Whole Curriculum,* London.

Newsom Report (1963) *Report of the Minister of Education's Central Advisory Council: 'Half our Future',* HMSO, London.

Nias, J. (1981) The nature of trust, in Elliott, *School Accountability,* Blackwell, Oxford.

Nuttall, D. (1991) An instrument to be honed, *The Times Educational Supplement,* p. 22, 13 September.

Omand, D. (1989) Towards a new management strategy for defence, *Journal of the Royal United Services Institution,* Autumn.

Open University (1980) *Classroom in Action: an Approach to Evaluation,* Open University in association with Schools Council.

Open University (1981) *Curriculum in Action – Practical Classroom Evaluation* (P533 UG), Open University Press, Milton Keynes.

Oxford Magazine (1991) Truth table? (editorial), no. 71, fourth week, Trinity term.

Peddiwell, J. (1939) *The Sabre-Tooth Curriculum,* McGraw-Hill, New York, NY. (A key chapter is reprinted in R. Hooper (ed.) (1971) *The Curriculum: Context, Design and Development,* Oliver & Boyd, London.)

Peters, J. S. (1977) *Education and the Education of Teachers,* Routledge & Kegan Paul, London.

Peters, T. (1988) *Thriving on Chaos: Handbook for a Management Revolution,* Macmillan, London.

Purkey, S. and Smith, M. (1982) Too soon to cheer?, *Educational Leadership,* December.

Queensland Education Department (1991) Advanced skills teacher (AST 1) positions, *Education Office Gazette*, Vol. 93, no. 19, p. 203, 4 October.

Rainsford, M. (1989) School development in the London Borough of Enfield (unpublished M. Ed. dissertation), Cambridge Institute of Education.

Randall, A. (1991) Quality control, *Managing Schools*, Vol. 1, pp. 26–7.

Ranson, S. (1991) *The New Management of Education: LEA Perspectives on the Implementation of the 1988 Education Reform Act*, Centre for Education Management and Policy Studies, INLOGOV, University of Birmingham.

Read, H. (1958) *Education through Art*, Faber & Faber, London (3rd edn).

Reynolds, D. (ed.) (1985) *Studying School Effectiveness,* Falmer Press, Lewes.

Reynolds, D. (1988) Research on school and organisational effectiveness: the end of the beginning? (keynote paper presented at the BEMAS Third Research Conference) April. Published in R. Saran (ed.) (1990) *Research in Educational Management and Policy: Retrospect and Prospect*, Falmer Press, Lewes.

Rogers, R. (1984) *Crowther to Warnock: How Fourteen Reports Tried to Change Children's Lives*, Heinemann, London (2nd edn).

Rutter, M., Maughan, B., Mortimore, P. and Ouston, J. (1979) *Fifteen Thousand Hours,* Open Books, Wells.

Sallis J. (1988) *Schools, Parents and Governors: A New Approach to Accountability*, Routledge, London.

Sams, B. (1991) Minister, let's be friends, *The Times Educational Supplement*, p. 14, 26 July.

Schon, D. (1987) *Educating the Reflective Practitioner,* Jossey-Bass, Oxford.

School Management Task Force (1990) *Developing School Management: The Way Forward*, DES/HMSO, London.

Sharron, H. (1991) Goodbye to all that: an interview with Michael Fallon, *Managing Schools,* Vol. 1, pp. 16–18.

Simons, H. (1987) *Getting to Know Schools in a Democracy*, Falmer Press, Lewes.

Skilbeck, M. (1984) *Evaluating the Curriculum in the Eighties*, Hodder & Stoughton, London.

Stenhouse, L. (1975) *An Introduction to Curriculum Research and Development*, Heinemann, London.

Stenhouse, L. (1977) Educational accountability and support for teachers, *The Times Educational Supplement*, 13 May.

Straw, J. (1991) Raising the standard: Labour's plan for an Education Standards Commission (Labour Party press release), London, 25 June.

Tawney, R. H. (1952) *The Acquisitive Society*, G. Bell & Sons, London.

Thomas, N. (1990) *Primary Education from Plowden to the 1990s,* Falmer Press, Lewes.

Tomlinson and Kilner (1991) *The Flexible Learning Framework and Current Educational Theory*, Department of Employment, London.

Unsworth, R. (1989) Under pressure, *Cherwell* (Oxford University's independent paper), 20 October.

Van Den Berg, R. M. and Vandenberghe, R. (1986) *ISIP (International School Improvement Project) – Strategies for Large Scale Change in Education: Dilemmas and Solutions*, ACCO, Leuven, Belgium.

Van Velzen, W., Miles, M. B., Ekholm, M., Harreyer, V. and Roben, D. (1985) *Making School Improvement Work: A Conceptual Guide to Practice*, ACCO, Leuven, Belgium.

Wallace, M. (1991) Whose development plan is it anyway?, *The Times Educational Supplement*, 18 January.

Weick, K. (1988) Educational organisations as loosely coupled systems, in A. Westoby (ed.) *Culture and Power in Educational Organisations,* Open University Press, Milton Keynes.

Wignall, A. (1990) Performance indicators as a management tool: their development, implementation and use (unpublished M.A. dissertation), Open University, Milton Keynes.

Williams, R. (1961) *The Long Revolution*, Chatto & Windus, London.

INDEX